AN ENCOUNTER WITH FIDEL

AN ENCOUNTER WITH FIDEL

An interview by Gianni Minà

Translated by Mary Todd

Ocean press
AUSTRALIA

The publisher grafefully acknowledges the assistance of the José Martí Publishing House of Havana, Cuba, in the preparation of this book.

Cover design by David Spratt

ISBN paper 1 875284 21 4
ISBN cloth 1 875284 22 2

First edition, 1991

Published by Ocean Press,
GPO Box 3279GG, Melbourne, Victoria 3001, Australia

Distributed in the USA by The Talman Company,
150 Fifth Avenue, New York, NY 10011, USA

Distributed in Britain and Europe by Central Books,
99 Wallis Road, London E9 5LN, Britain

Distributed in Southern Africa by Grassroots Books,
PO Box A267, Avondale, Harare, Zimbabwe

Distributed in Australia by Astam Books,
162–8 Parramatta Road, Stanmore, NSW 2048, Australia

Contents

Publisher's preface

"Fidel's devotion to the word is almost magical." The following marathon interview is certainly testimony to this comment by Gabriel García Márquez.

At the end of the interview, Fidel Castro observed, "I don't know if this is a world record or not, but 15 straight hours of dialogue with a television journalist is — for me, at least — a Caribbean record."

This book is the fruit of the interview with the President of Cuba by a well-known Italian television journalist, Gianni Minà.

Commenting later, Minà wrote, "I don't know why, among so many requests for interviews, Fidel Castro decided on this occasion to accede to mine. I think that displaying no conscious prejudices, as well as not having any preconceived truth that I would feel bound to reaffirm, helped to establish a professional credibility.

"The interview began at 2pm at the Center of Genetic Engineering and Biotechnology, one of the most advanced centers in this field in the world today. In all, the filming should have lasted around three or four hours. Instead, we wound up at dawn the next day in a corner of Fidel's office, which has his favorite armchair and a low table on whose edge he rested a foot every so often.

"At the end of this long and unexpected tour through Fidel's convictions, memories, theses, passions, analyses, tenderness, anecdotes, self-criticisms and occasional ironical remarks, we were all exhausted," wrote Minà.

On their first meeting, Fidel Castro had commented, "I've been told that you have a lot of questions, but I will answer all of them. How, with my history, could I be afraid of words?!" Some 120 questions and 15 hours later, emerged this panorama of Cuba and the world. It is as much a portrait of the Cuban revolution at the time of its 30th anniversary as it is of Fidel Castro himself.

This book is the most recent of a series of such lengthy sessions with visiting journalists. From Lee Lockwood's *Castro's Cuba, Cuba's Fidel* to Dymally and Elliot's *Nothing Can Stop The Course of History* and Frei Betto's *Fidel and Religion* — also published by Ocean Press — such endeavors have allowed Fidel Castro to directly present his perspective to a wide international audience.

Why publish such a book? Without a doubt, not since the early years of the revolution has there been such interest in Cuba. Ranging from the gleeful, if somewhat fanciful and premature, predictions of Fidel Castro's demise to profound interest in the continuing experiment of Cuba's revolution, the spotlight on Cuba rarely fades. Any visitor to the United States is struck by what Fidel himself has described as that country's "obsession" with Cuba.

In the interview Fidel frankly discusses such controversial issues as human rights; Khruschev, Kennedy and the Cuban missile crisis; Gorbachev and the Soviet Union; and US–Cuban relations in the Reagan and Bush years.

For the first time, Fidel speaks intimately of his relationship with Che Guevara and his decision to leave Cuba for Africa and Bolivia. He also reflects on his personal role in Cuba's revolution.

Since the interview was conducted much has happened to change the world in which Cuba exists. Events in Eastern Europe, Panama, the Soviet Union, Nicaragua and the Middle East have all had a great impact on Cuba.

To provide a more updated commentary, excerpts from three interviews and interventions by Fidel Castro during 1990 have been added as appendices to this book. These include an interview with Ted Turner of the Cable News Network conducted in June, a speech to more than one million Cubans at a rally in July, and a further speech to a national gathering of the Committees to Defend the Revolution in September.

These excerpts address the changes taking place in Eastern Europe and the Soviet Union and their impact on Cuba, the fall of the Berlin Wall and "the new walls being imposed by the United States," the Nicaraguan elections, the Gulf crisis and the need to avoid a military conflict, and renewed efforts by the US government to destabilize Cuba. Demonstrated once again is the consistency and coherency of Cuban foreign policy, as articulated by its central figure.

Agree or disagree, this volume provides a unique and complete insight into Fidel Castro's view of Cuba and the world.

The preparation of this English edition was assisted by the José Martí Publishing House of Havana, Cuba. Elena Rodríguez and Maribel Ibañez were always on call to assist in the organization and revision of the translation.

The translation of the book was prepared by Mary Todd.

Photographs were provided by Pedro Alvarez Tabio, director of the Office of Publications of the Cuban Council of State; the National Information Agency of Cuba; Prensa Latina; and the outstanding Cuban photographer, Osvaldo Salas.

Originally published in 1988 as *Un Encuentro con Fidel,* this book contains the transcript of the interview conducted on June 28 and 29, 1987. The interview with Fidel Castro was originally prepared for Italian television. For the purposes of presenting the material in book form, the interviewer has changed the order of some of the topics from their original sequence in the conversation. For that reason, readers will see some references to time that do not correspond to the placing of the chapters in the book. Minor deletions have been made from the original Spanish version for this English-language edition.

The interview and the subsequent publication of this book was made possible through the assistance and encouragement to Gianni Minà from Saverio Tutino, Paolo Caruso, María Citelli, Paolo Tufano, Romeo Ferrero, Paolo Sforzini, Antonio Fusco, Enzo Mina, Javier Ardizones, and Marianna and Georgina. "They all filled me with the desire," wrote Minà, "to struggle for the things in which I believe."

David Deutschmann
1990

Fidel Castro

Fidel Castro Ruz was born into a wealthy farming family in 1926 in Oriente Province, in the eastern part of Cuba. He got involved in politics as a student at the University of Havana, where he joined one of the student action groups, the Unión Insurreccional Revolucionaria — Revolutionary Insurrectional Union — in 1946. He was a founding member of the Partido del Pueblo Cubano — Cuban People's Party (the Ortodoxos) — in 1947, and became a leader of its left wing. That same year he was part of an aborted armed expedition that had planned to go to the Dominican Republic to overthrow the dictatorship of Rafael Trujillo. Attending a student conference in Bogotá, Colombia, in 1948, he participated in the *Bogotazo*, a massive upsurge that broke out while he was there.

After graduating from law school, Castro ran for representative on the Ortodoxo ticket in the 1952 elections, but these never took place because of a coup d'etat by Fulgencio Batista. Castro then began to map out plans for an insurrection. On July 26, 1953, he led an attack on the Moncada army barracks in Santiago de Cuba which was crushed. After being arrested and surviving an attempt to summarily execute him, he was tried and sentenced to fifteen years' imprisonment. Castro's defense speech, "History Will Absolve Me," later became the program of the July 26th Movement. After being released in 1955 as a result of a mass public pressure campaign, he went to Mexico, where he began to organize what was to become the Rebel Army. Sailing on the yacht *Granma* with eighty-one other guerrillas including his brother Raúl, Che

Guevara, Camilo Cienfuegos, and Juan Almeida, Castro landed in Oriente Province on December 2, 1956, where, from the Sierra Maestra, he led the revolutionary war to victory. With Batista's flight on January 1, 1959, the war came to an end, and Castro arrived triumphantly in Havana on January 8. He served as prime minister of the revolutionary government from February 1959 until December 1976, when he became president of the Council of State and the Council of Ministers. He has been first secretary of the Communist Party of Cuba since its founding in 1965.

Gianni Minà

Gianni Minà was born in the Italian city of Turin in 1938. A professional journalist since 1961, he was for many years special correspondent of Italian Radio Television (RAI). His reporting during these years include a four-part series on the history of jazz, programs on Latin American music and culture, a two-part series on Cuban music, a 14-part social history of boxing, and a series on modern soccer.

Among those personalities he has interviewed for Italian television are David Alfaro Siqueiros, Gabriel García Márquez, Federico Fellini, Sergio Leone, Muhammad Ali, the Beatles, and Robert De Niro.

Between 1981 and 1984 Minà hosted a weekly six-hour program on Italian television. In 1982 he won the Saint Vincent Prize, awarded to the most outstanding television reporter of the year. A collaborator of the daily *La República*, Minà regularly contributes to magazines and newspapers throughout Europe.

Introduction

Fidel — The craft of the word

Gabriel García Márquez

Speaking of a foreign visitor whom he had accompanied for a week on a tour around Cuba, Fidel Castro said: "How that man can talk — he talks even more than I do!" It is enough to know Fidel Castro just a little to realize this was an exaggeration, a great exaggeration, because it is impossible to find anyone more addicted than he to the habit of conversation.

His devotion to the word is almost magical. At the beginning of the revolution, hardly a week after his triumphal entry into Havana, he spoke on television for seven hours without respite. It must be a world record. During the first few hours, the people of Havana, not yet familiar with the hypnotic power of that voice, sat down to listen in the traditional way. But as time passed they went back to their daily routine, with one ear to their affairs and the other to the speech.

I had arrived the day before with a group of journalists from Caracas, and we started listening to the speech in our hotel rooms. Without a pause, we later continued listening in the elevator, in the taxi that took us to the business districts, on the cafe terraces blooming with flowers, in the freezing air-conditioned bars, and even walking down the streets where radios came full-blast through open windows. By evening we had carried out our day's schedule without missing a word.

Two things caught the attention of those of us hearing Fidel Castro for the first time. One was his terrible power to seduce his listeners; the other was the fragility of his voice. It was a hoarse voice which at times was reduced to a breathless whisper. A doctor, on hearing the hoarseness, concluded that even without the marathon speeches that seemed to flow as long as the River Amazon, Fidel Castro was doomed to lose his voice within five years. Shortly afterwards, in August 1962, this prognosis seemed to have its first alarming confirmation when he was left mute after having made a speech announcing the nationalization of US companies. But it was a transitory set-back which did not recur. Twenty six years have passed since then. Fidel Castro has just turned 61, and his voice sounds just as uncertain as ever; but it continues to be his most useful and irresistible instrument in the subtle craft of the spoken word.

Three hours, for him, are a good average for an ordinary conversation. And three hours at a time, the days speed by him. As he is not an academic leader entrenched in his offices, preferring to seek out problems wherever they may be, he can be seen in his discreet car, without the roar of accompanying motorcycles, slipping along the deserted avenues of Havana or on some out-of-the-way road at any time, even in the pre-dawn hours. All this has given rise to the legend that he is a drifting loner, a disorganized and unconventional insomniac, who may turn up for a visit at any hour and keep his hosts awake until dawn.

There was some truth behind that image in the early years of the revolution, when he retained many of his habits from the Sierra Maestra. Not only because of his lengthy speeches, but because he had no real home, nor an office for more than 15 years, nor did he have any fixed daily routine. The seat of government was wherever he might be, and power itself depended on chance, occasioned by his wanderings. Now it is quite different. Without detracting from his so characteristic impetuous inspiration he has finally imposed a certain order on his life. Previously, days and nights would pass with him snatching only a few winks here and there whenever exhaustion overcame him. Now he tries to allow himself a minimum of six hours' undisturbed sleep, although not even he himself knows when that might be. Depending on how things go, it could just as well be 10 at night or 7 the next morning.

He devotes several hours to routine matters in his office of the presidency of the Council of State, where there is a well-ordered desk, comfortable furniture of untanned leather and a bookshelf reflecting the breadth of his tastes: from treatises on hydroponics to romantic novels. From the half a box of cigars he used to smoke each day he became an absolute abstainer, just to have the moral authority to combat smoking in the country where Christopher Columbus discovered tobacco — still a major source of revenue for Cuba today.

The inclement ease with which he gains weight has obliged him to adhere to a permanent diet. This is an immense sacrifice, considering his large appetite and his insatiable pleasure in hunting recipes which he likes to prepare with a kind of scientific fervor. One Sunday, letting himself go, he finished off a good-sized lunch with 18 scoops of ice-cream. However, usually he picks at a fish fillet with boiled vegetables, and then only when hunger overcomes him, rather than according to set mealtimes. He stays in excellent physical condition with a few hours of gymnastics each day and frequent swimming. He limits himself to a glass of straight whisky consumed in almost invisible sips, and he has managed to control his weakness for the spaghetti he was taught to prepare by the first papal nuncio of the revolution, Monsignor Cesare Sacchi. His Homeric but momentary rages are now a thing of the past, and he has learnt to dissipate his dark moods in an invincible patience.

In sum: an iron discipline. But in any case this is never enough, considering how the inevitable scarcity of time imposes an irregular schedule and the force of his imagination may carry him off at any moment. With him, you know where you are starting from, but you never know where you will wind up. It is not unusual on any given night to find yourself flying in an airplane to some secret destination, to be best man at a wedding, fishing for lobsters on the open sea or tasting the first French cheeses made in Camagüey.

A long time ago he said: "As important as learning to work is learning to rest." But his methods of rest seem too original, and apparently do not exclude conversation. Once he left an intense work session close to midnight, with visible signs of exhaustion, and returned in the pre-dawn hours fully recovered after swimming for a couple of hours. Private parties run counter to his character, as he is one of the rare Cubans who neither sings nor dances, and the very few he does attend change in nature the moment he arrives. Perhaps he does not realize. Perhaps he is not aware of the power his presence imposes, a presence which immediately seems to fill all the space, although he is neither as tall nor as heavy-set as he appears at first glance. I have seen the most self-assured people lose their poise in his company, by contriving to look composed or adopting an exaggerated air of confidence, without ever imagining that he is as intimidated as they, and has to make the initial effort so that it is not noticed. I have always believed that the plural which he often uses when speaking of his own acts is not so majestic as it seems, but rather a poetic licence to conceal his shyness.

Inevitably the dancing is interrupted, the music stops, the dinner is put off, and the crowd gathers around him to join in the conversation which begins immediately. He can remain like that for any length of time, standing up, without drinking or eating anything. Sometimes, before going to bed, he will knock very late at the door of a close friend, where he can show up unannounced, and says he's staying only five minutes. He says it with such sincerity that he does not even take a seat. But little by little, he gets stimulated again by the new conversation, and after a while he collapses into an easy chair and stretches out his legs, saying: "I feel like a new man." That is how it is: weary of talking, he rests by talking.

Once he said: "In my next reincarnation I want to be a writer." In fact, he writes well and he enjoys it, even in a moving car in the notebooks he always has at hand for writing down whatever comes to mind, even personal letters. They are notebooks of ordinary paper, bound in blue plastic, which over the years have accumulated in his private files. His handwriting is small and intricate, although at first glance it looks as simple as a schoolboy's. He approaches writing like a professional. He corrects a phrase several times, crosses it out, tries it again in the margins, and it is not unusual for him to search for the right word for days, consulting dictionaries, asking around, until he finds what he wants.

In the 1970s he fell into the habit of writing out his speeches, so slowly and with such meticulousness that they were almost mechanical. But this same virtue spoilt them. Fidel Castro's personality seemed to change when he read them: the tone was different, the style, even the quality of his voice. In immense Revolution Square, before half a million people, he several times felt himself suffocating in the strait-jacket of the written word, and every chance he got he departed from the text. On other occasions he found that his typists had made an error, and rather than correcting it as he went along he would stop speaking and make the change with a ball-point pen, taking his time. He was never satisfied. Despite his efforts to liven them up, and despite the fact that he did succeed in many cases, those captive speeches left him feeling frustrated. They said everything he wanted to say, and perhaps they said it better, but they left out the greatest stimulus of his life, which is the excitement of risk.

The improvisor's stand, then, seems to be his perfect habitat, although he always has to overcome an initial inhibition which few people recognize and which he does not deny. In a note he sent me a few years ago asking me to participate in some public ceremony, he said: "Try for once to get over your stage fright, as I myself must do so often." Only in very special cases does he use a card with some notes which he unceremoniously takes out of his pocket before starting, and holds within view. He always begins in a nearly inaudible voice, quite hesitant, pushing forward in the fog on an uncertain course, but seizing upon any glimmer to gain ground inch by inch, until he lashes out with something like a great paw and grabs hold of the audience. Then a give and take is established, exciting them both and creating between them a kind of dialectical complicity, and in this unbearable tension lies the essence of his elation. It is inspiration: the irresistible and dazzling state of grace, which is denied only by those who have not had the glory of experiencing it.

In the beginning, public events commenced with his arrival, although that was as unpredictable as the rain. For some years now he has been arriving precisely on time, and the duration of his speech depends on the mood of the audience. But the infinite speeches of the early years belong to a past now confused with legend, because so much of what had to be explained at that time is now understood, and Fidel Castro's style itself has become more compact after so many sessions of oratorical pedagogy. He has never been heard to repeat any of the papier mache slogans of communist scholasticism nor make any use at all of the system's ritual dialectic, a fossil language which long ago lost contact with reality and which goes hand in glove with a laudatory and commemorative journalism which seems intended to conceal rather than to explain. He is the anti-dogmatist par excellence, whose creative imagination lives hovering over the abysses of heresy. He rarely quotes the phrases of others, neither in conversation nor on the rostrum, except those of José Martí, his favorite author. He knows the 28 volumes of Martí's work thoroughly, and has had the talent to incorporate his ideas into the bloodstream of a Marxist revolution. But the essence of his own philosophy is perhaps his conviction that mass work is above all a matter of being concerned with each individual.

This could explain his absolute confidence in direct contact. Even the most difficult speeches seem to be casual talks, like those he held with students in the courtyards of the university at the outset of the revolution. In fact, and especially outside Havana, it is not unusual for someone to call out to him from the crowd at a public meeting and a shouted dialogue will begin. He has a language for every occasion and a different form of persuasion depending on his different interlocutors, be they workers, farmers, students, scientists, politicians, writers or foreign visitors. He can reach each one at their own level with vast and varied information that allows him to move easily in any medium. But his personality is so complex and unpredictable that any one of them can form a different impression of him in the same encounter.

One thing is certain: wherever he may be, however and with whomever, Fidel Castro is there to win. I do not think anyone in this world could be a worse loser. His attitude in the face of defeat, even in the slightest events of daily life, seems to obey a private logic: he will not even admit it, and he does not have a moment's peace until he manages to invert the terms and turn it into a victory. But whatever it may be, and wherever, everything happens within the ambit of an inexhaustible conversation.

The subject can be anything, according to the interest of the audience, but the opposite often occurs when it is he who takes a single subject to all his audiences. This tends to happen during the periods in which he is exploring an idea which besieges him, and no one can be more obsessive than he when he has set out to get to the bottom of something. There is no project, however grandiose or minute, which he does not undertake with a fierce passion. And especially if he is facing adversity. Never than at such times does he look better, appear in a better mood, or in higher spirits. Someone who believes he knows him once commented: "Things must be going very badly, because you look radiant."

However, a foreign visitor who met him for the first time told me a few years ago: "Fidel is getting old; last night he went back to the same subject around seven times." I pointed out to him that these almost manic reiterations are one of his ways of working. The subject of Latin America's foreign debt, for example, had arisen in his conversations for the first time some two years before, and had been developing, branching out, growing more profound, until it became something very much like a recurring nightmare. The first thing he said, like a simple arithmetical conclusion, was that the debt was unpayable. Little by little, during three trips I made to Havana that year, I pieced together his latest variations on the theme: the repercussions of the debt on the countries' economies, its political and social impact, its decisive influence on international relations, its providential importance for a united Latin American policy. Finally, he convoked a major congress of experts in Havana and gave a speech in which he left out none of the salient questions from his preceding conversations. By then he had a comprehensive vision which the simple passage of time has borne out.

It seems to me that his most exceptional virtue as a politician is this faculty of discerning the evolution of a particular problem, all the way to its remotest conclusions, as if he could see not only the projecting mass of an iceberg but also the seven-eighths of it underwater. However, this faculty does not function by intuition, but rather as a result of arduous and tenacious reasoning. An assiduous interviewer could discover the first embryo of an idea and follow its development over many months though his persistent conversation, until it is finally made public in its completed form, as happened with the foreign debt. Then, once the subject is exhausted, it is as though a vital cycle had been completed, and he files it away forever.

Such a verbal mill requires, of course, the aid of an incessant flow of information, well-chewed and digested. His supreme aid is his memory, and he uses it to the point of abuse to sustain speeches and private conversations with overwhelming reasoning and arithmetic operations of incredible speed. This task of information accumulation begins when he wakes up. He breakfasts with no less than 200 pages of news from all over the world. During the day, despite his ceaseless mobility, they pursue him everywhere with urgent information. He himself calculates that every day he has to read some fifty documents. To this must be added the reports of his official services and of his visitors, and everything that could be of interest to his infinite curiosity. Any exaggeration about this can only be approximate, such as even in the extreme case of a trip in an airplane. He prefers not to fly, and does so only when there is no alternative. But when he does fly he is a bad passenger because of his anxiety to know everything: he neither sleeps nor reads, he hardly eats, he asks the crew for navigation maps every time he has some doubt, he makes them explain why this route is being taken and not the other one, why the noise of the turbines is changing, why the plane is bouncing in spite of the good weather. The replies, of course, must be precise, as he can discover the slightest inconsistency in a casual phrase.

Another vital source of information, of course, is books. Perhaps the aspect of Fidel Castro's personality least in keeping with the image created by his adversaries is that of being a voracious reader. No one can explain how he finds the time or what methods he uses to read so much and so quickly, although he insists that there is nothing special about it. In his cars, from the prehistoric Oldsmobile to successive Soviet Zils, up to the current Mercedes, there has always been a light for reading at night. Many times he has taken a book in the pre-dawn hours, and commented on it the following morning. He reads English, but does not speak it. In any case he prefers to read in Spanish, and at any hour is ready to read any piece of paper with letters on it that may fall into his hands. When he needs some very recent book which has not yet been translated, he has it translated. A doctor friend sent him, as a courtesy, his treatise on orthopedics which had just been published without, of course, any pretension that he read it, but a week later he received a letter from him with a long list of observations.

He is an habitual reader of economic and historical subjects. When he read the memoirs of Lee Iacocca, he discovered several errors that were so incredible that he sent to New York for the English version, to compare it with the Spanish. Indeed, the translator had once again confused the meaning of the word billion in the two languages. He is a good reader of literature, and follows it closely. I have on my conscience having initiated him in the addiction of quick-consumption best-sellers and then keeping him up to date as an antidote to official documents.

Still, his immediate and most fruitful source of information

Photo: Osvaldo Salas

continues to be conversation. He has the habit of quick interrogations which resemble a *matriushka,* the Russian doll from whose interior a similar, smaller one emerges, then another, until the smallest one possible is left. He asks successive questions in instantaneous bursts until he discovers the why of the why of the final why. It is difficult for his fellow conversationalist not to feel subjected to an inquisitorial examination. When a visitor from Latin America gave him a hasty statistic on the rice consumption of his compatriots, he did his mental calculations and said: "How strange, each one eats four pounds of rice a day." With time you learn that his master tactic is asking about things he already knows, in order to confirm his data. And in some cases to gauge the calibre of the person he is questioning, and treat him accordingly. He loses no opportunity to inform himself, Colombian President Belisario Betancur, with whom he maintained frequent telephone contact despite the fact that they had not met and that the two countries do not have diplomatic relations, once called him about some casual matter. Fidel Castro told me afterwards: "I took advantage of the fact that we both had time to ask him for some information that did not come in the cables about the coffee situation in Colombia."

He went to few countries before the revolution, and in those he has visited since on official trips he has been condemned to the narrow horizon of protocol. However, he also talks about them, and about many others he has not been to, as though he had. During the war in Angola he described a battle in such detail at an official reception that it was difficult to convince a European diplomat that Fidel Castro had not participated in it. The account he gave in a public speech of the capture and murder of Che Guevara, the one he gave on the storming of the Moneda Palace and the death of Salvador Allende, and the one he gave on the ravages of Hurricane Flora were great spoken réportages.

Spain, the land of his ancestors, is an obsession with him. His vision of Latin America in the future is the same as that of Bolívar and Martí: an integral and autonomous community capable of influencing the destiny of the world. But the country he knows most about, after Cuba, is the United States. He is thoroughly familiar with the nature of its people, its power structures, the ulterior motives of its governments, and this has helped him to steer his way through the incessant storm of the blockade. Despite the restrictions of the government of the United States there is a nearly daily flight between Havana and Miami, and not a day goes by without US visitors of every kind arriving in Cuba, on special flights or in private planes.

On the eve of elections there is an incessant influx of politicians of both parties. Fidel Castro sees as many as he can see, he makes sure that they are well cared for while they wait and does everything possible to give them sufficient time for an exhaustive exchange of new information. These are veritable talk-fests. He gives them a few home truths and puts up very well with the ones they give him. He conveys the impression that nothing amuses him more than showing his true face to those who arrive prepared by enemy propaganda to meet a barbaric caudillo. On one occasion, before a bipartisan group of congressmen and even a Pentagon official, he gave a very realistic account of how his Galician ancestors and his Jesuit teachers infused some moral principles in him which had proved very useful in the formation of his personality. And he concluded: "I am a Christian."

It hit the table like a bombshell. The people from the US, brought up in a culture that understands life only in black and white, skipped over his prior explanation. At the end of the visit, with the new day already dawning, they were left awed by his explosive conclusion. The most conservative of the legislators voiced the surprising view that he believed no one could be a more effective mediator between Latin America and the United States than Fidel Castro.

Everyone who goes to Cuba hopes to have the chance to see him in whatever circumstance, although there are many who dream of a private interview, especially the foreign journalists, who never consider their work finished until they can carry away the trophy of an interview with him. I believe he would oblige them all if it were not physically impossible: at this moment there are some 300 formal requests awaiting decision, a process which could take forever. There is always a journalist waiting in an Havana hotel, after having appealed to all kinds of sponsors to see him. Some wait for months. They get indignant about not knowing to whom to turn, because no one knows for sure what the right steps are for getting to him. The truth is that there are none. It is not unusual for some lucky journalist to ask him a casual question in the course of a public appearance and for the dialogue to end in an interview several hours' long on every conceivable subject. He takes a long time over each question, venturing out on the least-expected, most difficult terrain without ever neglecting precision, knowing that a single ill-used word can cause irreparable damage. In these rare formal interviews he tends to grant the time requested, however his unpredictable elasticity often prolongs the time, once stimulated by the dynamics of the dialogue. Only in very special cases does he ask to see the questions beforehand. He has never refused to answer any question, provocative though it may be, nor has he ever lost his patience. Sometimes the two hours planned turn into four, and nearly always into six. Or seventeen, as was the case in the interview with Gianni Minà for Italian television, one of the longest he has granted, and also one of the most complete.

Ultimately very few interviews please him, least of all the written transcripts, which in the interests of space tend to sacrifice the exactitude and the nuances particular to his personal style. He thinks that the television interviews end up unnatural because of the inevitable fragmentation, and it seems to him unjust to have given up to five hours of his life for a seven-minute program. But what is most regrettable, for both Fidel Castro and his listeners, is that even the best journalists, especially the Europeans, do not have even the curiosity to square their questions with reality. They aspire to the trophy with questions written according to the political obsessions and cultural prejudices of their own countries, without taking the trouble to find out for themselves what today's Cuba is really like, what the dreams and real frustrations of its people are: the truth of their lives. In this way they deprive the Cuban man in the street of an opportunity to talk to the world, and they deny themselves the professional achievement of questioning Fidel Castro, not about European suppositions, which are so distant, but about the anxieties of his own people, and especially in this time of great decisions.

In conclusion, listening to Fidel Castro in so many and diverse circumstances, I have asked myself many times if his zeal for conversation does not obey an organic need to hang on at all costs to the guiding thread of truth amid the hallucinatory mirages of power. I have asked myself that over the course of many dialogues, public and private. But above all in the most difficult and fruitless, with those who in his presence lose their naturalness and aplomb and speak to him in theoretical formulas that have nothing to do with reality. Or with those who whisk the truth out of his sight so as not to give him more reasons for concern than he already has. He knows it. To one official who did that to him he said: "You hide truths from me so as not to trouble me, but when at last I discover them I will die from the effects of facing so many truths that you will have failed to tell me." The most serious, however, are the truths they hide from him to conceal shortcomings, because alongside the enormous achievements which sustain the revolution — the political, scientific, sports, cultural achievements — there is a colossal bureaucratic incompetence which affects nearly every order of daily life, and most particularly domestic happiness, and which has obliged Fidel Castro himself, nearly 30 years after victory, to personally deal with such extraordinary matters as the making of bread and the distribution of beer.

Everything is different, on the other hand, when he talks to the people in the street. The conversation then recovers the expressiveness and crude frankness of real affection. Of his various civilian and military names, only one is left to him: Fidel. They surround him without risks, they use the familiar *tú* (you) form of address with him, they argue with him, they contradict him, they make demands of him, with a channel of immediate transmission through which the truth flows in torrents. It is then, rather than in privacy, that the rare human being shielded from sight by the brilliance of his own image is discovered. This is the Fidel Castro I believe I know, after innumerable hours of conversation, through which the phantom of politics does not often pass. A man of austere ways and insatiable illusions, with an old-fashioned formal education, of cautious words and simple manners and incapable of conceiving any idea which is not out of the ordinary. He dreams that his scientists will find the cure for cancer, and has created a world power foreign policy on an island without fresh water, 84 times smaller than its main enemy. Such is the discretion with which he protects his privacy that his intimate life has ended up being the most impenetrable enigma of his legend. He has the nearly mystical conviction that the greatest achievement of the human being is the proper formation of conscience and that moral incentives, rather than material ones, are capable of changing the world and moving history forward. I believe he is one of the greatest idealists of our time and perhaps this may be his greatest virtue, although it has also been his greatest danger.

Many times I have seen him arrive at my house very late at night, still trailing the last scraps of a limitless day. Many times I have asked him how things were going, and more than once he answered me: "Very well, we have all the reservoirs full." I have seen him open the refrigerator to eat a piece of cheese, which was perhaps the first thing he had eaten since breakfast. I have seen him telephone a friend in Mexico to ask her for the recipe for a dish he had liked, and I have seen him copy it down leaning against the counter, among the still unwashed pots and pans from dinner, while someone on television sang an ancient song: "Life is an Express Train That Travels Thousands of Leagues." I have heard him in his few moments of nostalgia evoking the pastoral dawns of his rural childhood, the sweetheart of his youth who left, the things he could have done differently to win more time from life. One night, while he was eating vanilla ice-cream in small slow spoonfuls, I saw him so overwhelmed by the weight of the destinies of so many people, so removed from himself, that for an instant he seemed different to me from the man he had always been. Then I asked him what he would most like to do in this world, and he answered immediately: "Just hang around on some street corner."

Chapter 1

My country

In order to encourage him to speak about his country, after nearly 30 years in government, I asked Fidel to go out on the balcony of his office in the Palace of the Revolution, from which you can get a beautiful view of the city. We had come to the Palace from the Center of Genetic Engineering after crossing the city in his black Mercedes, driven by one of the guards who have watched over Fidel's safety for many years. We had spoken about the standard of living of the people in Havana while passing the colonial architecture of an extremely beautiful city. "You can also live comfortably, with dignity, in a society where consumption isn't at the heart of daily life," Fidel commented as we drove down a long, clean avenue with little traffic. And he added, "What is more important: increasing consumption, or not spoiling the landscape and contaminating the health of a city?" The concerns of an intellectual head of state who, moreover, studied with the Jesuits. Themes that he would not forget in summing up the 30 years of the Cuban revolution, from its origins to today's difficult challenges, with great pride and perhaps a little rhetoric, but also with an indestructible passion.

G.M.

Gianni Minà: President Castro, Italians and other Europeans who are not burdened with prejudices say that the Cuban revolution survives because, even though a poor country, it freed itself from poverty, unlike the rest of Latin America. How was that possible?

Photo: Osvaldo Salas

Fidel Castro: I will have to try to synthesize so as not to go on at great length.

I think that, in essence, it could only be possible with a revolution — at least in a short historical period, or perhaps even in a long historical period. I don't know if others have solved it in another way, but it had to be a revolution because it had to overcome many interests and create a totally new power that wasn't pledged to those interests in order to carry out all the measures that made these achievements possible.

Because we created a new power with the support of all the people, we were able to implement revolutionary laws. It was just as we had imagined. Even before Batista's coup d'etat [in 1952], we had come to the conclusion that, if our problems were to be solved, a radical change was necessary — in short, a revolution.

That enabled us, for example, to recover all of the national wealth in our country. The mines, the best land, the best industries, the basic services — such as electricity, the railroad, the means of communication — the banks and foreign trade were owned by foreign companies. We had ceased to be a Spanish colony and had instead become a colony of the United States. So, if the country had not recovered those resources and placed them at its service, it would not have been able to carry out a program of that kind. It required the recovery of the national resources and a boost to agricultural development based on a radical agrarian reform, for hundreds of thousands of people in the countryside were landless and jobless. Some of the big US landholdings, for example, had 200,000 hectares of land. In all, the big US companies and the Cuban-owned large landholdings had millions of hectares of the best land. The agrarian reform gave a great boost to agricultural development.

We also had to stimulate the country's industrial development. Right from the beginning, it was necessary to achieve a better distribution of wealth. We had to carry out programs for developing education, with illiteracy at nearly 30 percent and semi-illiteracy around 80 percent — many people knew how to read a little but had not gone any farther than the second or third grade. We also had to develop health programs and a series of measures for housing construction; we had to create jobs for the population. We had to wipe out quite a few vices.

Gambling was quite widespread in the country, because many

people dreamed of having good luck, not of improving themselves, not of working, but of gambling, of winning a prize in the lottery. All the advertising was full of raffles and gambling; many commercial firms held raffles with a car or a house as a prize for their lucky clients. There was a soap factory that gave away a house every month, and all of those houses looked alike and had the name of the soap company on them.

All that had to be ended. Advertising itself was done away with, of course, because it is more characteristic of a capitalist consumer society than our Third World country.

In addition to all these measures, we had to develop programs for razing the poorest neighborhoods, the slums, the unsanitary neighborhoods, and for solving the problems of the beggars and homeless by giving them assistance, protection and a place to stay.

We also fought against drugs. Their use wasn't very widespread at that time, but right from the beginning we fought against them. Prostitution was another problem that was solved. Prostitution in our country was caused by unemployment, prejudices against women, the few possibilities of employment and a society that carried with it a lot of prejudices — a falsely puritanical society that, in order to preserve the virtue of some women, required the exploitation and prostitution of others. We didn't do this by decree, but carried out a program of searching for and distributing jobs. Political and social work continued to be done until prostitution was eliminated.

We had to pay attention to each of those problems until we reached our present situation, which is not one of great abundance or a consumer society — yes, I know that is one of the topics that worries you — but it is a society with social justice, where nobody goes hungry, all children have schools to go to, everybody who is ill has access to a doctor, every family has employment, there is no discrimination against women and there is no racial discrimination. In short, we have created a just society that is very advanced. I don't think that we have reached perfection yet, but we have solved many problems that few Third World countries and no other Latin American countries have yet solved.

Gianni Minà: Does the rest of Latin America have no hope of leaving poverty behind and reaching at least your level?

Fidel Castro: Naturally, you never lose hope. However, this is a matter not just of hope but of need, because the problems in Latin America are accumulating. I've seen the changes in the years since the triumph of the revolution. Latin America's present population is more than double what it was when our revolution triumphed, and in the course of these years its social problems have been aggravated. There is much unemployment, the health situation is more serious, and so are the housing and nutrition problems.

Gianni Minà: Drugs . . .

Fidel Castro: This is without mentioning drugs. In some Latin American countries, 70 percent of the people are undernourished; in some countries, 80 percent of the children are undernourished. These are tragic situations. I've seen these problems grow in our hemisphere; I've seen them accumulate. It's a matter not of hope but a social law, a law of history, that the accumulation of those problems tends to create crises, from which solutions emerge in one way or another.

Therefore, I think that, apart from the subjective factors and people's hopes, the objective factors inevitably promote the subjective conditions that make changes both necessary and unavoidable.

It is not that I'm preaching violence. I say, rather, that profound social changes are needed. Some attempts have been made to bring them about by political means alone as in the case of Chile. We shouldn't forget the efforts Salvador Allende made to solve all these problems through political means. But what was the end result? The overthrow of his government, the disappearance of thousands of people, murders and torture, a strong-arm regime that was imposed on the country and that has lasted for around 14 years already, destroying the noble effort of the Chilean left and President Allende to bring about profound changes through political means. But, one way or another, those profound changes are both necessary and inevitable.

Gianni Minà: What price have the Cuban people had to pay to reach the goal of being poor but not living in poverty?

Fidel Castro: Well, first of all, we aren't so poor — though we aren't rich either, by any means. For example, per capita consumption of calories is 3,000 per day. I believe that is what is necessary. Some nutritionists want to feed everybody as if they were stevedores in the ports, and everybody knows from their own experience that if you eat only 2,000 calories, it's hard to keep from losing weight, depending on the work you do. Cubans eat around 80 grams of protein per capita per day, around 50 percent of animal origin and the other 50 percent of vegetable origin; that's more than the required minimum. However, the average isn't the important thing — what's important is the distribution. In some countries where everybody speaks of averages, some consume 30 grams of protein while others consume 150. In Cuba, consumption is more or less the same for everybody.

Eighty-five percent of the people, including those living in rural areas, have electricity. In the next three years, that figure will be raised to 90 percent. Almost all families have a television set, and there's more than one radio per capita. A large percentage have refrigerators, fans, irons, electric sewing machines, blenders and washing machines. A large proportion of families have many household appliances that are related to the standard of living.

Housing has improved. Medical health services and the care that children receive in our country are comparable to what children of the wealthy receive in the Mayo Clinic in the United States. All of our children's hospitals offer intensive care; we have cardiovascular surgery for children; we have excellent maternity services; and almost all births take place in hospitals.

We don't have much individual transportation, many cars, but we do have an adequate system of public transportation. Every worker has the right to a month's paid vacation each year.

If you analyze the situation in terms of essential goods, you can't say that we're very poor. We aren't rich; we don't have the level of consumption that industrially developed countries have, such as in Europe, but we've managed things so that the people's basic needs are met. The children of workers can go to the university; depending on their ability, their merits in their studies, they will have access to any speciality. Women constitute nearly 54 percent of the country's technical workforce. That is, we can't say that our country is rich, but we have met our essential needs satisfactorily.

You ask about the price we've paid. That question is a little more complex: what is the price of a revolution? I might ask you, "What is the price you pay for a soccer team that participates in a championship and wins?" Its members had to make efforts through work, coordinate well, and use their intelligence and energies. But if you ask a player on the team about those great sacrifices, they hardly notice them, because they're thinking about the satisfaction of having won.

There have been great sacrifices. For example, there were great risks. We've had to confront the capitalist and imperialist country that is — if you allow me to use the term, and I hope you don't take it as a cliché — the most powerful one in the world. We've had to put up with the blockade, acts of aggression and threats of aggression. This has forced us to prepare ourselves — all the people — militarily to defend our country. Many Cubans died in the struggle against the dictatorship, in the struggle for the triumph of the revolution. After the victory of the revolution, some fellow Cubans died in the struggle against imperialist attacks and while on internationalist missions.

That is, we've made a great effort, run risks and made sacrifices. But you should compare our present situation with that of the past, when families didn't have jobs or any of these guaranteed services and possibilities and when many people had to work 14 or 15 hours a day. Now, all workers have to work only eight hours a day. When they work more than eight hours, they do so to cooperate on certain projects because greater efforts — in a sugarcane harvest or in construction — are requested of them. Or they're like the workers you saw at the Genetic Engineering Center, who put in 14 or 15 hours — not as an economic or material necessity but as a contribution to the revolution.

All workers have the right to a pension that enables them to live decently; all citizens have social assistance, which they didn't have before. In the past, some of the people who worked in the countryside for dozens of years received pensions of only six dollars a month — we now have guaranteed adequate pensions for all. That is, while there have been efforts, there have also been many spiritual, moral and material satisfactions to compensate for those efforts.

It's as if you were to ask me, "What sacrifices does a revolutionary make?" A revolutionary will tell you, "I've been doing what I like to do, I've done it with love, and I feel great satisfaction." Therefore, you can't use the term "sacrifice." I would say that our people made enormous, intolerable sacrifices — in exchange for nothing — *prior* to the revolution.

Gianni Minà: President Castro, aren't you afraid that, in an economically brighter future, the phenomenon called consumerism

— an element that could frustrate the achievement of many goals you seek — may develop?

Fidel Castro: I think that's improbable because the Third World countries are in a development phase. I consider it highly unlikely that we will have the material conditions for creating the habits that the industrialized capitalist countries have fomented in the West. As I already told you, we have some of the things you have, but not all of them. For example, we don't have as many cars. They are characteristic of developed capitalist society.

Gianni Minà: Who knows if they are good or bad?

Fidel Castro: I would say they aren't healthy. Moreover, it isn't feasible to have so many. Let's not think about Belgium, with a few million inhabitants, or about Sweden; let's think about China, with more than a billion inhabitants. Just imagine what it would be like if every family in China had one or two cars! How long would the raw materials for that industry last? I think — I read this the other day — the Chinese have one car for every 2,000 people. According to my calculations, this means they have around 500,000 cars — the same as in a province in Italy or France or a state in the United States. In China, there are lots of bicycles — they urge everybody to have a bicycle — and it is a model of Chinese development. It's more healthy. The Vietnamese use bicycles for transportation and thus get exercise every day.

It is impossible for everyone in China to have a Western lifestyle. Just imagine what it would be like if every family in India — with 570 million inhabitants — had a car, or if all of the African and other Third World countries set out on such a development program. The pollution that now exists in the world, the intolerable pollution with carbon dioxide and other things, would be multiplied a hundredfold, and the non-renewable energy resources would be exhausted much more rapidly. Thus, I don't see any real, objective possibility of the Third World countries being able to adopt that model of consumption.

In any case, they have to solve their problems of education, health, employment, housing, recreation, culture and food to achieve a diet that will enable their people to live healthily, with, as I said, the necessary proteins and calories. They also have to develop a much broader spiritual and cultural life. They can't even dream of other things. They must have enough clothes to meet

January 1959

their needs; when the people have 20 square meters of cloth per capita per year, they have enough and maybe some extra. They don't need a new style every month or year, requiring that they change the clothes they have; they don't need an enormous waste of cotton. If one person needs 20 square meters of cloth — and I don't know how many the Chinese have — why have 40 or 50? You'd have to get the raw material from agriculture, which should also produce foodstuffs, or you'd have to get it from oil, which may be needed to produce fertilizers or foodstuffs or for transportation.

Thus, I don't see any danger. We have so many investment and development needs that we can't allow ourselves the luxury of taking the resources we need to meet all of these basic needs and invest them in developing a consumer society.

I've suggested this. In the meeting I had recently with the heads of enterprises, I asked, "Why are we going to measure the efficiency of our enterprises in terms of sales volume? Wouldn't it be better for the people to save, and have the security of knowing they have money put away, than for us to strive, like capitalist companies, to sell more in order to make and hand out profits." We are analysing some of these problems in our system of economic management in terms of what our efforts for development should be.

In a socialist revolution the people are educated, and I, at least, have always been preoccupied in seeking other motivations. Even though raising the standard of living is one of our goals and we raise our people's standard of living whenever we can, we don't turn raising the standard of living into the leitmotif of our conduct; rather, we try to develop a broad sense of human solidarity.

Many countries are poorer than ours. We have an internationalist concept, not a narrow, selfish nationalism. We constantly remind our people of the situation in other countries, where life expectancy is 40 or 50 years and where the infant mortality is 100 for every 1,000 live births. We remind our people that we must help other countries as a matter of principle, that we must practice international solidarity. If we used only matters related to the standard of living to stimulate our people's efforts, then we couldn't also ask them to make sacrifices in order to help other countries.

Thus, in my speeches, I have been careful not to turn the level of consumption into the center of people's goals and motivations.

Actually, I don't see any real, objective possibilities for a Third World country seeking those models; what I do see is a need for education in this regard.

I don't know what future science and technology will determine. I don't know if, someday, it will be possible to use many more cars without contaminating the environment, if new forms of fuel will appear, if batteries that store larger amounts of electric energy for longer periods of time can be developed, if forms of non-contaminating liquid fuels may be created when the oil runs out. But these are still questions of fantasy, because you need energy, and you firstly have to use energy in industry and to meet top-priority social needs.

These limits of what we do or don't consume will depend not only on the possibilities of science and technology but also on the model of society that is drawn up. In socialism, we seek to program development and set goals. In capitalism, nobody programs development or sets goals; everything develops by virtue of spontaneous, blind laws. And it creates problems. Today, there are problems of unemployment that seriously concern the Europeans, problems of drugs and other situations that have made life hard for Europeans and North Americans — I don't know so much about the Japanese — but they have made life hard and very stressful in those conditions created by consumer societies.

Gianni Minà: Don't you think consumerism will be a problem in the future?

Fidel Castro: No, our problem is development.

Gianni Minà: President Castro, it's raining; shouldn't we go in?

Fidel Castro: What good luck you've brought us!

Gianni Minà: Why?

Fidel Castro: We've had some terrible droughts; it's a rare thing to see it raining. It has rained very little even in May and June, which are usually the months with the most rain. We've had several years of bad droughts, so this rain is a good omen.

Gianni Minà: A simple question: When you look at this city, do you look at it with tenderness, with pride . . .?

Fidel Castro: Well, I'll tell you: I almost never stand here on this balcony to look at the city. I see the city on the ground, because I visit many places: factories, hospitals . . . The best place from which to see the city is from the top of the monument to José Martí.

I don't think so much about what the city is like now; rather, I think about what it should be like in the future. We are carrying out a very intensive construction program; from 1989, we should complete 20,000 housing units a year in the capital. Some 250,000 new housing units will be built between 1987 and the year 2000.

What often worries me is how we can combine productivity with aesthetics, how we can combine prefabs with architectural elegance in building. We're no longer interested only in constructing a lot of housing units and meeting immediate housing needs; in my contacts with the planners and workers, I'm putting a lot of emphasis on the city's beauty.

As you know, we're rebuilding Old Havana, restoring it to how it once was. But we have to build hundreds of thousands of housing units, and we have to start thinking now about what the city will look like. This is an important problem. We have good architects and planners, but we can't say that we have good city construction strategists who know how to design them as an integral whole. We'll always have to strike a balance between productivity, large-scale prefabs and the economy on the one hand, and the aesthetic factors I'm talking about on the other. I'm upset by the idea that we'd have an ugly city after building hundreds of thousands of housing units and that future generations wouldn't consider the efforts that were made to solve a very pressing problem.

Gianni Minà: My question was an attempt to reach Fidel Castro, the man, not only the head of state, and I see that your concern as a revolutionary hasn't disappeared.

Fidel Castro: No, never. It is never satisfied and never disappears. When some problems are solved, others appear; you reach one goal and set yourself others.

Gianni Minà: The salt of life . . .

Fidel Castro: That's it.

Chapter 2

Human rights

It is always extremely delicate and difficult to find the correct way, the precise words, to ask a head of state about justice in their country, when there is a question of whether or not there are political prisoners and the unfounded or otherwise accusation of human rights violations. It is a topic that, for example, has placed members of the Italian government in difficulties with the foreign press when speaking of the "April 7 trial" or when, in the European Parliament, we were severely criticized because of our judicial system and the state of our prisons. All this is even more difficult when, as in the case of Cuba, there is a single, unquestionable ideology.

I took up the topic of human rights with Fidel, asking eight questions and digging so much that he said, "You ask me all the questions, even the ones I don't usually answer."

We were seated facing each other in the part of Fidel's office that contains his desk. We had been working for six or seven hours, and Fidel Castro, as readers will see from the tone of some answers, had become worked up for the first time in the interview.

I'd had the possibility of visiting and filming the Havana Prison, the largest one in the country, with a capacity for 10,000 prisoners. It has a hospital, a sports field and even private rooms where the prisoners' wives or fiancees can visit them. In our country, too, if a foreign journalist were to come, we would take him to visit a model prison, not one of the ones we're ashamed of. But the fact is that the Havana Prison is the largest one on the island. Armando Valladares, who was accused of terrorism in 1960, served the second part of his term there. He later became a poet and turned himself into an international "case" when, in order to end his imprisonment, he passed himself off as an invalid. Valladares was freed by the Cuban government in response to a petition by French President Mitterrand.

Readers may judge for themselves the credibility of what Fidel said. He never tried to evade the issue.

In my experience as a journalist in Latin America, I have encountered another kind of behavior, exhibited in that case by Argentinian General Videla during a disturbing interview that he granted to me in 1976. The military junta in power had unleashed repression, and citizens had begun to disappear. To an unexpected question about those happenings, details of which were already known in the United Nations, General Videla replied that he knew nothing about them and that, if irregularities in the behavior of the police and the military had been discovered, measures would have to be taken. I insisted: "You give me your word on that?" And Videla replied, "Absolutely."

But the next day I was advised to leave Argentina so as not to run risks. Later, we learned that, during those very years, more than 30,000 people "disappeared", were tortured and were murdered. By the end of the 1970s, the United Nations had published their names in a white book. I say this because, whatever opinion one may have about the degree of authoritarianism of the Cuban revolution, no international agency has ever been able to maintain anything more than what Fidel himself says, and the only discrepancies relate to the number of prisoners.

The problem, however — as may be noted from his replies — must touch the Cuban leader deeply; he is affected by ideological rigor, reasons of state and concerns as a humanist and intellectual.

G.M.

Gianni Minà: Recently, in Geneva, the Human Rights Commission of the United Nations rejected the proposal presented by the United States in which it sought to describe Cuba as a country that violated human rights. Former Cuban political prisoners such as Valladares and Gutiérrez Menoyo formed part of the US delegation. Felipe González, Prime Minister of Spain, presented a protest over the inclusion of Menoyo, who is of Spanish nationality. What do you think of all this?

VENCEREMOS

Fidel Castro: All of the US administrations have carried out major campaigns to discredit Cuba, but none of them until now had come up with the idea of accusing Cuba in Geneva of violating human rights. That hadn't occurred to them. The administration which did that was the one that was the least moral, the most reactionary and the most mendacious — frankly, the one with the least ethics and principles of all the administrations in the United States.

The others even drew up assassination plans. We'll exclude Carter from this. During Carter's term, I could see that he was a man of ethics based on a religious position. All of the others — including Reagan — took part in the assassination plans, in one way or another. I know that because we have some penetration and some intelligence and counter-intelligence activities, and therefore we know what our enemies are doing.

The Reagan government is the least scrupulous of all the US administrations. It used all of the influence of the United States — using its economic clout and its role in the International Monetary Fund and the World Bank — to apply pressure in support of such actions.

I can tell you this: no other US administration used so much influence or brought so much pressure to bear to obtain an agreement. It mobilized all of its NATO allies without exception — all of them. I know that some of the NATO governments weren't happy about it, because they didn't want that institution to be used for such a political maneuver. Eventually, however, they fell into line with the position of the United States. It obtained the more-or-less-willing support of some Third World governments that are entirely dependent on the United States. It did everything it could to break down the resistance, yet, in spite of that tremendous effort, it failed to achieve its goal.

It must be said that the Latin American governments set an example of dignity and national independence such as wasn't possible and wasn't even to be dreamed of in the era of the Alliance for Progress and the Playa Girón [Bay of Pigs] invasion. Latin America gave proof of its independence. Of course, this is a process that is advancing.

Earlier proof of this was shown at the time of the Malvinas crisis, when Latin America closed ranks with Argentina, even though it had a government that nobody accepted; but the other

Latin American countries stood by Argentina, the Argentinian people, in their claim to the Malvinas. The NATO countries sided to a greater or lesser degree with Britain, and the United States sided with it completely.

Now, there was another alignment of this kind, with all of the Latin American governments except Costa Rica — which voted against Cuba for obvious reasons of unbearable pressure by the United States — standing up to the US maneuver. It was something historic and quite amazing. The Brazilian government abstained, but most of the countries voted against the US proposal.

The US administration was mendacious because it lied unscrupulously. This administration has been characterized by lies, as we have said for a long time.

When it invaded Grenada, it issued many incredible lies; in its dirty war against Nicaragua, it has based itself on lies; all of its international policy is based on lies. It orchestrated a show in Geneva. It took those individuals — you mentioned Valladares and Menoyo — who are naked instruments of the United States, and it even took an individual who had lost a leg and had committed a crime, presenting him as someone who had lost a leg in prison. It turned Valladares into a US citizen — I don't know if it made Menoyo a US citizen, too — and it took them there as part of a delegation to lodge accusations against Cuba. But the attempt failed. No matter how powerful that empire may be, no matter how great its influence may be, it couldn't manufacture a lie of that kind, even though I know that there are people — many of them — who were confused as a result of that kind of campaign against Cuba.

Gianni Minà: Regarding this, I wanted to ask you a more precise question for our European audience and readers. Reliable sources state that the United States will do everything they can to get Cuba denounced for human rights violations. Why are there still conditions in Cuba that enable the United States to hope that they can achieve this goal? More succinctly, why are there still political prisoners in Cuba?

Fidel Castro: The conditions exist because the United States created them. It has made enormous efforts and invested many resources in all of the campaigns against the Cuban revolution, in which it has also had support from the reactionary sectors in Europe. We know what is going on in France, Spain and many other countries in which most of the press is rightist. It is often hard to find even one left newspaper, and the rightist press has a very determined, very clearly defined and very categorical position against the left, against the revolutionary movement. And, in general, those agencies have echoed the United States' campaigns against Cuba. That is, it has created an atmosphere, and insisted a thousand times in its lies and calumny, using fascist methods.

Hitler, too, made many people in Europe believe his theory of a superior race. Hitler always disguised his actions by surrounding them with lies and seeking pretexts. After invading Poland, he dressed up a few prisoners as Polish soldiers and murdered them; he always manufactured pretexts for all his adventures. I think that Europe knows this very well, since these means have been used many times to create certain states of mind.

Now, what can I say? What should I say? I say this honestly, with absolute sincerity. I would venture to speak with anybody about all these problems and to discuss them, because there is no other precedent in the history of the world, no other example of faithfulness to principles comparable to the Cuban revolution. It may well be the only revolutionary process in the world — and I know history — that never used violence against a prisoner, against a detainee. All of those slander campaigns accuse us of employing torture in our prisons. There was not a single case of a prisoner who was tortured, neither after the triumph of the revolution nor in our war of liberation — not even when anyone could have used the pretext of needing to obtain military information so as to save his own troops or to win a battle. Not a single case. There were hundreds of prisoners, and then thousands, before the war ended. You could look up the names of all of them; and not even one of those hundreds and thousands of prisoners was humiliated or even insulted. Nearly always, we set those prisoners free. That helped us to win the war, because it gave us great prestige, great authority in the eyes of the enemy soldiers. They trusted us. In the beginning, none of them surrendered; but by the end, they surrendered en masse.

Our revolution was carried out on the basis of a series of ideas and values, on the basis of awakening the people to oppose crime and torture. Our people were educated in this way and I think that one of the factors that has determined the success of the revolution and its ability to stand firm is its loyalty to principles.

Therefore, I can state something that I don't know if any other revolutionary process in the world can declare: not even once has there been a case of a prisoner being tortured or murdered in our country. And, of course, there have not been, in the history of the revolution, any cases of prisoners disappearing or anything such as that. This policy has been upheld with complete loyalty, without any exceptions at all. There isn't even one exception!

Something more: Cuba is the only country where, in a process such as this, the police have never, in 28 years, been used against the people. There isn't a single case of a people's demonstration being broken up by the police, not even one case of repression against the people in which a dog or tear gas or rubber bullets have been used. We see those things every day in the United States and Europe, against pacifists, strikers and blacks — methods which we have never used in 28 years.

How can this be explained without the people's full consensus and support for the revolution? These are daily occurrences in Europe and in the so-called democratic and super democratic world. Here, that has never been the case. There has never been a state of emergency or state of siege, and order has been maintained in our country. That is conceivable only with the people's support.

What is irritating about such calumny isn't that it attacks the revolutionary government but that it insults our people, because the people are the first not to permit any of the things claimed in that calumny — our people, not the government. The government, the revolution and the leaders of the revolution have played a role in the formation of this consciousness. But it is the people who wouldn't accept it. Go through the streets of the cities of Cuba and in the countryside and ask any citizens if they have ever heard of anyone being tortured or murdered or made to disappear in our country. All those incredible lies are used to slander the revolution.

Let me give you the example of the mercenaries at the Bay of Pigs: 68 hours of intensive combat, more than 100 Cubans killed and hundreds wounded while fighting against mercenaries organized and paid by and at the service of a foreign power who invaded our land within sight of a US fleet — the battles at the Bay of Pigs were fought within sight of a US squadron and aircraft carrier just three miles off-shore. We took around 1,200 prisoners. They didn't surrender in a formal capitulation by means of an agreement or document; they scattered and were captured in groups of two, three, five or 10, by the militia in the hours after the battles.

There wasn't even one case of a prisoner murdered, not even one case of a prisoner who was beaten or pistol-whipped — not even one case! They are there in Miami; you can study them case by case — their statements, what each one of them said. You can go and ask them. Nothing like that happened to even one of them. There was one accident with a small group when they were being taken to the capital — they were brought in closed vehicles — that was lamentable for all, because our people didn't want even one of them to die. The prisoners were our victory.

Now, what army in the world wages a battle against mercenary traitors without even one prisoner being murdered, not even one killed? Has that ever happened in the history of humankind? This is irrefutable proof of the principles in which our fighters are educated, principles that they have taken wherever they go, both here and on internationalist missions. Nobody can speak of even a single case of a prisoner being shot or treated with abuse by a Cuban. Those are the principles taught to our fighters, our people and all of the revolutionaries who are members of the Party.

Those gentlemen speak of torture, while the fact is that the healthiest prisoners in the world are the ones who come out of Cuban prisons. Cases such as Valladares, in perfect health. For years, he pretended to be an invalid. The day we proved to him it was a lie, using a movie we'd taken of him, we told him: OK, as long as you persist in this lie — his real condition had been confirmed scientifically — we can't set you free, in spite of whatever efforts are made and interest shown (for the French government, pressured by the rightist press with campaigns organized in Europe, had already taken an interest in his case). He stood up as soon as he saw the film of himself. Really, he didn't hold out at all when he saw the movie; he stood up and walked out on his own two feet. He did calisthenics every day in prison. All that was a lie, because he was neither an invalid nor a poet. Much of the literary material attributed to Valladares while he was in prison was written for him abroad.

The prisoners in Cuba are the healthiest in the world. They themselves are proof of the respect we have maintained for prisoners' health.

But I'm going to give you an even clearer example: some

prisoners are recalcitrant; they refuse to obey the rules or to wear prison uniforms. They have been there for years. In what other prisons in the world can a prisoner have the right not to obey the rules or not to wear a prison uniform? We prefer to accept that lack of discipline rather than employ physical violence. This is one more irrefutable proof that physical violence is not employed in our prisons. I wonder if that is so in the United States or Europe or anywhere else in the world.

We prefer to accept that rather than violate our principle of not using physical violence. We trained ourselves to reject and detest all manifestations of violence against prisoners in our struggle against the dictatorship, and we have upheld that principle, which took us to victory, ever since.

I think that history will record the truth, because a lie that big would be shown up. I think it was Lincoln who said that you can fool all of the people some of the time — we might apply this to world public opinion — but not all of the time.

Gianni Minà: In Cuba, where the least bloody revolution of the modern era took place almost three decades ago, there are still political adversaries who are imprisoned in the same conditions as the terrorists paid by the CIA. Why?

Fidel Castro: I don't accept the idea that anyone has been imprisoned because he is a political adversary, because all of the "political prisoners" have been convicted of having engaged in activities against the socialist state, against the revolution, of having broken the law. Nobody has been imprisoned simply because they are a political adversary of the revolution; no one can claim that of themselves. We have and will continue to have counter-revolutionary prisoners. Because as long as our country is harassed and blockaded by the United States; as long as the United States uses every means it can to instigate activities against the revolution; and as long as it doesn't renounce its plans for assassinating the leaders of the revolution, there will be people who will carry out activities against the revolution, and we will have to defend ourselves.

It isn't just in Cuba that activities are carried out against the state. I might ask you Italians or the French or the Spanish: "Why, after so many centuries and after so many decades, in highly developed countries with high standards of living and considerable resources, are there activities against the state?" In Spain, there are activities against the state every day, for one reason or another, and many people are in prison there, serving terms of dozens of years — in democratic Spain, in Western Europe.

I don't know how many prisoners there are in Italy; you should know that better than I, but there are dozens of prisoners serving terms of scores of years. If I'm not mistaken, they have prison terms of 30, 40, 50 — I don't know how many — years for activities against the system, for activities against the state. There are cases in Germany and France, too. And what happened in Sweden, a peaceful, neutral country? The Prime Minister was assassinated. The guilty parties haven't yet been captured, but that doesn't make it any less of an activity against the state of Sweden.

Now, why should it be strange that, in a radical revolution such as ours, which adversely affected many interests and is hated by the United States — which is doing everything in its power, using its radio stations every day, to promote activities against the Cuban socialist state, encouraging such activities and giving their perpetrators hope — such activities should take place, leading to sanctions against those crimes? This is the situation that exists and will continue to exist, because we have defended ourselves and are ready to go on doing so.

Whenever possible, we have been merciful and generous; the best proof of this was the way we treated the Bay of Pigs mercenaries: they were imprisoned for barely a year and a half, and then a ship took them to the United States as "heroes." Few others have been as generous as we have.

Our laws were tough; they weren't weak. They were promulgated when we were in the Sierra Maestra, and everyone was informed about them; they were the laws of the revolutionary movement, of the incipient revolutionary state, under which we later punished war crimes. The punishments were severe and included the death penalty or long years of imprisonment, depending on the nature of the crime. All of the individuals were punished only after irrefutable proof was presented in trials.

We've had hundreds of such prisoners. Why are most of them free? Because the revolution is generous. The United States didn't take any interest in the people who were imprisoned for having committed crimes under the dictatorship, but it took an interest in those who acted under US orders and were organized by the United States, because it felt morally more committed to them, to the CIA agents.

We have tried war criminals under laws issued prior to their crimes; Europe tried war criminals without any prior laws. The war criminals were judged and condemned at Nuremberg — and I'm not criticizing this, because they committed many crimes — under laws that didn't exist prior to their crimes; they were tried and punished. Some of them were hanged — and, really, they deserved it — and others were sentenced to life imprisonment. Some of them are still imprisoned, and more are being sentenced every year, whenever a Gestapo agent or criminal is discovered.

Klaus Barbie is being tried in France right now. More than 40 years have passed since the war; his crimes haven't been written off, because there isn't any statute of limitations on the crimes committed by war criminals.

France considers that it is fully entitled to try and punish Barbie, even though more than 40 years have passed; I don't know what punishment he will be given. But our right to defend ourselves — to try and punish war criminals, CIA spies, people who want to destroy the revolution and those who commit acts of sabotage that cause loss of life and property — is disputed.

The whole purpose of that US campaign is to guarantee impunity for the mercenaries who commit crimes in its service. Our right is disputed, and a terrorist is turned into a human rights case, yet there are people accused of terrorism in all the European countries.

Just imagine what it would be like if a huge campaign were to be launched in Latin America tomorrow in favour of Klaus Barbie, the Lyon war criminal! I think the French would feel very insulted and indignant, as would everybody else who denounced fascism. In Cuba, however, individuals who have engaged in treason — for example, there's the case of Menoyo, who invaded this country with arms in hand, sent by the United States — are supposed to be given every consideration, and we are told to be generous. Valladares was convicted of having engaged in acts of terrorism. If you want, I can tell you about Valladares, tell you just who he was.

Gianni Minà: Let's talk about Valladares. As an invalid poet, he tried to present his story on French and Italian television but wasn't very convincing. He seemed more like a man manipulated by someone as part of a campaign. But in Europe people don't understand why somebody like Valladares received a 25-year prison sentence.

Fidel Castro: The only reason Valladares deserves the importance we are giving him is because, simply, he has been turned into one of the key tools in the US government's campaign against Cuba. He is manipulated by the CIA, and not just now — he has been manipulated ever since he was sentenced. Knowing that we were going to talk about these unavoidable topics, I asked for some old newspapers. I'm going to go back to the period when Valladares was tried and sentenced and show you some interesting things.

This is a copy of the December 30, 1960, issue of *Revolución*. Here are two headlines: "Bomb Factory Seized" and "17 Terrorists Arrested." The text says, "A large amount of gelatinous dynamite made in the United States, plus arms and considerable supplies, were seized. Several groups in our capital are being prosecuted." Here are the photos of the dynamite.

The caption reads, "The high explosive power employed has enabled the terrorists to use packs of cigarettes for their attacks." They took the dynamite in packs of cigarettes and threw it in a store or theater, killing people and causing fires and other serious problems.

Gianni Minà: That was in 1960?

Fidel Castro: December 30, 1960.

Gianni Minà: Valladares wasn't yet . . . ?

Fidel Castro: Valladares wasn't yet the great invalid poet of the era.

Gianni Minà: You hadn't yet declared that the revolution was socialist?

Fidel Castro: No, it wasn't yet a socialist revolution. Those terrorist activities were organized mainly by Batista elements. In those early days, the activities were carried out by former policemen and Batista's men, mixed with some counter-revolutionaries who appeared after the triumph of the revolution, because the US government was already working intensively against Cuba. That was four months before the Bay of Pigs invasion; Cuba was already being blockaded economically. The CIA created a lot of organizations; in all, it created around 300 of them — I don't know if I told you this or not — some of which were more important than others.

Gianni Minà: What was the name of that newspaper?

Fidel Castro: *Revolución.* There are some other interesting things here. This is the explanation. "They followed instructions of the US Embassy. A large amount of gelatinous dynamite made in the United States, plus other war supplies, was seized by agents of the Ministry of the Revolutionary Armed Forces' Information Department. In the course of the investigations, which culminated in the arrest of 17 individuals who belonged to terrorist groups . . ." etc. It goes on to say, "Three arms factories were seized; a terrorist attack was planned for the end of the year." Those groups organized it. Note that they were captured on December 30, 1960, a few months before the mercenary invasion. It goes on to list those arrested: "Those arrested" — he's first in the list — "are Armando Valladares, Eduardo Miranda Ortiz, Raúl Sosa . . ." and some more. That is one of the groups.

"In another search, conducted in the grocery store on 35th Street that belongs to Olivero Obregón, a former sergeant in Batista's Navy . . ." There were many Batista elements in this group. The article lists what was seized.

"Also at the house on 88th Street and 3rd Avenue, Alfredo Carrión" — and several more individuals — "leaders of a counter-revolutionary organization that operates out of the United States, were arrested." Now it goes on to explain why they were arrested. It says that live phosphorus was seized on that occasion. And another curious thing: this group of terrorists who were arrested included Carlos Alberto Montaner, a gentleman who writes in Spain. He was arrested and sentenced, and later, thanks to the generosity of the revolution, he was freed.

So, there are the facts. Nobody had heard of Valladares. Valladares was a policeman under Batista. I don't say that he was a henchman or that he committed crimes, and nobody punished Valladares for having been one of Batista's police. Nobody here was punished for having been a functionary or policeman of Batista's. Valladares didn't have any problems; Valladares even got a job in the Ministry of Communications after the triumph of the revolution, as an investigation has shown. He stopped being a policeman and worked in the Ministry of Communications. I think that he was working there when he was arrested for these terrorist activities.

You'll see something interesting. Who was the editor of this newspaper, *Revolución,* when Valladares was arrested? None other than Carlos Franqui. Here it is: "*Revolución,* organ of the July 26 Movement. Editor, Carlos Franqui." This is the December 30, 1960, issue.

Now see what Carlos Franqui wrote at the time — Carlos Franqui, who I think is now a good friend and comrade of Valladares in his counter-revolutionary adventures. This article appeared on December 30.

Gianni Minà: You refer to the tour that Valladares made through Europe to launch his book. Carlos Franqui was his . . .

Fidel Castro: Carlos Franqui was his blindman's guide. On December 31, 1960 —

Gianni Minà: The next day?

Fidel Castro: — an editorial appeared in the newspaper — the editorials were the editor's responsibility — under the heading, "With their Action, the People will Crush the US TNT." It reads as follows: "'High Explosive' reads the label on one of the packages of materials that the Ministry of the Revolutionary Armed Forces' G-2 agents seized from the terrorist groups orchestrated and paid by US imperialism." The editorial, which has some very strong phrases, goes on to say, "In that sinister plan, they didn't even stop to consider the lives of women and children; in their sadism, they wanted to bathe the traditional end-of-year festivities in blood. But the brutal action didn't turn out as planned by the gentlemen of the Pentagon and carried out by the war criminals, mercenaries and cowards who receive their pay in blood-stained dollars."

Then it says, "Unhesitatingly, the people, together with their Revolutionary Government, have mobilized to crush the hyena of imperialist terrorism. In the factories and on the fields, in the workshops and in the offices, in the cities and in the countryside, the people are unanimously calling on their Revolutionary Government to take severe action against the dynamiters paid by the US monopolies, by the enemies of our revolution, by those who hate our homeland."

Revolucion, December 30, 1960

It even says here that this group was directly led by the US Embassy, and Carlos Franqui published an energetic editorial — I'm not going to tell you that he wrote it, because we'll speak of that later, of Carlos Franqui as a writer — that called for the severest punishment, and the penal code states that such crimes can be punished with the death penalty.

So, if the revolution hadn't been generous, if it had applied the punishment established by the law for that kind of crime, Valladares could have been shot. That is what Carlos Franqui was asking to be done in the editorial. This is to introduce you to the historical characters. I don't want to get ahead of your questions or other things that you want to take up in this regard.

Gianni Minà: OK, Valladares is a terrorist and an impostor. But Gustavo Arcos, Hubert Matos . . . . Arcos was a comrade of yours in the attack on the Moncada military garrison, and Hubert Matos fought in the Sierra on your side. In Europe, people say that the three served the same terms. What's the difference?

Fidel Castro: There's a difference: Valladares was a policeman under Batista; he didn't cooperate at all with the revolution. Arcos did cooperate with the revolution, even longer than Hubert Matos; from the beginning. Hubert Matos joined the war around April 1958, the last year of the war. He was in the war for seven or eight months. He had a good cultural level, some training, and I think he had skills as an organizer. In certain battles — that was the period when we were losing cadres — I assigned Hubert Matos the task of making some fortifications, and he made them well. Then, when we had to replace cadres who were killed, I promoted him. It would take too long to go into his characteristics; he was vain and ambitious. At one point, I was even about to remove him from the command of a column — he'd been named head of the column because of our forces' accelerated growth after the enemy's major offensive. I asked him for an explanation of his incorrect attitude in a discussion about some weapons that he shouldn't have had — distribution of weapons among the guerrillas was controlled rigorously, as there were few weapons and many who wanted them, and each column wanted to have more and better weapons. That was discussed later, but I'm telling you about it to give you a general picture of the man.

Hubert Matos did play a role, though it wasn't the one attributed to him later, when he was made out to be one of the big warriors, one of the important cadres of the revolution. He played a role of relative importance, or, rather, of little importance, that wasn't comparable to that of the people who came on the *Granma*, formed the Rebel Army and waged the main battles. What he did devote energy to was blowing his own horn. Wherever there was a radio station, he publicized himself. He took care to express rightist ideas — very anti-communist ideas — almost right from the beginning. That, naturally, won him immediate support in some sectors. The wealthy classes are intelligent and know how each person thinks; they label people rapidly.

That was what Hubert Matos did. When the revolution triumphed, he was the head of a military unit in Camagüey province.

Arcos couldn't come on the expedition because there was a last-minute mistake in the details, and some comrades weren't picked up. He didn't come to the Sierra Maestra, didn't take part in the war in the Sierra Maestra, but he did have a revolutionary background.

What happened with those two people who had been revolutionaries, who had been with the revolution? When the revolution went deeper and became more radical, they began to disagree with the revolution, to oppose it and to act against it.

Hubert Matos wasn't arrested for his opinions — he organized an uprising in Camagüey and was on the point of causing a bloody battle. He even confused some groups of people there, working subtly, using the prestige he had as a military chief in the days just after the triumph of the revolution. He manipulated public opinion that hadn't matured enough, where there were many prejudices against socialism and communism, where the favorite weapon was anti-communism. He began to foment that kind of campaign against the measures that were being taken in the social sphere. Certain bourgeois sectors echoed and supported him, and it is a fact that he organized an uprising. He even talked with a chief of the Central Army, trying to win him over; but that comrade reported what he was doing. He was trying to get people together to carry out an uprising.

There wasn't any uprising, because we stopped it. I stopped the uprising practically by telephone. There was a battalion in Camagüey. He had influenced the chiefs of the regiment, and I instructed a battalion that was doing economic work in the province that it should seize the radio stations, and right after that we denounced the conspiratorial activities. I was there. We didn't mobilize any military forces; it was a conspiracy, and we frustrated it with the masses.

In the morning, I flew to Camagüey. Camilo Cienfuegos went with me. I didn't move any troops. We landed and went to the city, and all the people were waiting there. In order to avoid any bloodshed, I went toward the regiment with the people but without any weapons. That was what happened. They wouldn't have fired on us; I know the moral consequences of such a situation.

But Camilo didn't let me get there while they were armed; he went ahead with a group of three or four. He went to the headquarters and disarmed Hubert Matos and the others. They didn't put up any resistance, but they were obviously on the verge of initiating a bloody battle, which was avoided by the way in which we tackled the problem. Matos's crime was very serious. That had never happened before among the revolutionaries, and it almost happened on that occasion. Those were the reasons for the punishments that were imposed.

That was when Camilo Cienfuegos, who was head of the army, died on his way back to Havana — flying from Camagüey in a small plane during the stormy season. Camilo became lost and disappeared. It may be said that, because of his activities, Hubert Matos was responsible for the death of one of the most beloved cadres of the revolution.

Hubert Matos had a public trial. I went to the trial to give my testimony and publicly discuss his slander and actions. He boasted of being somebody who had ideas, and moreover, that this was a political trial. He didn't even present a defense. He was demoralised, without any political integrity — he didn't even have sufficient to engage in a political discussion of his positions — and was sentenced to prison. The revolution was generous; many people were in favor of more severe punishment.

Gianni Minà: What happened to Arcos?

Fidel Castro: Arcos is another kind of person. Arcos has racist, fascist ideas; that is his philosophy. This became evident after the triumph of the revolution. At that time, Arcos began to conspire against it. He was punished, and, after he was freed, he went on conspiring. Hubert Matos's activities were of another sort, because he was about to cause a bloody confrontation.

Valladares has no revolutionary background; rather, he was a member of one of the counter-revolutionary organizations. Nobody had heard of Valladares, nobody knew who Valladares was; Valladares simply appeared in the group of 17 heading the list of those arrested and was given a stiff sentence, but not that insisted by Carlos Franqui.

What happened concerning Hubert Matos and Valladares? For a long time, there was a huge campaign outside the country about Hubert Matos. We were subjected to pressure, but the revolution has never given in and will never give into pressure. All that nearly became a test of the revolution's morale, the revolution's dignity, its capacity to withstand huge international campaigns. They set about manufacturing the figure of a counter-revolutionary leader and pressuring us to set him free; this was in the period when imperialism was going around looking for figureheads. He served his sentence; when completed, we set him free.

There are few individuals here who have served their sentences in full. At one time, in the early years, there were thousands of prisoners — 5,000, 10,000, close to 15,000 counter-revolutionary prisoners. There were, as I told you, 300 organizations, and, of course, we infiltrated many of those organizations; with popular support, we uncovered and neutralized them. At the Bay of Pigs alone, some 1,200 prisoners were taken in just a few days. How were those people freed? As a result of imperialism's pressure? No, it was thanks to the revolution's generosity.

There were counter-revolutionary bands in all the provinces, and hundreds of people were imprisoned for having taken part in the activities of armed bands — like those in Nicaragua. We had many counter-revolutionary prisoners. That is the truth, and we don't deny it. It was thanks to the revolution's initiatives that the vast majority of those prisoners were released from prison. The vast majority were freed long before completing their sentences — when they had served a third or a half of their terms. Only when they were turned into tools for pressuring the country, when they were turned into "leaders" and figureheads, did the revolution refrain from granting clemency.

Hubert Matos served his full sentence, but Valladares didn't. There were many campaigns and finally the French government — which was also subjected to great pressure — made a rather strong request that we release him. It was the leftist government in France. Régis Debray came here on a visit and told us that the French government's situation was untenable; he practically said that the French government would fall and that it was a great tragedy. In the end, I told him, "But look who this individual is; look what he did. He's a sham and a liar." In fact, as we saw, they made him a tool; he was a fraud. Our doctors proved that it was a lie, that he had no problems; he was one of the healthiest prisoners we've ever had in this country. He walked out on his own two feet, and he did calisthenics every day. I said, "OK, we'll send him to Mitterrand."

We showed him the movie a few days before setting him free. As soon as he saw it, he got up — these are the facts — and walked out on his own two feet. The great myth of the invalid was completely destroyed.

I don't criticize him so much for pretending to be an invalid, because I think that, no matter what a person's motivations are or the reasons for their being in prison, they always try to invent something, to do something. So I don't see anything particularly bad in his trying to pretend; but rather, in his lying, creating a pathetic scene and saying it was because we didn't give him medical care, whereas, within 15 days in Miami, he was immediately cured, thanks to the nobility and excellent medical care of the United States. Really, the only condition we set was that he walk out, abandoning pretence, and that's how he left.

Gianni Minà: At the Havana Prison we filmed the cell in the prison hospital used by Valladares. Both Valladares and Hubert Matos complained about the living conditions they had to put up with for 20 years. What can you say about the things they published about their "living hell in Fidel Castro's jails"?

Fidel Castro: Not even an individual's own home can be good when it is a jail; you can make a cage of gold, and it will always be a cage. I don't think prison is agreeable for anyone, no matter what material conditions it may have. I was in prison.

Gianni Minà: We also filmed the place where you were in prison.

Fidel Castro: I was there for two years, and I had a rebellious attitude. They put me in solitary; they kept me in isolation for many months.

Gianni Minà: They kept you in isolation, alone?

Fidel Castro: Yes, alone. At the beginning, they tried to treat us well, to neutralize us. I maintained a very rebellious attitude as a prisoner, and I was subjected to isolation. That is, I had the inner strength you get from the conviction that you are defending a just cause.

I imagine that counter-revolutionary prisoners have to manufacture a motivation and somehow convince themselves that what they are doing is just. When there isn't such a motivation in fact, I imagine that the prisoners manufacture it. They were the kind of prisoners who refuse to accept discipline, all those things, but they had the same prison conditions as the other prisoners.

The food couldn't be the same as in a tourist hotel, but they had the same things the workers got in the workers' dining rooms. That was what we had, the resources available to us. Of course, there are disciplinary measures; it is true that the prisons have disciplinary measures: visiting privileges can be withdrawn for bad behavior. Often, however, the prisoners' relatives left the country. If an individual refuses to obey the regulations, you aren't going to employ violence to make him do so; if he doesn't want to get dressed, you aren't going to employ violence; you have to use some disciplinary measures, but not violence. They may have had that kind of difficulty. But, when they talk about physical punishment, that's nothing but an outright lie. When they talk about torture, that's nothing but a lie.

Gianni Minà: Hubert Matos spoke of the heat in his cell, that it had a metal roof, saying it was like a Turkish bath.

Fidel Castro: Then how come he was so healthy when he got out, after 20 years in prison? He had good medical attention and good food, and has been organizing counter-revolution for the last 10 years. Not only did we free him, but we let him leave the country; we could have set him free and told him not to leave the country, so imperialism wouldn't have a little counter-revolutionary cadre, a little leader, a "hero" who had survived the revolution's jails. He didn't worry us; he served his term and left. There can be a thousand "heroes" of that kind who are impotent against the revolution. But I was referring to his excellent health when he left prison after serving his term and the activities that he and Menoyo — and all the others who have left — have been carrying out.

You can be sure that no prisoner in US jails has conditions as good as those in Cuban jails. All of the counter-revolutionary prisoners had the right to work and to be paid normal wages for their work. We gave the prisoners the opportunity to work, and they were paid 100 percent of their wages, the same as a worker outside prison. Those who wanted to work did so; nobody was obliged to work — not Hubert Matos or Menoyo or anybody else. They were "personalities"; they'd been turned into personalities by propaganda abroad. But the prisoners even had the right to work.

Compare a US jail — I don't know of those in Europe — with one in Cuba, and you'll see that the treatment here is a thousand times more humane and just than the treatment prisoners get in US jails.

Gianni Minà: Several years ago, the National Guard killed more than 30 prisoners, members of the Black Panther organization, during a supposed rebellion in the prison in Attica, New York.

Fidel Castro: That has never happened here in our prisons; there has never been a case like that. If we make a comparative analysis with the prisons in other countries, I think it will show that no other country has these prison conditions and work possibilities, with prisoners receiving 100 percent of the normal wage for the work they do. You can tour the United States, Europe and Latin America, and I doubt that you'll find a more humane penitentiary system. Now, a prison isn't a tourist hotel; being in prison isn't anything like being on a vacation, in Cuba or anywhere else.

Gianni Minà: On our visit to the Havana Prison, we were very surprised to see that the prison guards aren't armed. Now, I'd like to ask you something else: how many political prisoners does Cuba still have?

Fidel Castro: You ask me all the questions, even the ones I don't usually answer. I'm not going to tell you the exact figure, because I'd have to make a phone call and ask, "Hey, how many prisoners are there for counter-revolutionary activities?" But I will say that around 800 individuals are in prison now for having carried out counter-revolutionary activities of greater or lesser importance; there are a few dozen in for serious crimes, serving long terms for crimes committed under the dictatorship, but there aren't many of them, because we've been setting them free. There are a few dozen undisciplined prisoners, who have refused to obey the regulations, and there are some others who are in for more recent but less important activities.

When Carter was president, there were around 3,000, and we set more than 2,000 free. But individuals still keep getting sent to prison; there are people who enter the country along the coast, sent by counter-revolutionary organizations in the United States to engage in sabotage or attempt to carry out assassination, and we have to arrest, sentence and punish them. There are people who try to hijack a plane — an attempt was made not long ago — and drop a bomb among the passengers; they even hurt and kill people, and we must punish some of them. There are people who receive instructions every day to engage in sabotage against the economy. Others engage in espionage — the CIA recruits them from among the Cubans who go for family visits and then return; there aren't many of them, but the United States recruits some of them through its agents. What should we do with a spy when we find him? We have to punish him. And so, over the years, they have accumulated.

I can give you some more information on this. Some of these prisoners who have been here the longest and who still have many years of their terms to serve, especially the ones who are imprisoned for having committed crimes during Batista's era and some of those who received heavy sentences for being CIA spies and engaging in acts of terrorism — how has their freedom been arranged? Representatives of the US churches have even intervened (a representative of the Catholic Church was here a short while ago), and we have systematically followed a policy of releasing them before they have served their full terms. We told the representatives of the churches, "Alright, if you obtain visas for the following prisoners, we're willing to set them free." We make a selection, keeping in mind their age, time served and length of term. But we must be careful, because they go to the United States and begin to organize activities against Cuba again when we set them free — in our act of generosity. They may infiltrate Cuba along our coasts, and it may cost the life of a compatriot of ours. And who would be responsible? We would.

We were opposed to setting Menoyo free, because he was the head of Alfa 66, a counter-revolutionary organization that still operates in the United States. Sometimes you set those counter-revolutionaries free and they carry out terrorist attacks, such as the one against the plane near Barbados, which cost the lives of more than 70 people. Some of the members of that organization were in prison; mercenaries from the Bay of Pigs intervened there. Some of those counter-revolutionaries go to Nicaragua to train mercenaries and wage the dirty war; they go to El Salvador and commit other crimes of that nature. So we have to think not only about ourselves but also about other countries when we set free a dangerous counter-revolutionary of that kind, because they go, at the service of the CIA, to engage in counter-revolution in other countries. We have no reason to be generous with them at the cost of others.

We follow these criteria in deciding which prisoners to free before they've served their full terms. We don't choose the most dangerous cases, those who, in our opinion, are very dangerous and may be useful to the enemy. But, talking with a representative of the Church who visited us recently and brought lists of requests, I told him that we were ready to free several hundred of those counter-revolutionary prisoners if the Church could get visas for them. This has already been done several times. Why? For example, in the case of a prisoner who committed crimes in the Batista era, it's very difficult to send him back to the town he came from, among the relatives of his victim or where a school or a factory has been named after his victim. It isn't easy.

The people oppose the counter-revolutionary elements; it isn't easy to find work for them, to place them in jobs. So we told the Church people, "If you get visas and jobs for them, we'll send them to the United States." And, not long ago, we sent the Catholic Church of the United States lists of those we were willing to free. The Church is working on several problems, not only that of the prisoners, but also that of reuniting families and other similar humanitarian problems.

I like to talk with representatives of the churches, because they aren't political; they don't go in for politicking and aren't demagogues. I wouldn't talk about these things with US government officials, but I do with Church representatives, for they have a constructive position, a sincere concern about human matters. In addition, they have what I consider a correct position on the issues of peace, underdevelopment and poverty. In my opinion, the US churches have progressive positions, and I prefer to deal with their representatives than with those of the US government — they constitute a moral force in the United States, it's easy to talk with them, and they have an interest in some of these problems.

Gianni Minà: President Castro, to conclude with this topic, which is a sensitive one for you . . . .

Fidel Castro: It's true, I may get a bit worked up when I talk about these things.

Gianni Minà: I'd like to take up another delicate subject. In 1980, thousands of Cubans wanted to leave for the United States through Mariel after having forced their way into and occupying the Peruvian Embassy in Cuba. People say that, among those who left, you also sent a large number of criminals and social misfits who were in jail or mental clinics. How did the matter end with the United States? Who rejected these people? Is all this true?

Fidel Castro: This had its origins in several factors.

Throughout these years, the United States' policy has been to deny visas to those who want to move there. Its initial policy was to take away our doctors and administrators, taking as many people as it could away from the country. It opened its doors wide in the beginning, and many people left — some because they didn't like socialism or the revolution (the wealthy, large landowners, owners of large blocks of real estate and members of the bourgeoisie) and others who were professionals and wanted to leave. We always opened our doors and accepted the challenge.

There were other people who wanted to go to the United States because they thought only about their own personal interests and were drawn by the propaganda about its standard of living. That happened not only in Cuba but all over the world. In Latin America, millions of Mexicans, Venezuelans, Colombians, Haitians, Peruvians and Dominicans — people from all of the Latin American countries — have gone in one way or another to the United States to look for work, and the United States closed its doors to them as much as possible. When the revolution triumphed, the United States opened its doors wide to everybody who wanted to leave Cuba, and we said that anybody who wanted to leave should do so, for we uphold the principle that the construction of socialism is the task of free men who want to make a new society. The United

States opened its doors and took in tens of thousands. Later, those who already left urged through their propaganda for others to leave. Many families were separated. That is a fact.

Then, during the October Missile Crisis, the United States stopped granting visas and fomented illegal departures, because they served as propaganda material. Whenever anybody stole a boat and left, they received a lot of publicity.

That led us to say, "If you don't patrol your coasts, we aren't going to do it for you. And if you don't take measures against those who leave illegally, breaking the law — since you don't want to give them legal permission — we're going to authorize people to come get them." We'd already done that some years ago, and the Cubans living in the United States — who, it seems, aren't very disciplined and have great confidence in the word of the revolution — sent hundreds of boats to Camarioca and picked up many of their relatives. That led to an agreement, by virtue of which the US government allowed a number of Cubans to go to the United States. Time passed, and the United States shut its doors again. For years, it prohibited legal entry there but fomented illegal departures and accepted people who arrived illegally. That happened for a second time.

We have a policy of open doors: anyone who wants to travel may do so, though sometimes we impose some restrictions. If it's a specialist and there isn't anybody to take his place, we say, "OK, but you have to wait until we have a cadre to take your place." It depends on the work he is doing. Doctors have had to wait a while, because we have our medical program. We have some restrictions of this kind, but no hard-and-fast prohibitions on leaving. The rule is to maintain an open door for those who want to emigrate and travel.

Many families were divided in that period. Then problems arose in some embassies, caused by the demagogy of politicians. If an individual went to a Latin American embassy and requested a visa for traveling, they wouldn't give it to him. But if the individual forced his way in and made a scandal, then, yes, they gave him a visa. This happened at the embassies of some countries.

Several times, we decided, "Alright, we're going to end this problem and give those people permission to leave." But every time attempts to leave this way were successful, the same thing was immediately repeated, and we were conscious that this stimulated illegal departures.

Who were they? They weren't people with political problems; they were people who wanted to emigrate, to be with their families, or lumpen elements. There is always some lumpen element, some person who refuses to accept social discipline, who likes to sponge on others, criminals or people who like gambling and other such activities. All over the world there are people who don't want to work and who hate discipline — in our country, as well. The confrontation with the United States has encouraged such people. Any criminal, lumpen element, or classless person who wants to go to the United States — because it's the paradise of gambling, prostitution, drugs, etc. and because of the stories they have heard — gets into an embassy and says they can't stand communism.

We told those governments, "Give them permission. We don't oppose their going, but we can't give them permission if they use force to enter." This had happened in various embassies, and it was happening in the Peruvian Embassy: a group forced its way in. We urged the Peruvians not to encourage those actions, because those people didn't have any problems and should be sent home, where they would have full guarantees, and they did that. But, because of pressures in their own country — it's the same old story of the rightist press accusing the government of being weak — after sending them home, they asked them to come back, and back they came. We told the Embassy people that they were responsible for what was happening.

A few days later, trying to force their way in, a few individuals caused an accident that resulted in the death of a policeman, and then we said, "OK, it's your responsibility. We can't risk the lives of our men while you maintain a policy of encouraging acts of violence." And we removed the guards from the Embassy.

We knew what would happen, of course, just as we knew what would happen at the time of the Camarioca departures when we said, "Come and get them . . ." Everybody came to collect friends and relatives, because they believed what the revolution said.

Many of those elements, declassed people and lumpen elements, saw that as the opportunity they'd been waiting for to go to the United States — none of them wanted to go to Haiti, Santo

Domingo, Colombia, Central America or even Peru. No, they wanted to go to the United States, to their friends and relatives there, to their image of the US and its consumer society. So we removed the guards. Those people knew the revolution, trusted the word of the revolution and knew the revolution's laws, and thousands of those elements went there, into the Peruvian Embassy. There were nearly 10,000 of them and they filled the Embassy. We told the Peruvians, "Well, there you have the consequences. Now you solve the problem." That's what we told the Peruvian government, a military government that was in cahoots with the oligarchy: "Now you solve the problem. Do you want them? Fine, now welcome them there . . ." We said that everybody who wanted to leave had permission to do so. But Peru found that it couldn't take in 10,000 of those elements — it accepted around 1,000, who have been causing it headaches for years.

When that happened, it was given a lot of publicity, and Carter said that the 10,000 would be welcomed with open arms. We were delighted, and we gave them all exit passes. We told them, "You can return to your homes; you won't have any problems, for we'll give you passports so you can leave."

We warned the United States what was happening. The United States turned it into a great publicity stunt, saying that we didn't authorize them to leave. When the US said that they would be welcomed with open arms, we said, "Fine, we're ready to authorize them to go to the United States, and their relatives can collect them." It was logical that from that moment dozens — hundreds — of boats came with their relatives to collect those people, some of whom were in the Peruvian Embassy, and some other relatives. We stated that those who wanted to go, could — first of all, many of those from the Peruvian Embassy.

When a study was made of all those people, none of them had any political problems. There were many criminals who had earlier been released from jail and were free, but who had committed crimes. We told them, "Don't be mistaken: they aren't dissidents, they're criminals. The vast majority of these people are lumpen elements." We said, "Yes, we'll give passports to those who want to go to the United States." And we gave them passports, and tens of thousands of them went to the United States. Naturally, who were the ones who left? Were they university professors or skilled workers? It was the lumpen elements who left that way.

Afterwards, campaigns were launched. Then the United States realized that the people it was receiving weren't patriots or dissidents but were irresponsible, antisocial adventurers. I don't say that all were like that, but most of them. We gave them all permission to leave.

Then came the different theories: that we had sent murderers, mental patients, etc.

Gianni Minà: Drug addicts . . .

Fidel Castro: I tell you out of respect for the country and domestic security — not only as an ethical matter and basic respect for the US people — we couldn't send murderers there. That theory is utterly false. There may have been a few who had committed crimes of violence. Some of those who left were former prisoners, but they weren't sent deliberately.

Perhaps the worst accusation was their saying that we had sent mental patients. Our country has too much respect for the sick — and has made too many efforts to help the sick — to send them to the United States. To do so would be absurd. This is one of the few countries where the mentally ill are cured. Our mental hospitals set an example in the world and are admired by all visitors who come here and see them. It was utterly inconceivable that we would send mental patients to the United States — it's a lie that our people would agree to use the sick and send them there.

When we had the discussions about the migratory agreements, we told the US government that they should tell us what patients had left — that they should name even one case — and they couldn't name even one mentally ill person who had been in hospital and had gone there. Among all the people who went with their families or were claimed by their relatives, there may have been one or two cases of mentally retarded people, but there wasn't even one case of a mentally ill patient leaving a hospital.

We told them, "Tell us about the murderers, the people punished for having committed crimes of violence; how many are there?" There were a few cases of people who had committed earlier crimes of violence, a few cases — six or seven of them — mixed in with the lumpen elements. An insignificant number, and not even one mental patient. We told the US government to send them to us with their records; to tell us how many were mentally ill. They didn't even find one. All of those charges were false.

But lumpen elements did go, along with thieves and other people of that sort, people who wanted a consumer society. They went of their own free will. We didn't send them. When they saw the opportunity, they left.

Gianni Minà: Did any of them return?

Fidel Castro: Later, when they saw the reality, many felt deceived and wanted to come back, but the people didn't want them to return. It wasn't even easy to reach an agreement, because the US authorities wanted over 2,000 to return, as some of them were stealing planes and boats in which to come back. We said that in exceptional cases, some of those who left may return; but in order to do so, they must have authorization. The US authorities had a list, which we accepted around 2,700 people who wanted to return. With that migratory agreement, a family reunification program was drawn up. Many former counter-revolutionary prisoners — the ones who were in the streets — and their relatives, could go to the United States as part of a family reunification program. An annual quota of 20,000 other citizens was part of this agreement, in line with certain categories of people who had that right according to US law.

There will always be some people here — irresponsible adventurers and former prisoners — who will want to go to the United States. Many of those who go of their own volition and subsequently welcomed as heroes, are lumpen elements. My view was, "This has now happened twice. If you don't look to your laws and guard your coasts, you can't expect us to take measures here to uphold US laws and to protect US coasts." That's what I said.

All this is still to be discussed. Those agreements were suspended when suddenly, without any advance notice, and with only 24 hours' warning, the United States started broadcasting through its subversive, anti-Cuban station which — insulting our people — it called José Martí. It's as if a radio station in a country that is Italy's enemy were to be called Garibaldi — a station created "to inform and guide" Italians. That was what the United States did.

We declared that we weren't opposed to their broadcasting to Cuba, but we claim our right to broadcast to the United States. We have stations that can reach all of the United States, and we have suggested that we discuss this.

We told the United States that the agreement that we made can be renewed if a technical formula is sought for our broadcasting to all of the United States. We don't use interference, but we claim our rights. Since they want to debate and polemicize, we'll broadcast to all of the United States. I had also spoken about this problem with the representatives of the Church in the United States. As regards the divided families, we explained that we weren't opposed to their leaving. We aren't the ones who don't want them to go.

I also said this to a French journalist from *L'Humanité* who asked about it. I said, "No, we're not the ones; Cuba's doors are open for all who wish to leave. It's the United States that doesn't give them permission to travel, while fomenting illegal departures."

This is what I can tell you about this matter, with precise and reliable data.

Gianni Minà: The ones who want to return from the United States now — do they feel deceived because they didn't find the paradise they'd expected?

Fidel Castro: Many people wanted to return, but we don't accept them. We accept family reunification there, not here, because the United States has more resources than Cuba. We don't have enough housing. We have to construct housing for the workers and those newly married. If we were to agree to having 10,000 families return, there would be 10,000 fewer houses available. We would have to take them away from the workers who are struggling here to help their country advance. We accept the principle of reunification, but it must be there. Reunification can be here only in exceptional cases, when the people who return have housing waiting for them and those problems are solved. We can't accept a massive influx of returnees, because we don't have enough housing for those families. We must give priority to the workers, to those who are working for their country here — not those who left and went to the United States.

Gianni Minà: You very briefly mentioned an episode that was tragic but about which very little is known in Italy and the rest of Europe. In 1976, a Cubana Airlines plane en route from Caracas to Havana exploded in mid-flight because of a bomb placed on board by counter-revolutionary elements during a stopover on the island of Barbados. Many people were killed in that attack, including all the members of Cuba's junior fencing team. When such an action as this is carried out, what do you think is the purpose behind it? Why haven't other, similar attacks taken place?

Fidel Castro: It was a monstrous thing to do. Just remembering it makes one mad. All members of the junior fencing team, who had won the gold medals in a Pan American competition, were killed along with the other passengers. They included some foreigners: Koreans and Guyanese.

Gianni Minà: I was here the day you spoke in Revolution Square, and I filmed the funeral ceremony. It is a truly tragic memory.

Fidel Castro: It was something that shocked our people. The plane flew from Caracas to Trinidad and Tobago. It was a plane we had rented from Canada using one of our crews.

Gianni Minà: The crew members were Cubans?

Fidel Castro: Cubans.

The plane landed in Trinidad and Tobago, and the two men who carried out the act of sabotage — two Venezuelans — boarded, prepared the bomb, and left the plane in Barbados. They boarded the plane and then got off it. Soon after the plane took off from Barbados the bomb exploded and the tragedy took place. The pilot tried to return. Over the radio he reported that there was fire and smoke. He made a superhuman effort to return — the whole conversation was taped — and then the plane plunged into the sea, killing everyone on board.

The two individuals who had set the bomb returned to Trinidad. It seemed that the authorities noted something suspicious and arrested them. Two Cubans, prominent counter-revolutionaries, had sent those two Venezuelans to carry out the act of sabotage.

Gianni Minà: Their names?

Fidel Castro: Orlando Bosch and Luis Posada Carriles. They were CIA agents. They had worked for the CIA and even had relations with Pinochet in Chile. They were quite well-known terrorist elements. They had an office in the Venezuelan capital and organized it all from Caracas. Carlos Andrés Pérez was president and arrested them and put them on trial. The fair thing would have been to send them to the country that had been their victim or perhaps to put them on trial where they committed the crime. But the Venezuelans claimed jurisdiction and tried them.

It must be said that Carlos Andrés Pérez upheld a firm position in that case, demanding that justice be done.

But some of those Cubans worked with a collaborator named Uzcátegui, a Venezuelan who had been in the Christian-Social-Democratic government (it has another name, but it's the same thing). One of them — Posada Carriles, who worked for the CIA — had also worked in the Venezuelan political police. He had close ties with the man who had been chief of that institution. When there was a change of government, Uzcátegui once again had an important position and made a great effort to clean the record and destroy the evidence against Bosch and Posada. A great effort was made, and an arbitrary trial was held in which they were declared innocent. Cuba made an energetic protest, and relations were nearly broken. The verdict was appealed and taken to other courts. They took it to the military court again, and it was there for a long time. It was a scandalous, sordid process in which the CIA worked through some of those characters, such as Uzcátegui, to clear those individuals of all blame.

Not only that. One of them, Posada Carriles, managed to escape, helped by the US government and the CIA. They sent large amounts of money to Venezuela and bribed a lot of people until they enabled Posada Carriles to escape and then go abroad. When did we hear of him again? Recently, when the Nicaraguans shot down a plane that was transporting arms for the counter-revolution, they captured a crew member named Hasenfus, who talked and explained how the supply of arms was organized from El Salvador. Among the people who were there, he identified Posada Carriles, working with the CIA in El Salvador sending supplies to the counter-revolution.

When we denounced the fact that the CIA had taken part in the sabotage of the Cuban plane, it seemed unfounded. We presented as evidence the information we had. It was necessary to use one of our agents who had infiltrated the CIA to show proof of its activities in those acts of terrorism.

A few years later, one of those primarily responsible for the crime appeared in El Salvador working for the CIA, protected by the United States.

Bosch is still in prison. A lot of evidence has been destroyed and a lot of money changed hands. And, even though I know that the

Venezuelan government is concerned about all this, nobody knows what is going to happen. There are many reports saying that the verdict absolving Bosch has already been written, and also that the two Venezuelans are going to be punished with Orlando Bosch acquitted for lack of evidence. That news is known all over, and there are reports that a residence is being prepared for him in Miami. That is the situation.

Really, all kinds of tricks, machinations and bribes have been used to ensure that the crime will go unpunished. One of the two people who were mainly responsible for it escaped, and the other, according to reports, is about to be absolved.

Gianni Minà: What nationality are Bosch and Posada Carriles?

Fidel Castro: Cuban. They were born in Cuba, trained by the CIA in the United States and worked for the CIA — more "heroes" of the counter-revolution who have killed dozens of people — and there is a monstrous possibility that they will be absolved.

I'm not criticizing the Venezuelan government. The current president of Venezuela has an honest attitude toward this problem. It isn't something that's in his hands, but rather those of the courts. Carlos Andrés has always opposed those individuals being absolved, because he knew all the facts — he saw all the records and all the evidence. Later, efforts were made to destroy all traces of what happened.

Gianni Minà: President Castro, one more detail before we move to another topic. When you spoke of those tragic days of the terrorist attack off Barbados, you said that the CIA's best agent in Cuba was, in fact, a faithful supporter and cadre of the revolution.

Fidel Castro: It was a very serious case, and we wanted to present the evidence we had of the CIA's plans. That evidence came from exchanges of information between the CIA and the agent on subjects the CIA requested. Because of the importance of the case we had to use that evidence to support our denunciation. It is true that we sacrificed the cover of an agent who had been an important source of information. We have had to do that possibly more than once, sacrificing what we might call operational advantages or sources of information in order to prove a point. That has always happened.

The loss of those *compañeros* was irreparable. More than a

million people gathered in Revolution Square to denounce that crime.

Gianni Minà: I remember.

Fidel Castro: There was tremendous indignation. It was a moment of national shock that is still fresh in people's minds. That was why we decided to use that agent.

Gianni Minà: How many other times, over the years, have you responded to this kind of provocation?

Fidel Castro: Well, there is no response to those acts of provocation. What response could there be? Are we going to take reprisals against someone, against the people of the United States? It isn't conceivable that we do that. In this case, our response was essentially political, denouncing the crime before international public opinion. That was what we did; it was a political response. But there is no possible reparation for such actions, the deaths of those innocent people.

1. A few weeks following this interview, Orlando Bosch was released by a Venezuelan court. Bosch was subsequently placed on trial in the United States but acquitted by a Miami court in July 1990.

Fidel Castro with Maurice Bishop of Grenada and Daniel Ortega of Nicaragua, May Day, 1980

Chapter 3

Defense and diplomacy

Foreign policy is certainly one of Fidel's passions — one so strong that it offers his adversaries the possibility of attempting to draw out supposed contradictions. Discussion is generated by the revolution's capacity over more than three decades to confront the United States, the most powerful nation in the world, and its allegiance to the Soviet Union, even underlined in the Constitution. But Cuban foreign policy also highlights the role of Cuba in the region: Fidel was the first statesman to declare that Latin America would be unable to pay its foreign debt under the present international economic conditions.

Fidel took up these foreign policy issues well into the night. Right from the beginning it became apparent that the passage of time has given the revolutionary a diplomatic streak I hadn't expected. He dropped this stance and employed sarcasm only during a few moments when referring to Ronald Reagan's strategies.

Fidel is very well-informed about everything that goes on in the world and is up-to-date on nearly all events and their interpretation. He makes no mystery of this: "Every day I receive and read hundreds of cables from all over the world and try to interpret what lies behind the words. This frequently takes me all morning." But Fidel's foreign policy is much more subtle and pragmatic. Confirming his role as a leader of the Third World, Fidel not only has over 1,000 Cuban doctors on missions in the poorest countries, but also receives 22,000 students from Latin America, Africa and Asia — of these 16,000 are on the Isle of Youth, where we went to film. The same is true at the cinema school of San Antonio de los Baños, where those from Cuba join students from Namibia, India, the Cameroons and Mexico, to qualify as directors, scriptwriters, cinematographers and sound technicians.

A good part of the future ruling classes of those countries will be grateful to the Cuban revolution.

This too is foreign policy.

G.M.

Gianni Minà: President Castro, speaking of foreign policy with you inevitably means talking about the United States . . .

Fidel Castro: I'd like to tell you something. The various US administrations have always tried to create an unfavorable image of the Cuban revolution. This was to stem the influence of revolutionary ideas, knowing that very favorable objective conditions for the revolutionary movement existed in Latin America. For this reason, they have made tremendous efforts to isolate Cuba, adopting measures to blockade our economy and managing to coerce all the Latin American countries — with the exception of Mexico — to support a policy of blockade and isolation. From the start this has all been accompanied by great propaganda campaigns against the Cuban revolution.

It was the same with the revolution of Arbenz in Guatemala and with the Mexican revolution in the era of Lázaro Cárdenas when they said terrible things only because he had nationalized oil. Later it did the same against the Sandinista revolution — in fact, against all revolutions.

Kennedy inherited Eisenhower's policy. The invasion plans to destroy the revolution had already been agreed upon even before the revolution became socialist. The most important measure we had taken had been the agrarian reform. Other measures included the confiscation of the unlawful gains of embezzlers, the reduction of electricity and telephone rates, the law governing rents and the urban reform. But it wasn't yet a socialist program. Kennedy therefore inherited the plan of action of Eisenhower and Nixon and with some misgiving and hesitation he put it into effect — bringing about the mercenary invasion of the Bay of Pigs, which ended in defeat. People call that the first great defeat of US imperialism in the Americas.

Gianni Minà: Why did Kennedy back out at the last moment?

Fidel Castro: Although Kennedy was having some doubts, he went ahead with the plan. He had believed the CIA evaluation of the situation. He accepted the wisdom of the Pentagon and CIA, and their military expertise and professionalism. He had believed the propaganda and was convinced that the people would join the mercenaries and invaders. He thought that the militias wouldn't put up much resistance and would turn their arms against the government. He had believed all that, even though his strategy, which I have studied very carefully, did not reflect this theory. They had chosen an isolated place, cut off from the rest of Cuban territory by a large swamp which made it difficult to maneuver. It was very difficult to counter-attack, since the only access was along two highways crossing 10 kilometers of swamp. It created a kind of pass of Thermopylae where it was impossible to attack from the flanks. They counted on total air domination. They had bombed our planes — the few we had — at their bases with a surprise attack and using Cuban identification markings. They did all that, but the cause of their defeat was to underestimate the people.

Kennedy vacillated. Let's not forget that his administration had only just begun. He was afraid of the consequences of a confrontation with the Latin American people and of the genocide of a Latin American people. We already had hundreds of thousands of weapons and were ready to fight. We, who had learnt to fight when we were only a handful of six or seven, 10 or 12, 20 or 30, were already hundreds of thousands at that point. It therefore meant facing an armed people in a people's war, and Kennedy was having his doubts. I don't criticise him for this, I believe he was judicious. No one knows how many human lives would have been sacrificed. The Cuban people would never have surrendered. There still hadn't been the drama of Vietnam but Kennedy knew that there would have been an enormous price to pay.

Kennedy finally agreed to provide air support but when they took that decision there wasn't anyone left to support the mercenaries. In 68 hours our counter-attack had dispersed, confused and liquidated the entire expedition, something that the instigators of that landing would never have imagined. The defeat was severe for the empire. It was taken as a great humiliation and drove the US government to contemplate revenge. It was this reaction that led to the measures which brought about the October Missile Crisis, which only just stopped short of triggering a nuclear war.

In the period following the invasion of the Bay of Pigs, Kennedy limited himself to promoting the dirty war, the economic blockade and pirate attacks. But his reaction was also intelligent: drafting a program of social reform and economic assistance for Latin America. It was a shrewd strategy aimed at curbing the revolution.

Gianni Minà: It is now said, however, that this program cost Kennedy his life: that he was assassinated for having "betrayed" the Cuban counter-revolutionaries at the Bay of Pigs and for the policy followed in Latin America. The Mafia and other organizations made him pay for those two mistakes.

Fidel Castro: What mistake — for not having intervened directly?

Gianni Minà: For not having intervened to help the counter-revolutionaries and for having chosen a program for Latin America that wasn't in the interests of some multinational corporations.

Fidel Castro: Well, all of this could have damaged some US economic interests.

I don't believe that the Cuban counter-revolutionaries had the force to organize a conspiracy against Kennedy. Moreover, Kennedy had relations with them. He helped them, he had met with them in Miami, held a big meeting there and made promises to them. If there was a conspiracy against Kennedy, it had to have been promoted by powerful US economic interests. At most they could have used some Cuban mercenaries to carry out the plan.

Actually, I don't have the evidence to ascertain whether the counter-revolution was directly responsible for the assassination of Kennedy. Up until now no proof has emerged to indicate the responsibility of one group. Only suspicions exist and this has been written and talked about.

Gianni Minà: The Mafia had huge interests in Cuba which the revolution had destroyed. It is said that Sam Giancana was entrusted with the job of assassinating both you and Kennedy.

Fidel Castro: The Mafia did take part in plans to assassinate me, plans designed by the United States' government and the CIA.

I wouldn't go so far as to say — in fact, I don't have any basis for saying — that it was the Mafia or a lunatic that assassinated Kennedy. Reagan only just missed being killed by an individual who wanted to pull off a spectacular act only to gain attention from an actor he was in love with. That individual had fascist ideas but you can't accuse a certain group of having a plan to assassinate Reagan for this.

I have no interest in excusing reactionary groups or counter-revolutionaries of historic responsibility, but neither have I facts or evidence to point a finger at those who are guilty. When the inquiries began we collaborated by supplying all the information we had in our possession. After all, that individual had asked to visit Cuba but hadn't been given permission. There were times when I thought that it could all have even been a vast provocation and that they could have manipulated a fanatic in order to blame Cuba and the Soviet Union considering that that individual had been married to a Soviet citizen and that he had asked to visit Cuba.

Gianni Minà: Lee Oswald.

Fidel Castro: I have often said that if this individual had come to Cuba, had spent some time here and then returned to the United States and killed Kennedy, they would have tried to implicate us.

Anyway, let's come back to what Kennedy was trying to do in Latin America, with a program to halt the revolution. I think it was an intelligent initiative. It was a true political program. I wish it had such a program now, but it doesn't. It is now faced with a much greater catastrophe and it doesn't have any program.

At the time of the Alliance for Progress, Kennedy proposed a plan of collaboration which anticipated the allocation of $20 billion over 10 years and an agrarian reform program, fiscal reforms, housing development, education and health — what we have done. What happened was that many people appropriated the money, there wasn't any program, and the Alliance for Progress didn't solve anything.

Today, after more than 25 years, the Latin American countries owe $400 billion, 20 times the sum Kennedy had proposed at the time of the Alliance for Progress. Every year they pay the developed capitalist countries more than $20 billion in interest. We now have an inverted alliance: the bankrupt countries are helping in the development of the developed capitalist countries. This is today's reality and as far as I know the United States doesn't have any program.

Gianni Minà: President Castro, in 1964 you said: "We can wait 20 years to resume diplomatic and commercial relations with the United States." You have always kept your word on this. But now, in the midst of an economic crisis created by the foreign debt, would you be able to put off the renewal of diplomatic relations with the United States for another 20 years?

Fidel Castro: These years have passed — almost three decades — and we have made some progress. In Washington we have an office which protects our interests. They've got one in Havana. In actual fact a sort of diplomatic relation exists. However, political relations are very bad and there are no economic relations of any kind. The United States continues to be very hostile toward Cuba.

If I said then that we could go on without relations with the United States for 20 years, I now add that we can let another 20 years pass because they have forced us to do without them and to look for solutions to our problems without having any relations with them. In this sense we are the freest country in the world, a country which is not economically dependent on the United States. All other countries, to a greater or lesser degree, depend on the United States. We don't. I think this is quite a privilege in today's world.

We are not unwilling, however, to have normal diplomatic and economic relations. These would be useful for us, although neither are vital nor essential despite our economic difficulties. We have the same problems as the whole Third World, but fewer of them because our economic relations with the socialist countries give us a solid base for economic development. We are partially affected by the international economic crisis, to the extent of our trade with the Western world from which we acquire important products to transform raw materials that we receive from the other socialist countries. This is important and we don't underestimate it. But it is neither vital nor essential. We wouldn't like to go 20 or 28 more years without relations, but are ready to do so.

Gianni Minà: You do, however, have cultural and sporting relations. There are contacts between the two peoples.

Fidel Castro: Yes, its true, we do have relations in sport. There are competitions between volleyball, baseball and boxing teams. Furthermore we are soon going to take part in the Pan American Games in Indianapolis. The United States wants Cuba to be there because it increases competition, given the fact we are the only ones to challenge their supremacy of sport in this part of the world.

We also have cultural relations. Writers and other intellectuals visit us. It is one thing the United States hasn't forbidden so as not to provoke reaction at home. There are also relations between scientists, even though the United States has adopted measures to curb this type of exchange.

Gianni Minà: Let's turn to another country. The Sandinista leaders visit you frequently and you have also been to Managua a number of times. What advice did you give them in a situation as complicated as theirs?

Fidel Castro: No advice. I know revolutionaries and their psychology very well, and anyone who knows the psychology of revolutionaries doesn't make the mistake of trying to give advice. My relations with revolutionaries are very good.

I set out from a principle: we give our opinion only when they ask us to. We may have an opinion on a matter but if they don't ask us we don't give it. We respect the independence and criteria of the revolutionary organizations. We are careful never to dictate or dominate. Our relations are very respectful and fraternal. When we are asked we exchange many opinions and we have relations of trust and friendship.

I have been to Nicaragua twice. The Sandinista leaders have been here many times. Our countries are very near, there are numerous flights every week. There are frequent contacts. But these aren't relations in which we are the old and expert revolutionaries trying to teach the others or telling them what to do. Relations are excellent, based on respect, trust and the exchange of opinions. They don't consist of giving them advice.

Gianni Minà: President Castro, there are many in Europe who don't understand your policy on Africa. They ask how it is possible to justify the presence of 10,000 Cubans in Angola and Ethiopia. Nor can they explain why Ethiopia is a friend and the Eritrean Liberation Front an enemy.

Fidel Castro: There are many more than 10,000 Cubans in Angola. In Ethiopia, there is only a small force, which is symbolic more than anything else.[1]

Ethiopia, a country well-known to the Italians, was one of the poorest African states in the world, and it had one of the most backward and reactionary regimes of our time. Slavery still existed there. Different political forces, including the Eritreans, had struggled against that regime. Then the revolution triumphed — one of the most important events in the history of Africa. Slavery, feudalism and countless other social injustices disappeared. What happened in Ethiopia was comparable to the French revolution of 1789. Haile Selassie's anachronistic empire disappeared, and the peasants' conditions changed from those of slaves to owners of the earth. A revolutionary government has been installed there whose social works and international position make it one of the most prestigious and progressive governments in the Third World.

The Ethiopian revolutionaries are very sensitive to any form of secession or division of the country. Their nation is composed of more than 80 different ethnic groups and they can't agree to having their multinational cohesion disintegrate. The same is true of many other African states composed of a large number of ethnic groups or nations or tribes — whatever you wish to call them, depending on the level of development of these communities. They want unity. And you Italians, who were divided for hundreds of years, should know the value of unity, even more so today, when after a long series of frontier conflicts and bloody wars European integration and unity is talked about. Instead of encouraging the friction between the various components of Ethiopia, we should strive for a just and peaceful political solution for the conflict in Eritrea, without sacrificing the unity and integrity of the Ethiopian state.

Moreover, our cooperation and assistance to Ethiopia isn't only of a military nature, as there are also a large number of doctors and civilian technicians. Our military assistance began when the revolution was attacked from the outside by Somalia, whose troops penetrated hundreds of kilometers into Ethiopian territory. The problem of Eritrea is an internal one and we have never interfered in this conflict nor any other internal Ethiopian affair.

As for Angola, its history is well known. Our compatriots went there to help a people who had struggled intensely against Portuguese colonialism. We began to cooperate with the Angolan patriots at that time and continued to do so for the entire period of that struggle. It was the [1975] invasion of Angola by the South African racist and fascist troops — who penetrated nearly 1,000 kilometers into Angolan territory — in the days before the total independence of the country, that led us to send Cuban internationalist combatants there. The fact our small country, 10,000 kilometers from Angola, gave decisive help is without doubt one of the most noble acts of solidarity in our times. What was Europe doing at that time? Nothing! What can we be accused of? How can it criticise us?

Gianni Minà: You have always maintained that a victorious revolution must never be used to incite revolutions in other countries, because the revolution is tied to the internal situation of every country. You have, however, during the past years helped in some way both the Sandinistas and the People's Movement for the Liberation of Angola (MPLA) to take power. But now you seem to caution the revolutionaries of other countries not to believe in the miraculous powers of the revolution in a world controlled, as you say, by the International Monetary Fund and the military-industrial power of the Pentagon. What do you now think of revolution?

Fidel Castro: Revolution cannot be exported. We have always held this view and continue to think so. At times we judged that objective conditions for revolutionary change did exist, but on those occasions the subjective conditions were lacking. If we analyze the conditions in which the Cuban revolution developed, we note that the subjective factor had an important role. In other countries the objective conditions were even greater than in Cuba. We have noted that. But this is not in contradiction with the principle that the revolution cannot be exported. No one can export the conditions that make a revolution possible. No one can export Somoza, the 50 years of his domination, the plundering of the country, the appropriation of all the wealth, the repression and finally the economic crisis. All of these factors constituted the objective conditions. They gave rise to the development of the revolutionary movement. The subjective conditions therefore arose which produced the revolution.

We have expressed our solidarity with the Sandinista revolutionaries and as much as possible gave them our modest cooperation. But without the objective conditions, without the effort of the

Sandinistas and without the struggle of the Nicaraguan people, a revolutionary victory in Nicaragua would have been impossible.

Thus, expressing solidarity and giving some form of cooperation to a revolutionary movement, a revolutionary process, does not mean exporting the revolution.

The same thing happened in El Salvador: a heroic, extraordinary and impressive struggle. The Salvadoran revolutionaries have written an indelible page of history in a tiny country measuring only 20,000 square kilometres and inundated by a river of vehicles, arms, technology and military "consultants" from the United States. They resisted for more than six years and the United States was unable to crush a revolution which for all intents and purposes received practically no help from abroad, especially given that the conditions for receiving such help did not exist. They had to make do with their own resources. What could we export under such conditions? In truth, the revolution cannot be exported anywhere.

Not even to Angola, where by now the struggle of the patriots has lasted for 20 years. It is true that we gave political support for a long time. We trained some of their cadres and offered modest cooperation. We gave the greatest help when they had practically already won their independence and Angola was invaded by the racist South Africans who penetrated into the south of the country and were rapidly advancing towards Luanda. Up to that point, our help had been modest — we were assisting the MPLA to train some cadres in Angola.

Gianni Minà: Military cadres?

Fidel Castro: Yes, some military cadres. Several dozen of our officers trained them. It was the continuation of a commitment which had been going on for quite some time. We sent some military units when the South African troops advanced rapidly toward Luanda. That was the assistance, but the Angolans had already achieved their independence. At that point the South African fascists and racists invaded the country. We offered our help to defend their independence, not to achieve it. They had already ended the struggle for independence by themselves and had won.

I maintain, therefore, that revolution cannot be exported. This doesn't contradict the assistance and solidarity that can be offered.

Cuban internationalists farewelled by one million Angolans, January 10, 1989

As for the debate on the economic crisis and the foreign debts, we have underlined that the most urgent task for Latin America and the countries of the Third World is to unite in order to confront the economic crisis and debt. We must unite to struggle against unequal terms of trade, protectionist measures, dumping and the other factors which hold back development. We must unite to implement the resolution of the United Nations on the New International Economic Order, which we consider essential. Social changes are important, but at this moment it is fundamental to create the minimum conditions for development. A country making a revolution needs the minimum conditions to develop.

This is the most urgent thing to be done. In effect, I have proposed a policy of unity among all the forces to resolve the great economic crisis and I consider this task even more important than the social changes which will have to take place sooner or later. All of this doesn't imply a change in my point of view, but a realistic analysis of the times in which we live. This seemed a greater priority for the future of the countries of Latin America.

Gianni Minà: El Salvador has never been as close to victory as in January 1981, when the so-called final offensive was announced.

Fidel Castro: Not precisely at that moment, but a short time later. No government could have resisted the attacks of the revolutionary movement. Yet I'd like to tell you something: the government in El Salvador is like a jacket on a hanger; you beat it on one side or the other but it doesn't fall, because it is held up at the shoulders. The government of El Salvador is like a jacket held up at the shoulders by the United States. Without the presence and intervention of the United States that government would have collapsed some time ago, and the revolution, in my opinion, would have triumphed.

Gianni Minà: Keeping to the theme of revolution, I'd like to ask you something that is of interest to Italians. Many years ago you seemed to be of the opinion that the revolution could take place anywhere in the world. All that was necessary was to unite all the forces that had the will to make the revolution. Now you argue that things have changed, that the world has changed and so too, probably, the balance of power. Do you believe that in Italy, at a given moment, it would have been possible to have or that we should have made a revolution in Italy as in Cuba — that is, with an armed struggle?

Fidel Castro: Actually, I have never said that the revolution could take place anywhere in the world. I have never imagined how one could bring about the revolution in the United States, Great Britain, West Germany or many other countries. I referred to countries with similar situations to that of Cuba, countries of the Third World where objective conditions existed which, in theory, permitted the possibility of a revolution. This depended on the subjective factors — since, if these aren't present, it is impossible. I was referring to this kind of situation.

Western Europe never crossed my mind. However, you ask about Italy . . .

Gianni Minà: I have asked you this question about Italy because you met Feltrinelli and perhaps other Italians who have considered making a Cuban-type revolution in Italy. What do you think of these attempts? More exactly, what do you think of the Red Brigades?

Fidel Castro: I'll answer you in order.

First of all, it is possible that the conditions may have existed for a social revolution in Italy in the years immediately after the First World War — and even the revolutionary seizure of power. They were years of great convulsions: the disastrous consequences of that war for many countries, the reality of the revolution in the old empire of the Tsars and other factors had probably created the objective conditions. But at that time the forces on the right prevailed and fascism triumphed. The left could have won. I say this even if I do not know Italian history in depth, but I am trying to imagine a situation in which the objective conditions for a revolution could have arisen.

Gianni Minà: The left could have won?

Fidel Castro: I don't think this could have happened after the Second World War. I wouldn't say the same for that period, the strategic situation was very complicated. And anyway, the US army had occupied Italy. I wouldn't venture to say that the objective conditions existed, even though there was a powerful leftist and popular movement for the revolutionary seizure of power.

At the moment I don't think the ideal conditions exist for taking power in a revolutionary struggle: not in Italy, nor in any highly developed capitalist state of Europe in which the workers most certainly don't have the same conditions as those who lived at the time when Engels wrote about the suffering of the working class or at the time when Marx wrote. It is part of an extremely rich world which, benefiting from the privilege of cheaply acquiring our raw materials, sells to us its products ever more expensively and buys our raw materials and export articles at lower and lower prices. It didn't occur to me, and I really don't think that it would occur to me, to suggest such a thing.

I have the impression that the social changes in Europe will continue to come about through political means. This is my opinion. I don't see another way, unless some great catastrophe, some great crisis, takes place. I don't know, but I can't see it. What I do see very clearly, and it seems to me to be correct, is political struggle for those who want to change the social order. This is my point of view and I say so quite honestly. I'm not giving advice to anyone, I'm simply expressing my opinion.

I knew Feltrinelli, and I liked him. He seemed a likable and interesting person. We only had dealings for a short time, but I felt he was a friend. But Feltrinelli never spoke to me about revolutionary plans in Italy — nor did he mention the idea of armed actions or seizing power through a revolutionary struggle. He never spoke to me about this. Our conversations instead were mostly on a book about the Cuban revolution. He had come to Cuba as a publisher. Later on I heard how he had died, but I don't have the necessary facts to analyze his thought, nor his actions. I don't even know whether his death really happened the way they say it did. I neither reject nor accept this version. The truth is that I don't have enough information concerning the circumstances of Feltrinelli's death.

I met his widow who came to visit us. We have a good and respectful — very respectful — and friendly relationship. She usually comes to the Latin American Film Festival. She has already been to our country on numerous occasions.

You have asked me about the Red Brigades. I can you tell that I know very little about them. I don't know their plans, their ideas, objectives, or projects. I don't know the Red Brigades nor do I believe I should take it upon myself to be their judge. I have never met any member of the Red Brigades and the information I have is too little to allow me to formulate an opinion concerning this phenomenon. I don't even know if they are a national or international group. I have only read reports and cables about them.

Gianni Minà: I have asked you about the Red Brigades since they are the fruit of the illusion of some young Europeans of 1968 to bring about an armed revolution, not only in Italy but also in France and Germany. I have also asked you about the Red Brigades since there has been a recent rumor in Italy that after their defeat in the last few years, some of the members of this organization have found refuge in Cuba. What do you know about this? Is this only propaganda?

Fidel Castro: That's all we need, to be accused of having members of the Red Brigades living here! I already told you before when you asked me that question, that I have never met a member of the Red Brigades. I have never even heard that a member of the Italian Red Brigades has ever been here. I don't know whether any of them have ever been here as tourists, since tourists from Italy, France, West Germany, Sweden and all over, come here, and none of them are asked about their political affiliations. Should any of them have come here it would perhaps have been as a tourist, probably with an Italian passport, and legally. But as far as I know, no member of the Red Brigades has visited Cuba; we have never had any relations with them.

Gianni Minà: Twenty years later there is still talk of 1968 as a moment in which something could really have changed Europe. In certain sections of the European left this period is still seen as a frustrated dream.

Fidel Castro: Those events surprised the whole world. The phenomenon had a considerable effect. Undoubtedly subjective factors had an enormous influence. You would need to analyze whether or not the other factors which would have allowed a change to take place existed there. Everything seems to indicate that De Gaulle was worried by the demonstrations and strikes. Some say that, in order to have support, he even called back French troops stationed in West Germany. News about those events awakened great interest all over the world. I do not know whether a systematic, serious and thorough study has been done of those events. Just as Europe isn't aware of many of this world's problems, we, too, are somewhat ignorant about what goes on in Europe.

Gianni Minà: In 1968 the young people took to the streets with pictures of Fidel and Che.

Fidel Castro: I was told that they carried pictures of Che. Che created a great aura, a great mystique. I can say that Che set a tremendous example and symbolized the highest human values. Anyone who carries a picture of Che in good faith may be mistaken, but those who carry Che's picture honestly will always be deserving of respect. That's what I think, and it may be proof of the high degree of idealism and the noble intentions of those who supported that movement. However, I repeat, it is a theme on which we are not well enough informed. In that period we had many problems. Our attention has been concentrated on the problems of the Third World and we have little information about the developed capitalist world. We would really be surprised to hear that in any developed European country a sudden revolutionary change had taken place.

Gianni Minà: Let's go on to another topic. In Europe, and even in the most progressive circles, many people have criticized that fact that the allegiance of Cuba to the Soviet Union has been sanctified by the Cuban Constitution. What can you say concerning this?

Fidel Castro: We are friends of the Soviet Union and don't deny it. We are very grateful to the Soviet Union which offered us decisive solidarity during the economic blockade and aggression from the United States. We would be the most ungrateful people in the world if we didn't recognize this and claimed all the merit for our successes and progress. The economic relations — the equal terms of trade and its credits — which we have with the Soviet Union have helped us to achieve our economic and social development. We are friends, but friends on the basis of principles.

I knew you were concerned about this, and I asked for the text of the Constitution so as to reread what it has to say. I have thought about this problem and of your concern. Perhaps it isn't necessary, but I'll read them to you to show you there is no article in which allegiance to the Soviet Union is decreed.

The Soviet Union is mentioned in the preamble, in an introduction. It reads: "Guided by the victorious doctrine of Marxism . . . basing ourselves on the principles of proletarian internationalism, of fraternal friendship, of the assistance and cooperation of the Soviet Union and the other socialist countries" — note that we refer to all the socialist countries — "and on the solidarity of the workers and peoples of Latin America and of the world . . ."

It is a declaration in the preamble that says: "We base ourselves on the principles of proletarian internationalism." It clarifies the forces in the world we rely on. It is not a declaration of allegiance, since friendship and allegiance cannot be decreed.

And then, in article 12, the Soviet Union is mentioned once again: "It is based on the principles of proletarian internationalism and on the militant solidarity of the people." It is a declaration of principles. "It denounces imperialism, it denounces direct or indirect imperialist intervention, describes wars of aggression and conquest as international crimes, recognizes the peoples' right to repulse imperialist and reactionary violence, works for a lasting peace with dignity based on respect, and establishes its international relations on the principles of equal rights and the sovereignty and independence of states and on mutual interest. It bases its relations with the Soviet Union and the other socialist countries on socialist internationalism, on the shared goals of the construction of a new society, on fraternal friendship, cooperation and mutual assistance." In other words, this article defines the basis of our relationship with the USSR and the other socialist states.

This declaration may not be necessary. In a world in which there are many prejudices, the very mention of another country in the Constitution could appear as an act of rubber-stamping or of blind allegiance. In fact, it is the expression of a principle and of trust within the socialist community. This declaration is, from my point of view, unobjectionable, even if — I repeat — it is not absolutely necessary. It may have created some prejudices of that kind, but no one who is in good faith could doubt the independence of our country, its choices, and the principles on which it bases its relations with other states.

Gianni Minà: You have confirmed in this interview that Cuba survives on its own merits, but in Europe many people think that this is only possible because of the million dollars a day you receive from the Soviet Union.

Fidel Castro: Not a million dollars. The United States calculates the difference between the price the USSR and the other socialist countries pay us for sugar and the price of sugar on the marginal world market — not the price of sugar in Europe or the price the United States pays for its imports of sugar. It then calls the difference a subsidy. Having succeeded in establishing fair, equitable relations of trade, such as should exist between all underdeveloped and developed countries, and having established the kind of relationship which we're suggesting to all the underdeveloped countries in the world in their relations with the developed capitalist world, a goal that even forms part of the concept of the New International Economic Order . . . these are all used to create false, arbitrary and manipulated calculations. Sugar is usually sold at a much higher price than that of the marginal prices of the world market, which is depressed as a result of the dumping by the EEC and protectionist measures by the United States. These calculations are made and then the United States speaks of subsidies.

We have received credits, just as many countries in the world have. We don't get loans from the World Bank, the International Monetary Fund, nor the Inter-American Development Bank. The only countries which have provided us with credit, at favorable conditions, have been the socialist countries. We receive their loans and invest them, just as other countries do. The subsidy theory is ridiculous, and yet they never get tired of repeating it.

We don't underestimate the importance of these economic relations, but the revolution survives above all thanks to its political and military merits. It survives because of our people's strength, organization, determination to defend themselves and capacity to struggle — to make aggressors pay too high a price to make aggression worthwhile. All of that is certain.

Gianni Minà: And also thanks to its economic organization.

Fidel Castro: We have been here for almost three decades. That would not have been possible any other way. History will judge it. How could we hold on? Cuba has shown that no nation, no matter how small it may be, can be scorned in today's world. I already told you about El Salvador, how the US forces have become bogged down.

We greatly appreciate the economic relations we have with the socialist countries and feel most satisfied for having reached a certain degree of understanding with them. This is the origin of the subsidy theory.

Gianni Minà: You have met Khruschev, Brezhnev, Andropov, and now Gorbachev. What impression do you have of him? How does he differ from his predecessors?

Fidel Castro: It is delicate to speak about the leaders of states friendly to us. I will tell you frankly that Khruschev was a good friend. He was the premier when we began our relationship with the Soviet Union. When the Yankees closed the sugar market to us, the USSR decided to buy it; when they stopped supplying us with oil — the United States controlled the tankers, the multinationals and the refineries — the USSR supplied us with petroleum. Khruschev was very friendly toward us. Therefore, I consider it obvious to express our gratitude.

Personally, he was like a Russian peasant: very astute, very alive, very energetic. He liked joking, sometimes too much. On certain occasions his jokes were too ironic — not towards us, but towards his own comrades. He was a man full of initiatives. I remember him with gratitude for his attitude toward us. I shouldn't judge all the other things he did.

There were problems at one point, during the time of the October Missile Crisis. He made a mistake in his relations with us, and it hurt us a great deal. But that doesn't obscure, much less wipe out, the gratitude we owe him.

Gianni Minà: What was the mistake?

Fidel Castro: It stemmed from the October Missile Crisis. He wounded us, and it caused a lot of irritation at one point. It was a very tense international situation. We thought that a conflict was inevitable and were resigned and determined to face it. It was sad and painful, but we had to acquiesce. That was our position, not mine or that of the Party, but that of the whole nation. Our people went through the experience of a nuclear confrontation, and the people were serene, very serene. It was a very tense moment and of course something could have happened at any moment that would have unleashed the war.

We were already shooting at the US planes, which had begun to fly low. We didn't have any surface-to-air missiles, but we did have anti-aircraft artillery, hundreds of batteries, manned by Cubans.

We explained our position to those in charge of the Soviet units stationed in Cuba. We thought that we shouldn't allow the US planes to fly so low since this could have facilitated a surprise attack. We made our decision and told the Soviets we were going to shoot. The next day we opened fire on all the low-flying planes.

It was in those circumstances that one of the anti-aircraft batteries of the Oriente province shot down a U-2 plane. It was the moment of greatest tension. Actual fighting was in fact taking place. I think that was where Carlos Franqui got his theory that I wanted to unleash a war, whereas we were simply stating that we couldn't allow foreign planes to fly low over our territory and that we had to respond. That was our position and I'm convinced that it was correct. The flights were suspended. Later, we were forced to shoot once again after the crisis was settled.

At that moment of tension, Khruschev took some initiatives. Perhaps under pressure due to the delicacy of the situation, he presented the United States with a proposal without consulting with us first. We didn't find out about the proposal to withdraw the missiles — which hadn't been discussed with us — until it was made public. That seemed unnecessary to us. I think that the crisis could have been solved better with a little more equanimity and firmness. At least he could have discussed it with us and told the US authorities that they would have to discuss it with us, and perhaps the conditions would have improved. Not that we were against a solution — what counts from the point of view of history is that a nuclear conflict was averted.

However, the US naval base remained on our territory and they began high-altitude spy flights out of reach of our artillery. When, during the following days they once again tried low level flights, we still shot at them. Since the US government didn't want to complicate the situation, it ordered the suspension of these low-altitude flights.

I am convinced that, at least as a matter of principle, Khruschev ought to have consulted with us, but he didn't do so. We thought that was absolutely incorrect; it provoked irritation and we lodged a protest. It influenced Cuban-Soviet relations for years. That was the incident that really affected our relations with the Soviets. But that is a thing of the past, water under the bridge.

Of course, we are grateful to not only Khruschev, but also to the Communist Party of the USSR and all Soviet people, who have always maintained an attitude of cooperation, solidarity, and selflessness toward us. I certainly cannot attribute all the merit to one man, but I think that Khruschev played an important role in this process.

Gianni Minà: Then came Brezhnev.

Fidel Castro: Brezhnev replaced Khruschev. I knew him. When I went to the Soviet Union in 1963, Brezhnev was president of the Soviet, and he impressed me greatly as a person. He was very affable and intelligent, with great authority. He wasn't the top authority at the time.

Then Brezhnev was elected to replace Khruschev. Brezhnev still appeared young and energetic. He served for many years, but when he took up office he was at the height of his faculties. His relations with us were very friendly and cooperative. He visited our country, was well-received and our relations with him were always good. I have said that we remember Brezhnev that way. I shouldn't judge him since no one has the right to set himself up as judge of the leaders of other countries.

Gianni Minà: And Andropov?

Fidel Castro: I didn't know Andropov as well. I only met him once, after the death of Brezhnev, when he was elected. He served a very short time, but unquestionably he had great authority and prestige in the Soviet Union. Nevertheless, he didn't have the opportunity to develop his policy.

Gianni Minà: Now, for Gorbachev.

Fidel Castro: Well, I've had an opportunity to see Gorbachev. I hadn't known him before he became General Secretary of the Party in the Soviet Union. Raúl knew him, having met him while on vacation in the USSR, when nobody imagined he would have the responsibilities he now holds.

I was in contact with him after he was appointed. At that time, we had a hurricane that caused a great deal of damage. The hurricane went from one end of the country to the other. Gorbachev phoned, offering us cooperation. He offered considerable material assistance in wheat and rice — the hurricane had destroyed banana groves, flattened the sugar-cane, and caused a lot of damage throughout agriculture. He sent us a donation of merchandise worth tens of millions of dollars. We would have spent dollars to obtain those resources if it had not been for that assistance. That was his first spontaneous gesture.

There was another one. I saw him in the Soviet Union during a Party Congress. He told me that he wanted to talk with me. Naturally, I saw he was very busy; I know how much work a leader has in a Congress. Then he had a free Sunday; it was his birthday. I told him he should rest that day, but he insisted and we had a nearly three-hour discussion in the Kremlin.

We have kept in touch.

Gianni Minà: The Soviet Union has now allowed the publication of books such as *Doctor Zhivago,* which used to be banned in the Soviet Union. Was that a mistake in the past?

Fidel Castro: It's a change in policy toward a greater openness. I don't want to make judgements about such developments. I don't want to assume the role of judge.

In such matters, in our relations with friendly countries, the other socialist countries — I also told you this when we were speaking of Nicaragua — we are very careful about voicing opinions and making judgements. Therefore, I don't want to say it was a mistake. But I can say that I entirely agree with the openness and with the large-scale publication of those books.

Gianni Minà: Why are certain books censored at given times in the socialist countries, and then it is said that a mistake was made and that there wasn't any reason for censoring them?

Fidel Castro: Look, I think you're going to have to talk with other leaders of socialist countries — of the Soviet Union, China, other countries — and ask them, so they can answer questions about those problems. I can answer only for us.

Rather than establishing censorship, we are selective about what we publish. We don't have enough resources, such as paper, so we make a selection, trying to ensure that the best, most interesting books in science, literature and everything are made available. I won't say that we're going to waste money and paper publishing trash; there's a limit to our economic resources.

In addition, I tell you frankly that we aren't going to publish a counter-revolutionary book. That is our privilege. We are in favor of spreading literary works, artistic works, works in a wide range of currents and styles of cultural thought. But don't tell me that a counter-revolutionary book deserves our publishing it. That is something else. We select what we publish. I'm not going to tell you that we're going to publish *Mein Kampf* here, although we should publish it so the history students may know what the theories of Nazism were.

There are many books, in both literature and politics, that aren't any good. I wouldn't have any fear about publishing a serious book, but we have no reason for publishing trash.

We are in favor of a wide range of publications, but not all of them. And we aren't going to waste money, materials and hard currency on buying and publishing those books when we don't have enough paper for all the textbooks and books on science and literature. We have a few thousand titles here waiting to be published. There is a long list of young writers and poets who are waiting for a chance to see their books published. It wouldn't make sense for us to bring in a libelous counter-revolutionary book and put it ahead of the list.

As for the rest, any book on any topic is alright, be it religion — we are Marxist-Leninists and we are glad that the Church brings in tens of thousands of Bibles every year because the Bible is a very interesting book, a book that can enrich people's culture — or capitalism. There are many books that speak of capitalism and other such things. As long as they are serious analyses, we are willing to publish them. But no libel or trash.

I am speaking for us Cubans. As for the others, you should ask other socialist leaders when you have the opportunity to do so.

Gianni Minà: Agreed. Let's now go on to another leader who, in the Mediterranean is very important. What do you, Fidel Castro, think of Muammar El-Qaddafi?

Fidel Castro: We have always followed events in Libya with great interest even though at the beginning Qaddafi had many prejudices towards communist theory and there wasn't much mutual understanding between us. At the Nonaligned conference of Algiers in 1974 he had made some statements critical of me, having perhaps misinterpreted some of our declarations, which were not intended to refer to him. In actual fact, we have always been supportive of events in Libya: the creation of a revolutionary movement, the overthrow of the feudal monarchy and the establishment of an independent government.

I recognize that there are differences between the philosophical ideas of Qaddafi and myself. When you are going to analyze a political leader at a given time you have to be guided by the facts. Firstly, it is of great importance that Qaddafi freed Libya from colonialism — we must describe the foreign rule that existed as colonialism, as it wasn't even a semi-colony. Libya was a Western colony. Secondly, he freed his country from NATO rule, from the military bases. Qaddafi has recovered the basic wealth of the country — oil — and carried out social changes, initiated important development programmes and tried to invest the resources. I could see that. He has even tried cultivation in the desert by using water found at great depths.

I had an opportunity of seeing the effort which is being made in Libya to produce foodstuffs. I have even tried to calculate its cost: amounts of water, cubic miles of deep underground water, for there is an enormous quantity of water some 800 or 1,000 meters down. I was calculating this. This water has an enormous value and in the future it could well be worth more than oil as we are dealing here with pure water in a world which is ever more polluted. In all sincerity, I have admired his efforts and I have come to know it as a country with a great sense of honor and dignity. All of this is a product of the political movement and the changes Qaddafi brought about in his country. His international policy has always supported peoples who have been victims of US aggression, to support the liberation movement. His anti-imperialist politics has earned Qaddafi the hostility of the United States and Libya has been a victim of their aggression. One of the most incredible actions of our era was the attempt to murder a head of state and his family, using military means, with a surprise bombing attack.

We know today that the plan of the Unites States Security Council and Colonel North was to kill him, even if this meant killing his entire family. Some of his relatives were in fact killed in that attack. I don't believe there are precedents to such aggression.

All these facts have led me to conclude that Qaddafi is a patriot and a revolutionary. Others may have different ideas; whoever wants to may criticize this or that aspect. But the opinion I have formed of him, and I say this frankly, is that he is a patriot and a revolutionary — two essential qualities — and I think that he has given his country prestige and dignity and has demonstrated courage in facing imperialism, earning himself the hatred of the empire.

I think that these features constitute the unquestionable historical merit of Qaddafi as a political leader whom the United States have tried to destroy and overthrow. It wanted to wipe him out physically and has done everything possible to destabilize him politically. Why? Because the United States tries to destroy its adversaries, those men whose conduct becomes an obstacle to its policies. Since you ask my opinion, this is what I think, what I consider to be the essential aspects of Qaddafi's personality.

Gianni Minà: Yet, he's very emotional. His politics are not as well thought out and rational as those of Fidel Castro; he is often emotional.

Fidel Castro: Our politics, also, have emotional moments and as you have seen there are occasions when I too allow myself to be overcome by passion when expounding certain opinions.

Gianni Minà: As with Khruschev, in that situation . . .

Fidel Castro: And I have been a head of state longer than he has. But I believe — I've read his *Green Book* — that he has thought ahead and set forth more advanced social ideas in what he proposes. I don't share his point of view, but I respect it.

I also think that someone doesn't have to be a Marxist-Leninist to be considered a revolutionary. There are several leaders in various countries who aren't Marxist-Leninists but who have played important roles in achieving their countries' independence, in freeing their countries. Being a revolutionary depends on the time, the place, the circumstances.

The changes that Qaddafi has carried out in the conditions of his country are truly revolutionary — nobody can deny that.

Gianni Minà: And Khomeini?

Fidel Castro: I consider Khomeini, also, to be a revolutionary. I have no doubts about that. Khomeini is an ayatollah, a religious leader. But how can I judge the fact of the Shah's overthrow? The Shah was a henchman, a tyrant, an ally of imperialism in that area, armed to the teeth. The Iranian people overthrew him without arms. It was one of the best-armed governments in the world, yet the heroism of the people — under Khomeini's spiritual and political leadership — overthrew him. That movement has played an important revolutionary role. I say this objectively. Thus, objectively, I believe that the Shah's fall and the elimination of an extremely repressive, reactionary regime, which was one of the most powerful allies of imperialism in the region, was a great event.

I promised you that I was going to answer all your questions, but I really don't like being turned into a judge, judging everybody. However, I know that all these matters are discussed at length in many places and I am giving you my opinion. I try to analyze such matters objectively.

1. On December 22, 1988, accords on Angola and Namibia were signed at the United Nations. The accords established conditions to guarantee the sovereignty of Angola and the independence of Namibia. The withdrawal of Cuban internationalist forces began in January 1989 and is expected to be completed in 1991. For the text of the 1988 accords and the background to Cuba's involvement in Southern Africa see *Angola and Namibia: Changing the History of Africa* published by Ocean Press.

   Cuban forces were also withdrawn from Ethiopia during 1989 and 1990 following a series of negotiations aimed at finding a peaceful solution to the conflict in Ethiopia.

Chapter 4

Debt, dependence and the Third World

I had left my questions about the economy and the Latin American foreign debt until the end, thinking they would be the most complex for the television audience and would break the rhythm of an interview which I thought, somewhat prematurely, would last around three or four hours. Therefore, when we got to this topic dawn was fast approaching. When I asked Fidel one of my endless requests for clarification, those who were present say he looked at me for the first time with a rather unfriendly expression. However, even at that moment, in spite of how tired we all were, Fidel was able to make a lucid, precise and rational explanation, without forgetting any details or making any mistakes in dates, figures or projections.

I don't know if it's a matter of memory or familiarity with the material, or his custom of controlling his physical and mental fatigue, but the fact is that, in his approach to and explanation of the economic topics at close to 5 o'clock in the morning, I discovered, as a journalist, one of the most eloquent aspects of Fidel's famous character: his tenacity, his determination.

When you spend many hours together in an exhausting intellectual exercise, a kind of complicity, intimacy, is created in the work team. Thus, jokingly, in the breaks for changing the film, the members of the team called my attention to the very Latin way Fidel tapped me on the shoulder to give more emphasis to what he was saying, claiming that, in fact, he was tapping to keep me awake, to encourage me to have his resistance.

I should say in my defense that, when we came to the reflections on

Mexico *Photo: Osvaldo Salas*

the economy, many of us, Cubans and Italians alike, lost some of our concentration. Only Fidel showed no signs of fatigue.

When I told Fidel about this on the day we returned to Italy, he laughed a lot. And then, jokingly, he added, "You should do like me: run every morning."

G.M.

Gianni Minà: President Castro, according to *The Wall Street Journal*, you have called on the politicians and businessmen of the West to help Latin America. You have stated that if there isn't a moratorium on debts, the Latin American subcontinent will be faced with a revolutionary wave of unprecedented magnitude. Do you consider that this revolution would have a local character in the different countries, or could it become unified and triumph in several countries at the same time? Is *The Wall Street Journal* correct when it says you issued such a call?

Fidel Castro: I have spoken quite a lot about the debt. We have had some important meetings about it. Essentially, what I have maintained is that Latin America's economic and social problems have multiplied; that they have accumulated and have reached unbearable limits. If the problem of the debt isn't solved through the cancellation of the debt — which wouldn't be enough by itself; it would also be necessary to implement the New International Economic Order — the situation of the Latin American countries is going to become untenable. The democratic processes — all of those democratic processes that have taken place — are going to find themselves in a dead-end street. If the creditors are bent on collecting that debt and if there is no solution for those economic problems, social outbreaks will take place in various Latin American countries. I am absolutely certain of this.

I have tried to convince people that I am not preaching that the banks be ruined. I have simply been suggesting that a part of the enormous sums that are spent on the arms race be used by the governments of the industrialized capitalist countries to pay the debts to their own banks, to shoulder the debts of the entire Third World. I'm not suggesting any new taxes or proposing that the banks be ruined — I'm simply suggesting that a rational use be made of those enormous resources, which would suffice to solve the problem of the debt, the problems of unequal terms of trade and the New International Economic Order.

I have suggested that, for example, if the Third World countries had $300 billion more to spend every year, the unemployment rate in the developed capitalist countries would drop, trade would increase, the international economic situation would benefit considerably and they could get out of the vicious cycle and stagnation in which they are bogged. The West has under-utilized industries, an under-utilized work force and under-utilized productive capacity, and the Third World has enormous needs but lacks the required purchasing power. This solution would even benefit the economies of the industrialized countries. That is what I am suggesting. Now, what is going to happen? It is inevitable. Underground forces are going to accumulate in the volcano until it erupts.

I have even said that I prefer solutions. I want solutions for problems; I am not advocating eruptions. I am simply saying that, in my view, this is going to happen. I have been warning about these realities. Those, I think, are the statements that *The Wall Street Journal* has reported and interpreted. Once it even wanted to interview me, and I may meet with its journalists some time — but more briefly than in this interview: for two or three hours . . . .

Gianni Minà: The fact that many countries are in debt to US banks appears to have its negative aspects for the banks, as well. For example, the US bank that holds the largest slice of Brazil's debt has been faced with serious problems and was on the point of bankruptcy. Does this seem ironical or tragic to you?

Fidel Castro: For the bank it's tragic. For history, it's ironical, because many of those banks pursued, went running after, potential debtors, offering them loans.

Those banks are now realizing that the debt is unpayable. Many US politicians and other people are beginning to understand this reality and are talking about looking for formulas for solving these problems. Some of the banks are taking measures and setting up reserves to offset those losses. Now, nobody really talks about paying the debt. What they talk about is the interest — and not even the interest. I would say that, now, they're talking about how they *aren't* going to pay the debt. A government that owes $700 million, between repayment of the principal and interest payments, is asking for a loan of $750 million — $50 million more of fresh money. It formally acknowledges the debt, but it's growing. That is what is happening. It would be better to solve this problem frankly and wipe the slate clean.

Naturally, the creditors aren't resigned to this and try to collect on the debt, using any means. That's why they are suggesting such dangerous, harmful formulas as the so-called capitalization of the debt, which means converting the debt into rights to the debtor country's national assets — that is, turning over to foreign capital a part of the nation's patrimony in payment of the debt. In the long run, it promotes a process of denationalization in the debtor country, which then loses the ability to guide the course of its economy.

The countries not only need the debt to be annulled but also need fresh money. If they don't get it, the crisis will grow even more acute. I think that, now, everybody realizes that the debt is unpayable and uncollectable. How are they going to collect the debt: by killing people, making people disappear and murdering people? There's no way anybody can collect that debt, and no government would be willing to ruin itself politically by imposing the extremely harsh conditions which payment of the debt would entail; it would decapitate itself politically and would be utterly ruined in political terms. That is a fact, and all we have to do is sit back and see what happens.

I have been making these suggestions for some time and I paid a lot of attention to the problem throughout 1985, when we held Latin American meetings of students, workers, women, political figures and journalists. I dedicated nearly all of that year to this problem of the foreign debt. We worked, planting the seed — now, we must wait until everybody is persuaded that this is a reality.

Gianni Minà: Let's talk about how, at certain moments, the capitalist system creates difficulties for the Cuban economy. In the summer of 1986, the Paris Club recommended that Cuba take readjustment measures in its economy so as to avoid bankruptcy. How did Cuba respond?

Fidel Castro: We have negotiated the problem of the debt with our creditors, but nobody has imposed any measures on us. We determine the economic measures we take, depending on the situation and needs. We aren't under anybody's protection, nor can we allow any group of creditors or any international organization to impose measures on us. Unquestionably, we analyze the situation and take measures which are beneficial to our economy to increase exports, reduce imports, etc. But these measures aren't guidelines or models imposed by the Paris Club.

Gianni Minà: Two years ago, you advised all countries with large foreign debts not to pay them, because, in view of the conditions imposed, it was impossible to do so. Nevertheless, as Peruvian President Alan García has pointed out, Cuba honors its commitments and pays its debt punctually. Yet, in the summer of 1986, Cuba suspended its payments for three months. Could you clarify this important point of Cuban economic policy?

Fidel Castro: Our theses and positions cannot be portrayed in that way.

I already told you that it is an objective fact that the Third World's foreign debt is unpayable. In strictly mathematical terms, no formula is possible — even assuming variants that are so benign and optimistic that they are utterly unrealistic. There is no rational evidence that allows us to accept the idea that the Third World's debt can be paid.

As an example, let's take the most favorable variant that can be imagined: let's suppose that the present debt isn't increased by even one cent, that a 20-year grace period is granted for repayment of the principal, that the present interest rate of 6 percent is maintained, that interest payments are limited to 10 percent of the value of exports and that exports grow by an amazing annual average of 10 percent for 20 consecutive years. In this quite improbable case, at the end of 20 years the Third World countries as a whole would have paid their creditors more than $1.2 trillion in interest, and their debt would still amount to more than a trillion dollars. That is, in 20 years, the underdeveloped countries would have paid an amount greater than their present total debt, and they would then still have a debt approximately equal to what they now owe. For 20 years, the Third World would have been turning over more than $60 billion a year just to maintain an ever-growing debt.

I think that this simple calculation will show you how illusory is the idea that technical formulas for solving the problem may exist. If, in their efforts to pay their debt servicing, some debtor countries have obtained larger positive balances of trade, it has been at the cost of cutting back their imports to subsistence levels. The prices of the products they export have plummeted and the markets where they sell them have been closed following the imposition of high protectionist barriers by the same countries that demand complete, punctual payment of their obligations.

The underdeveloped countries owe more while they pay more,

because the monetary manipulations of the big capitalist powers plunder their few resources: transnational banks cut off their credits when they most need them or grant credits only on terms similar to those imposed by medieval usurers. The framework of international economic relations in which the phenomenon of the debt is developing, its internal structure and the dynamics of its growth — take on new debts so you can pay your old debts — explain the mathematical and economic impossibility of ever being able to pay it.

But the debt is unpayable not only for mathematical or economic reasons — it is also unpayable for political reasons. The debt is one of the most important world political topics of today. For the creditors, there is the real fact that it cannot be paid and the risk of the bottom dropping out of the international financial system. For the debtors, the magnitude of the debt is so great that the crisis caused by its payment could be the beginning of the transformation of the international economic order now in force. The application of the International Monetary Fund's restrictive measures has, as you know, caused serious economic and social conflicts in many countries. Every day, it is increasingly evident that without the use of repression and violence the people won't accept greater privations and sacrifices. It is a political cost which the democratic processes in the Third World cannot assume. That is why I say that unless a real, definitive solution for the present debt crisis is sought, serious social upheavals may occur that will lead to violent political changes in many countries.

I could go on giving you other reasons — moral, juridical and historical reasons — for why the debt is unpayable, but I don't want to speak too much on this topic. I would only like to add that I have raised the need for all countries to unite and support one another in the search for a solution for the problem of the debt — and not only for the problem of the debt but also for the economic crisis and unequal terms of trade, dumping and protectionism and in the struggle for the New International Economic Order. That is what I have suggested — united, not isolated, actions. What I have said is that, if a country finds itself in a situation in which it has to suspend payments, it shouldn't have to stand alone; we should give it our utmost support. I haven't been proposing isolated actions.

Our debt is small and has no influence. I have stated that our debt is a special case, that the loans which were extended to Cuba were made in spite of pressure by the United States — which, throughout the revolution, has made all kinds of efforts to impose a credit blockade against Cuba. Our debt isn't to US banks, which are the hub of private transnational banking. Rather, our debt is to banks that defied US pressure and even to some credit sources in other underdeveloped countries. Our relations with our creditors aren't exactly the same as the rest of Latin America's relations with the banks. We have to keep that factor in mind, and we have always tried to meet our obligations as much as possible. I wasn't afraid that anybody would think our position was in response to selfish interests. I was analyzing the situation and problems of the Latin American and Third World countries as a whole.

Moreover, the money we received was invested in programs for developing the country or in social programs. That money wasn't misappropriated or sent abroad. Even though we are victims of all those problems of dumping, protectionism, unequal terms of trade and the manipulation of the interest rates — of all those devices — in our trade with the West, the resources we received were invested in conditions very different from those, for example, in the rest of Latin America and Third World. In the other countries, the banks ran after the governments, trying to lend them money; there were big commissions and very high interest rates. Much of that money was misspent; much of it fled back to its country of origin; much of it was misappropriated. Very bad use was made of it.

Alan García had a position that isn't very different from ours. While I was saying that the debt was unpayable, Alan García said that no more than 10 percent of the country's exports should be used to pay it, and that was the policy he applied, based on the experiences of his own country. Certain wire services and newspapers tried to stir up contradictions between Peru and Cuba over this difference of opinion.

What I say and what Alan says lead to the same conclusion: the debt is unpayable. There aren't any substantial differences between Peru's position and that of Cuba.

I had an opportunity to talk with Alan in Harare at the Nonaligned Summit. I spoke with him at length about all these problems, and our relations were good, very friendly; there isn't any quarrel. I support his position, and I have supported similar statements — which aren't extreme. However, I believe the debt is unpayable, and I have supported the formulation that, in the present conditions, the debt is unpayable. I am absolutely convinced that the debt is not only unpayable but also uncollectable.

The debt keeps growing larger and larger every year, and, if you make a mathematical projection such as the one I explained, you find that, at the end of 20 years, the debt has multiplied considerably, and an impossible rate of economic growth would be needed, with an impossible growth in exports, to obtain the resources needed to pay that debt. And, even if all that is achieved, based on the best variants, far from being reduced, the debt will continue to grow.

Chapter 5

Reflections on the revolution

In the last few years, every time I have returned from Cuba after filming a special feature on sports or music or attending the Varadero Music Festival or the Film Festival, many people have asked me, "What's the atmosphere like in Cuba?" Obviously, they weren't asking about the climate. Instead, this question has been and is used to disguise prejudices or at least a lack of information.

Nobody asks such a question, for example, when you come back from Brazil, where nearly half the population still live in conditions of tragic poverty, at the lowest limits of human dignity, or when you return from Mexico or Central America. Nobody asked this in the late '70s when somebody came back from Argentina, where thousands of people began to disappear and were assassinated at the time the world soccer championship was held. What was the atmosphere like in Argentina then? Nobody asked. And the interesting thing is that, for quite some time, people haven't asked this question when friends have come back from the Soviet Union.

Now, I don't know what kind of concern, reaction or sense of guilt is unleashed by Cuban reality. What is true is that for decades Cuba has been the victim of information — or disinformation — and of an attitude that isn't expressed about other countries.

I don't believe that I hold such prejudices. Nor did I experience any Marxist ideological raptures in the past. I can say with the modesty of an old journalist that, for someone who comes from opulent Western Europe sinking in consumerism, it is true that Cuba has a rigorous, authoritarian atmosphere, although Cubans sing, dance and enjoy themselves as it must surely be difficult to do in the Eastern European countries. Cubans are unquestionably freer and less inhibited. This is so because of their culture, geographic position, history and traditions — but also, perhaps, because they have a cultured leader who has adapted Marxism to his people's special characteristics.

The pages that follow, both those concerning domestic policy and those on "the new human being," help to explain the society of which Fidel dreamed and the contradictions that may exist between that dream and the Cuban people's aspirations.

We Europeans who come from developed capitalist nations where the standard of living is certainly higher even than that of the United States probably wouldn't like the Cuban "atmosphere" if we didn't come as tourists with money in our pockets. But perhaps the millions of disinherited who live in the rest of Latin America, not only without freedom but also without human dignity, would have another opinion.

The fact that the Cuban revolution has survived for the past three decades may probably also be explained in the light of this truth.

G.M.

Gianni Minà: More than 30 years ago, President Castro, you left a prison on an island south of Cuba. At that time, it was called the Isle of Pines; since then, you have baptized it the Isle of Youth. During those subsequent years, you carried out a revolution and have ever since governed a rejuvenated country. Don't you feel satisfied with your historic role, and haven't you thought that you should turn your post over to someone younger?

Fidel Castro: What are you saying, suggesting that I retire?

Gianni Minà: No . . .

Fidel Castro: I'll answer. These are two topics, two interesting topics. They are somewhat related to what I think, deep down inside, about these matters.

First, you ask me if I'm satisfied. I would say, yes, I am fully satisfied with the work to which I have dedicated my life. But I still have a critical spirit and will always be unsatisfied in the sense that I usually analyze what I have done, trying to see if I could have done it better.

I think it's good never to be satisfied. It seems to me that this is proper and essential for a revolutionary. However, I assess work objectively, and I know that I have dedicated my efforts and my life to a noble goal and that we have advanced along that path, in spite of whatever imperfections that revolutionary work may have.

Now, you talk of age. I am over 60, but the years have passed without my realizing it. I still test my reactions a lot, and they are the same as when the revolution triumphed, when I was 32. I have to remind myself every so often that I am over 60. I feel very well, both physically and mentally — we have to watch ourselves in that, too. My habit of exercising may have contributed to this. I think that physical exercise helps not only your muscles but also your mind; I even think it keeps your mind relatively young, because exercise helps the blood to circulate, carrying oxygen to all the cells, including the ones in your brain. So, as I say, I feel in excellent physical and mental condition.

I think I dedicate more time every day to the revolution. I think I pay it more attention, because I meditate and reflect more on this subject as time goes by. That may be why Plato wrote in *The Republic* — the first utopia ever conceived — that the ideal age for people in government posts was after 55. So, you could say that for a wise man such as Plato, 60 years was the nearly perfect age for exercising the functions of government. And I imagine that 60 years in Plato's time would be around 80 nowadays.

Gianni Minà: For sure.

Fidel Castro: You'd have to analyze the life expectancy and average age in Plato's era.

Gianni Minà: That's right.

Fidel Castro: Certainly, they were less. It seems that Plato left the tasks of government to great-grandfathers.

I don't share all of Plato's ideas, because I know that the tasks we carried out when we began the struggle against the dictatorship and drew up a program, a concept, required a tremendous amount of energy: first in the underground struggle, then in the Sierra Maestra and later in leading the victorious process and the defense of the revolution. Throughout this long history it required an enormous amount of energy, which only young people could have. I couldn't do many of those tasks now. I would have to be a strategist working from an office, contributing in some practical way with my experience, helping to decide how to do things.

Now, I have other responsibilities of government that require reflection and maturity. In fact, I make these comparisons because I've experienced both stages: the one when I was 32, 33 and 35, which is unquestionably more impulsive, and now that of my 50s and 60s, which is more reflective. Experience plays a great role. I would even say that the training of a leader is too expensive, for it requires a learning process, and society loses if it trains one leader with great experience and then replaces them with somebody else who then has to begin the learning process.

It seems to me that I can carry out my functions — which also require some physical effort, strong physical work and great mental effort — perfectly well. They can be carried out at my age. That is what I think. It isn't ridiculous, nor am I an anachronism.

When we celebrated some of the anniversaries of the revolution — for example, the 25th anniversary — I said that I was armed with the experience of 25 years and the enthusiasm of the first day. I think that this is very important: the amount of enthusiasm a person has for what they are doing. Some people have the ability to preserve their enthusiasm. You are a journalist and have been one for years, yet you may have just as much enthusiasm as when you began to work as a journalist — or even more. It seems to me that the same is true of artists and writers. There are scientific theories which state that great works are accomplished in a given age range — when you're in your 30s, which is the time when your neurons, your brain cells, have the greatest potential. But I know artists, scientists, doctors and researchers who still have great enthusiasm at 60, 65 and 75.

A few days ago, I read that a great Spanish guitarist had died at age 95 and he had been playing the guitar at that age. I think that 95, 90 or even 80 is very old for tasks of government. But these people often keep on working.

Now, how long will I remain on the job? I'll tell you: even though I may have an influence, this isn't a decision that I can or should make. The Party and the National Assembly should make this decision on behalf of the people. In short, the people should decide.

It is a fact that, in all epochs, those who start revolutions acquire great authority. Often, that great authority has been misused or has led to an abuse of power. We have seen that; I don't want to give examples, but there are quite a few in the history of the revolutionary movement. I have always been very aware of that problem, even though I have had great authority. All the democratic machinery may exist, but people who have started revolutions influence things. These situations give rise to cults of the personality, excesses of authority and abuses of authority.

I have tried to prevent this by using some mechanisms: first, by being aware of the problem, and second, by fighting all manifestations of cult of the personality from the very beginning of the revolution. We passed a law that forbids naming streets or projects after leaders or erecting statues or putting up portraits of leaders. You will find very few countries in the world like Cuba, where leaders' portraits aren't in all the offices. When you do find a photo of a leader, it's because the people cut it out of a magazine or looked for a photo and put it there, as there are no official pictures in public offices. We have always been against the cult of the personality, right from the start.

Gianni Minà: But isn't it true that, when you go anywhere, it is the most important event for every Cuban — something like a victory in the Olympics?

Fidel Castro: I can explain.

But to finish with the other idea, let me say that I have made a practice of sharing the work, distributing the authority and powers. Remember that when our struggle began we had an army that was being created, and there's a single command in the army; the chief assumes the responsibilities — in the military, at least. We have had a collective leadership for policy-making. Ever since we began to work, in the first days of the struggle against Batista, we had a small leadership group, and we maintained a collective leadership throughout our history. Although the revolution had a victorious army in command when it came to power, one that had tremendous authority and support, I always distributed the responsibility and emphasized that the merits belonged not to one person but to many and to an entire people. I was lucky to have clear ideas and correct concepts on this problem, which helped greatly to avoid one-person-rule trends, the abuse of power and all those things. We have a collective leadership, in which I have an influence — unquestionably, I do have influence. Even in matters related to how long a leader should continue to assume his responsibilities, the main leadership cadre does have an influence.

In this regard, I think that you have to be very alert to the circumstances or the moment when you really begin to lose your ability to carry out your responsibilities, because I think that no honest person — no matter how attached they are to a project — will try to go beyond that point to carry out functions which they are aware cannot be performed well. There may be many people — and certainly there are many — who are more capable, more intelligent and better trained than any of our present leaders. They lack the authority we have, the prestige that comes from a history of struggle; they may lack the experience we have.

In these cases, I believe that the transition shouldn't be abrupt. Of course, if an individual has an accident and dies, there is an abrupt transition. The ideal situation is for the cadres to be trained and for the transition to be made gradually, progressively. That is the best way, the ideal way, but I don't know how it will come about. I'm just telling you what I think.

You ask me if I like my work. Yes, I like it. I'm very enthusiastic about everything I do. I would like to see projects completed, as has already been the case many times. I would like to keep physically and mentally fit as long as possible to do this work.

Moreover, I am aware of the large numbers of new cadres who have emerged. There's a Spanish poem that speaks of the genius hidden in every human being, just waiting for the farmer, the sculptor of that hidden genius, to appear. I think that there is hidden genius in millions of people. I learned that in our revolutionary history, fighting in the mountains. How many brilliant leaders appeared whom we had never imagined? What made them leaders? The tasks, the opportunity to be put to the test. I am one of those who think that there are many hidden geniuses in the masses.

On one occasion, when a comrade of the revolution, Camilo Cienfuegos, died — which was a very painful loss — I said, "There are many Camilos in the people." Camilo sprang from the people, from a group, and from a group of a few dozen people many brilliant leaders arose. That shows that there are many potentially brilliant leaders who need only the responsibility and the opportunity to develop. I am far from imagining that I am more capable than others. The most I can say is that I have a little more experience than others and that I have experienced this whole revolutionary history — and experience should not be belittled.

I hope that many cadres who are more brilliant and more capable than I will appear. The last Congress of the Union of Young Communists showed that we have some exceptionally capable young people. That makes me feel very satisfied.

Gianni Minà: The book by Tad Szulc, *Fidel Castro, A Critical Portrait,* states that you were always a Marxist. Others say that his interpretation isn't correct. What do you think about this interpretation of your political personality?

Fidel Castro: First of all, I should tell you about the book of Tad Szulc; it has a history.

He came here as a journalist for some US magazine, conducted one or two interviews and then insisted on writing a book. He came here, asked for a tourist visa, rented a house and set himself up. I had many doubts. He visited me and we talked. I think he says — I've been told this — that we had a discussion, I asked him what guarantees there were that his book would be objective and he replied that his prestige as a writer guaranteed it.

I had seen some of the other things he had written. I had seen a history of the revolution in Santo Domingo and the US intervention, and it seemed very superficial. There is another, longer book on other subjects. I haven't read it, and it may be a more serious book.

He insisted on my participating and providing him with all the information for writing the book. I agreed in principle and he began to work on the book, to gather information and data in various places. But the basic element was lacking — long conversations between us, so I could present my views and relate my experiences. During that period, certain attitudes shown by Tad Szulc made me feel less than eager to cooperate, to participate in providing the information needed for creating the book. In the end, some things happened that led me to distrust what he was doing. The confidence that he tried to create, the arguments he employed, fell apart in practice. He had many links with the US Interests' Office, and he even had many contacts with people we had identified as CIA agents in the US Interests' Office here in Havana.

Later, some other episodes occurred that led him to decide to leave. We didn't ask him to go, but some difficulties arose with him. I don't want to go into this aspect in detail, but he left Cuba before conducting the interviews and conversations that were required so I could present my point of view on a whole range of topics.

He spoke with many people, both adversaries and friends, but he and I didn't have even one interview about the content of the book. He tried to give that biography an official character which it doesn't have. I had nothing to do with the writing of that book. And I think there are some things which only I know or remember or which I may view from a different angle, and which are necessary to interpret the historical events in which a person has participated. That was what happened.

I haven't spoken about this before; I haven't wanted to speak about it, actually. I can't judge the book, because there isn't any Spanish translation. I haven't read Tad Szulc's book and therefore I can't make an analysis of the book. I can only refer to the circumstances in which it was written. I had nothing at all to do with the book.

I think that once this is stated — since I can't judge the book, I can neither denounce nor accept it — I can say that if he upheld that thesis about my political training, I don't know if he did so with good intentions or bad. I can't judge. It seems that the book is polemical. I know that some enemies of the revolution have contested and even criticized the book. In the end, I'll have to read it to see what he said. If he stated that I already had Marxist-Leninist thinking and training, that is true, and it's nothing new. I've explained how that thinking was formed and developed, what my concepts were. If you ask me for proof, I would say that the revolution itself is proof of this, because someone who did not have Marxist-Leninist training could not have interpreted Cuba's events and could have drawn up a strategy for making the revolution. I think it was precisely that concept and those ideas that enabled me to prepare a strategy that led to our success, because I had a scientific conception of our society and country, what their problems were and what was the only path for making a revolution. I have explained that.

Now, I don't know what it is the people want to deny the revolution — everything? They want to deny the work of the revolution and even its ideology.

Gianni Minà: They say —

Fidel Castro: That's the last straw! What do they accuse me of, then, if they say I don't have an ideology?

Gianni Minà: They say the revolution wasn't loyal, because at the beginning the United States helped the revolution.

Fidel Castro: That it "wasn't loyal"?!

Gianni Minà: That the revolution wasn't loyal, because at the beginning the United States helped it.

Fidel Castro: Now, wait a minute! First of all, as far as I know, the United States helped Batista's government. Secondly, Batista's army had many US advisers right up to the end of the war. Not only that. At the end of the war the US Embassy and the government of the United States conspired to try to destroy the revolution and bring about a coup d'etat, to unleash events that would hold back the triumph of the revolution. All those plans failed.

I remember that I met with the US advisers a few days after the victory of the revolution, at what had been the main camp of Batista's army, and asked them, "What are you doing here?" I told them, "You can't teach us anything, because you advised Batista's army and we have defeated Batista's army." And, with those words, the military collaboration of the United States in Cuba came to an end. Those individuals had to leave. There wasn't even a document, a letter or anything else in writing. I talked with them and told them, "You advised the enemy army, lost the war, have nothing to teach us and may withdraw". That is how it ended.

I don't know where that theory came from. The United States, with its characteristic opportunism, saw that there was a major conflict, that Batista was defeated, that its tool was no longer useful and tried to maneuver — but it couldn't influence the outcome. By the time it realized how things were, Batista's army had been defeated and disarmed, and the people had the weapons in their hands. That was what happened. And all the people supported the revolution. Then it tried to use political and diplomatic measures to tame the revolution.

Naturally, our program was not yet socialist; it was a program of national liberation. It is contained in *History Will Absolve Me*, my address in which I defended myself following the attack on the Moncada barracks in 1953. The program and all the arguments are there, and anyone who takes the trouble to read that material will see that it contains all the premises for the subsequent development of a socialist revolution. It is very clear.

In that era, there were many prejudices, a lot of anti-communism. It wouldn't have been correct or timely to launch a socialist program, because our country wasn't ready for such a radical, advanced revolution. Our country was ready for that program of national liberation, which was very ambitious.

Many people may have thought that we were just one more revolutionary group such as the others that had existed in Cuba's history, which drafted programs and never carried out any of them. Perhaps they thought that in the end they could dominate, control and tame the revolution. Many sectors thought that way.

In that period, the struggle mainly centered around overthrowing the dictatorship and establishing or re-establishing the people's rights. But the program contained very advanced social measures, talking about an agrarian reform and many more of those programs I just told you about — for health, education and even reforestation. We had stated clearly that we weren't going to depend on capitalist development, that the country's development wasn't going to depend on free enterprise and supply and demand. Instead, it was going to depend, fundamentally, on using the country's resources in development programs. It contained the bases for an agrarian reform, an urban reform and a program for developing the country — all the conditions for socialism. The people accepted that program.

We set about carrying out that program, and we did so. But when the United States expressed its hostility toward Cuba, it was not against a socialist program. It was against a national liberation program that included an agrarian reform — similar to those of many other countries, including that carried out by the United States in Japan. When MacArthur was there he broke up the large landholdings, carved up the land and turned over small plots of land to many Japanese farmers who had small amounts of land. That's why the Japanese now have to farm the land in small plots and use mini-tractors and mini-combines for their rice crop. In this case, the Japanese, who are very hard-working, manage to make it productive. But because we carried out an agrarian reform that was less radical than the one MacArthur imposed in Japan, the United States decided to overthrow the Cuban revolutionary government — as it had already decided to overthrow the Arbenz government in Guatemala in 1954, because it too had carried out an agrarian reform. Our agrarian reform adversely affected the interests of big US companies.

It waged war against us because we carried out an agrarian reform, yet Kennedy promoted an agrarian reform in Latin America later on, to avoid radical revolutions. The United States practically declared war on us, not because we had proclaimed socialism or set ourselves a socialist program or openly proclaimed the Marxist-Leninist doctrine; it declared war on us because we carried out an agrarian reform as part of an advanced national liberation program of developing the country, a program which was not yet socialist. That is the historic truth. If we had launched a socialist program in those years, it would have been a mistake; we wouldn't have been effective revolutionaries or Marxist-Leninists. I think that we did what revolutionaries should do, because nobody should aspire to a program that is beyond what the objective conditions in a country allow. An ambitious revolutionary program also requires the formation of the necessary subjective conditions, and that was what we did. I think we showed that we really were conscientious revolutionaries who were mature enough to take the correct steps in each of those circumstances.

I've spoken at length about this. If that is Tad Szulc's thesis, it makes me begin to think that he was written some objective things.

I don't want to express an opinion of the book, because I haven't read it, but I know that he was rather annoyed with Cuba when he left because of a problem that arose with some people who were close to him who carried out underground journalism. We were quite offended by the fact that people would engage in underground journalism in our country, and the person responsible for that was very close to him. Those activities caused us to protest, which created some unhappiness. We didn't ask him to leave the country. He went as he had come: he came as a tourist, on his own, and rented a house. I might say that he imposed his book. I saw so much interest that, even though I had some reservations, I agreed to cooperate with him on the project. I assumed that he would gather information in many places, talk with many people, and then, as the key part of the book, interview me. Those interviews never took place. Those were the conditions in which he wrote the book.

I have the duty to tell the truth, which isn't an opinion about the book. I'm simply telling you how the book was written. The book never had official backing — or, at least, my cooperation. The least you can say about the procedure of writing the biography of someone with whom you haven't spoken even one word is that it isn't very rational. If you are going to interpret an historical period and someone's thinking, you have to speak with that person, if they are still alive.

I think that you and I have spoken much more. I did speak with him earlier, on a visit he made to Cuba when he came with a photographer — a very outstanding photographer, who, during the war in Vietnam, took a photograph that made him famous: the photo of a policeman killing a prisoner. During that visit, he interviewed me and asked questions about several topics. I wasn't very pleased with the articles he wrote at that time. They were objective, but they were also quite preconceived. I would say that he tried to adapt the interview to the criteria, opinions and prejudices he had brought to the interview. Therefore, I didn't trust him very much. That's the truth.

Since you asked me about it, I felt that I had to speak clearly in this regard.

Gianni Minà: Was there anything in the past 30 years that was your responsibility that you now think could have been better implemented? In other words, is there anything that you would not have done if you'd had the experience then that you have now?

Fidel Castro: I think that everything could have been done better — not one thing, but everything, even the best things we've done. And we have had to tackle many tasks.

State leadership is a very difficult thing. It's much easier to lead guerrillas, create an army, lead an army and win a war. It's even easier to consider all factors, draw up a revolutionary strategy, see a possibility and carry it out. It's easier to carry out political and military tasks than to manage a state. That's very difficult.

All the members of our team were very new, very young. I was one of the oldest, and I was 32; others were 30, 28 or 27. I think Che was one or two years younger than I; Raúl was around four and a half years younger; Camilo was younger; many were younger than I was. We lacked experience in these tasks. What we had was theoretical preparation and many ideas. I think that we interpreted the basic ideas well and that our strategy was correct. The revolution didn't commit any strategic mistakes, but I would say it committed tactical mistakes.

We carried out many programs. I've already explained how we promoted agricultural and industrial development. We implemented new, really successful measures in the agrarian reform itself, something we didn't copy. And that was true of many of our activities. We had the task of promoting development and building socialism, of creating a socialist economy, starting with an underdeveloped country and people who didn't have an industrial culture — we had to go from that phase to one of industrialization.

In the countryside, almost all activities were carried out with oxen, with animals — the preparation of the land, transportation, manual activities. The revolution introduced machinery. There were a few hundred tractors, perhaps 1,000 or 2,000. Later, there were tens of thousands of tractors; machines were brought in to handle all activities related to the preparation of the land, the planting and the harvesting. Productivity was greatly increased. But when we started many of the people were illiterate. Those workers who replaced oxen with tractors didn't know anything about mechanics. They used to take the oxen to a pasture where they drank water and ate; they didn't have to maintain the oxen or grease, oil or repair them. The tractors had to have water, oil and fuel; they had to have parts replaced. The workers often treated the machines the same way they treated animals. That made it necessary to set up a network of repair shops.

The factories were nationalized and many of the management personnel left the country. Sometimes the manager of one of the nationalized industries was a worker with a fifth or sixth-grade education. All of the cadres who took charge of the economy had very little training.

Analyzing the conditions under which we began doing all this, I would say it was nearly a miracle. We didn't have any experience. The most difficult task may well have been that of drawing up the economic development programs, the economic management programs. We made mistakes in that. I am responsible for the mistakes, either directly or indirectly — either because I had an idea that wasn't the most appropriate or because I accepted ideas from those who had theoretical, not practical, knowledge.

Over the years, we have gained considerable experience in all these matters. I knew this was going to happen, because when the war ended I felt a kind of sudden vacuum — a great joy, but also an awareness that a new stage was beginning. We had learned how to wage a war, and it was over. If you analyze our resources in terms of the men with whom we carried out that task, we were extraordinarily effective. But I knew that an even more difficult task was beginning and I presented it to the people as such. I didn't imagine how difficult it would be, and I don't think anybody did, because it seemed that ideas and actions, theory and the practical application of theory, would not be so far apart. If I had had the experience I have today, that was the sphere in which I would have exerted greater control. But that's utopian; I'm talking about hypotheses. I think the same thing has happened to all revolutionaries.

Gianni Minà: Is there anything about which you would say now, "I shouldn't have done that?" A mistake that you wouldn't repeat now?

Fidel Castro: I think that at one point we were too ambitious. We wanted to skip stages, to leap over the stage of the construction of socialism, and we tried, as Marx said of the Paris Commune, to storm the heavens. We almost wanted to build a communist society immediately — when the productive forces for the construction of the communist society had to be developed, and a phase was required in which you had to apply the principles of socialist distribution established by Marx. He said that in socialism, each one should contribute according to their ability and receive according to their work — that is, in accordance with the quantity and quality of their work. We didn't pay as much attention as we should to that stage. I think that if we had it to do over again, we would not make those mistakes.

Then we committed mistakes of another kind. It was somewhat the fault of the technocrats. I am responsible because I didn't foresee all of the consequences. Perhaps also, I had the idea of using other experiences. Some of those technocrats simply copied.

We also went through a phase of rejecting the experience of other countries, which is just as incorrect. We had suffered from a stage of thinking that we knew more than we did, of thinking that we were doing things better than others. Then we went through another stage in which we tended to copy — although I, personally, didn't participate in that — and I have said that we copied both good and bad features.

Photo: Osvaldo Salas

I believe that we now have a more balanced view of this. We value the experience of others, we analyze everything more calmly, and we reaffirm our criteria, our own criteria, and develop them without chauvinism, without an arrogant attitude. I would say that we have reached the ideal point for applying and making the best use of our own ideas, at the same time as also making better use of the experience of other countries. We do what suits our conditions and don't do what doesn't.

You attended the assembly in which I met with thousands of people, including the representatives of all the enterprises in the provinces of Havana and City of Havana. We analyzed in depth many matters.

We have reached the ideal point when making decisions. The political leadership should go deeply into each question, not simply rubber-stamp what a group of experts, technocrats — I call them the "tribal witch-doctors," those who have boned up on the subject, the ones who know because they've had theoretical training but who don't see the overall picture . . . Scientists and economists should help the political leaders, who are those who set the goals and know how to achieve results.

Sometimes there is too much specialization in the world. The technocrats have influence over those in government. They don't know anything about politics, and often their ideas are alien to politics. They may not even care about the consequences of their ideas.

They also tend to believe in mechanisms too much. We in government tend to believe more in the people, in men and women — especially in a socialist process, in which development is programmed and goals are set. This is a very interesting question. I don't want to go into it too much, but we have gone from the mistakes of idealism to other mistakes because of technocratic influences, in which we began to place too much importance on money. Yes, we went from a period in which it was given very little importance to a period in which it was given too much importance. From a period in which we began to promote conscious efforts to the maximum to a period in which we were beginning, unwittingly, to corrupt people by paying them for everything. Voluntary work began to be weakened, as were certain values that cannot be renounced in a revolution.

That is the kind of experience I can discuss with you, for which all of us were to blame. I have my share of responsibility for it. If we had to begin again now with this experience, unquestionably we would do things much better in this field. There may be some consolation. "Misery loves company" is the consolation of fools, and these mistakes have provided lots of company in misery, but this is no consolation. Rather, we should take it as an explanation of what has happened to revolutionaries all over the world.

I think that you can't be a revolutionary without a large dose of idealism and tremendous confidence in human beings. A sceptic can't be a revolutionary. A revolutionary is an optimist, someone who believes in human beings.

I know many people who don't believe in humans, who think they are animals governed only by instinct and personal ambition. Capitalist society has viewed human beings that way more than any other. It always viewed them as economic animals governed only by selfishness. But I know that human beings are capable of great efforts, great altruism and great solidarity, and I know this not because I read it in a book but because I saw it in this struggle. I saw many generous, splendid people who gave their lives for ideas, running all kinds of risks. I saw it in the war, in many comrades, who made enormous efforts and sacrifices — and they weren't even paid. They had nothing — nothing but an idea — yet we managed to defeat an army that was who knows how many times larger than ours. Even at the end of the war, the enemy had 25 soldiers for every armed combatant of ours. How could that be done? That is why I have always been inclined to put more faith in the moral factors, in the conscience of human beings, because I've seen what they are capable of achieving. I have had many lessons of this throughout our history.

I'll tell you: the people have confidence, and the people know history.

You said that many people look forward to my appearances. That depends on how often I speak. At the beginning of the revolution, I spoke very frequently. There was always a need to guide the people, waging an ideological battle. Now that the people have acquired a political culture, with more solid knowledge, it isn't as necessary for me to make public appearances. I speak at rallies and on anniversaries; I speak in meetings a lot, and some of those speeches are televised and published. I am always working in groups, holding meetings. But in the big mass meetings, on anniversaries, I speak only when the circumstances warrant it, and, of course, that always awakens expectation, interest — it's a habit that has been created.

Gianni Minà: Let's take up some questions that Europeans would describe as more delicate.

Fidel Castro: You can ask whatever you want.

Gianni Minà: Thirty years ago, your revolution described itself as a national, patriotic revolution. The legitimate government of Cuba can now allow itself to give the people weapons without their being used against the constituted government, even though, as you say, not everything has been done in the best possible way. Does this mean that the revolution kept its word? Or, as its enemies say, does it mean that one half of the population controls the other half through the Committees for the Defense of the Revolution?

Fidel Castro: Let me begin with the first part. Our revolution was nationalist and patriotic, and it is still a nationalist and patriotic revolution. This isn't a narrow nationalism — rather, it is a healthy nationalism, because it is also internationalist, and internationalism doesn't deny patriotism or nationalism.

The revolution, as you say, has allowed itself the luxury of arming the people. The workers in their factories have weapons. There are millions of men and women who are organized, trained and armed. That is the strength of our defense: to apply our concept of war of all the people in case of a direct military attack on Cuba. The workers, farmers and students are trained and armed. Each one knows what they must do in case of attack — who should remain in production, in the factories — and the whole country is organized for that eventuality.

I think that this is the supreme test of the people's support for the revolution and of consensus and participation. I might ask if in the United States the government can arm the people — if it can arm the workers, the Chicanos, the blacks, the students, all the population. I wonder if Europe ever gave arms to the workers, if it ever gave arms to the people. No, the use of arms is exclusively the domain of professionals.

Luis XIV said, "L'Etat c'est moi." That was the maximum expression of absolutism. Now in that same country only a part of the population, certain institutions and forces, can say, "I am the state."

In our country, however, every citizen can say "I am the state," because of their participation in all activities. Among other things, they defend that state and are a part of that state. I think that the supreme test of a citizen's identification with the state or with a political process is their total dedication to that process, their readiness to defend it with their life. I think that the supreme test of confidence in the people and of identification with the people is when the state arms and trains the people and the country's defense stops being an exclusive function of a group of professionals. That is a reality which any visitor can see in our country.

As for the theory that the revolution only continues because one half is keeping an eye on the other, that would surely give rise to an interminable civil war. Those divisions and polarizations are what give rise to civil wars, and we have never had a civil war in our country, simply because the vast majority of the people support the revolution and defend it. A half of the people didn't have to confront the other half. Just imagine what would happen if a half of the people, supported by the United States, were against socialism and the revolution: they would wipe out the revolution. The revolution has been able to defend itself because the vast majority has supported it, and only a tiny minority — a militant but very small minority — has opposed it. Moreover, nobody is neutral in a revolution. We had 90, 91 or 92 percent in favor and only from 8 to 10 percent against. That was enough of a base to organize counter-revolutionary activities, as was the case.

The CIA and the United States not only organized mercenary invasions — such as the one at the Bay of Pigs — and threatened to attack directly, but also created hundreds of counter-revolutionary organizations here in the first few years. As I told you, I think we recorded 300 of those organizations. Five, six or 10 people would get together and create an organization under the inspiration and guidance of the United States. The revolution managed to defend itself because it represented the vast majority, and the minority was controlled by the vast majority.

One day, after returning from the United Nations, I was at a rally when four bombs went off in the city. And I said, if we have all the people, let's organize all the people, because it isn't the same for all the people to conspire against an oppressing minority as for a counter-revolutionary minority to conspire against the people. And we organized the people, block by block, in all the cities and the countryside.

We have powerful mass organizations: for the workers, the women, the farmers, the residents in each area, the students and even the children, and all of the mass organizations support the revolution. They are the ones who have crushed all counter-revolutionary activities and made them completely ineffective. The other theory is very simplistic. I don't really think that a European can be taken in by such a simplistic version, that tries to ignore the fact that a revolution in Cuba's conditions, confronted by a country as powerful as the United States, had to have the support of the vast majority of the people in order to defend itself and survive.

Gianni Minà: That block, or neighborhood, organization is often considered an attack on individual liberty.

Fidel Castro: We needed it because we were confronted with counter-revolutionary activities. The counter-revolutionaries had cars, garages and houses and carried out activities. The police, alone, couldn't control it. And since the people were militant revolutionaries, we asked for and organized their cooperation. So the people had control — not of what an individual did, but of the activities against the revolution.

That's how the Committees for the Defense of the Revolution were created in the early years. There were hard years, years of struggle, such as those in Nicaragua, engaged in a struggle against a dirty war. We, too, were confronted with a dirty war, with bands of men armed by the United States in all the provinces, in the mountains and the cities — all over — and the CDRs played a very important role in the struggle against the counter-revolution.

Then the counter-revolution was defeated. It didn't disappear entirely, because as long as there is harassment by the United States, there will be counter-revolutionary activities generated from abroad. Our CDRs later tackled other activities. They still have the function of defending the revolution, and we remind them of it, but the organized people set about all kinds of activities: the literacy campaign, the vaccination and other health campaigns, the organization of the electoral districts, the assemblies for nominating candidates and many other important activities.

You have to see what our assemblies are like. The Party doesn't nominate the candidates for delegate in each voting area. The delegates have the power and later elect the members of the other state bodies. The Party doesn't even participate in the nomination of the candidates. Those assemblies are open to all the people, and the regulations state that there must be from two to eight candidates, any one of whom, to be elected, must receive more than 50 percent of the votes. A run-off election is held when, in the first round, no candidate has more than 50 percent of the votes.

All of the mass organizations help to carry out the various tasks: combating epidemics, striving to wipe out a kind of mosquito, cleaning up the city, painting and constructing. These institutions were created at different historic moments and now carry out other tasks, because the enemy has mainly taken refuge abroad. And even though it has its sympathizers, enemies of socialism inside our country, they are an insignificant minority. This mass organization has other tasks and we aren't going to dissolve it. But of course, there is propaganda about it, because the enemy has to explain the failure of all its offensives and all of its counterrevolutionary plans.

Gianni Minà: Many people say that you are the only real head of the opposition in Cuba. Now that the economic situation has become more critical, where do you, as head of the opposition, think the most emphasis must be placed?

Fidel Castro: That has its history. The revolution has always been critical and self-critical. If the revolutionary processes are analyzed, it will be hard to find an example similar to that of the Cuban revolution in the practice of public criticism and self-criticism. We have often criticized ourselves frankly, without any demagogy: "This was a mistake"; "That's what happened." That has been a feature of the revolution ever since the beginning. Of course, because of my influence on public opinion, my criticisms are echoed. I don't hesitate to speak out when things are going wrong. I often prefer to talk about what's wrong rather than what's going smoothly, and I'm very frank, very open, to everyone in meetings. I believe that men and women have a sense of honor.

I remember how the men reacted to criticism during the war. There were units that were in one position and then, when the enemy withdrew, they did also. Then I had to call together a whole squad or a whole platoon that abandoned a position and criticize its members severely and choose between disarming them and giving their weapons to the recruits — there were always some recruits without weapons — or giving them another chance. More often than not, the next day, when they clashed with the enemy, they carried out heroic feats.

I've always had the custom of appealing to the honor and dignity of human beings. Therefore, I've had the habit of criticism. I even criticize groups: whole groups, entire factories, the people as a whole, when there is something that's wrong, a negative trend. I also have a lot of criticism of the government, for my own tasks, for the work of the revolution. That's why some people say that I'm the opposition.

In our conditions, the Party itself, the revolutionary cadres, each at his own level, must be the opposition. And we do this frankly and honestly. There isn't even the shadow of demagogy in this, for nobody can be a demagogue with the people. As the refrain puts it, a liar is easier to spot than a lame man. Ever since the triumph of the revolution, people have said that they can distinguish between speakers who are shams and those who are speaking frankly.

If you ask me what the problems are — and we have difficulties, all of us have them, although we have fewer than others — I would say that our main effort now is to reduce the wasting of resources, to make the best possible use of our material and human resources and seek maximum economic efficiency, to optimize our plans. We are engaged in that effort right now: doing more things with fewer resources by making better use of the technical, human and material resources we have.

Gianni Minà: For us Europeans, what we saw last Thursday, for example, was quite sensational: you went on television and admitted that a high-ranking official, a minister, had acted incorrectly. You mentioned him by name: Luis Orlando Domínguez. You even said more: you admitted that you yourself had chosen and believed in him. Nevertheless, using documentary proof, with dates and times, you showed his errors. You didn't judge him. You said, "The judges will do that; these are the facts." For us, that is a singular, new way of communicating with the people. Is this part of your philosophy, of your relations with the people and with the revolution?

Fidel Castro: The best thing, with a comrade who begins to make mistakes, is to discover their mistakes in time, point them out and criticize them. That is what is done with many comrades. That is one of the Party's tasks. Every Party member, in their Party nucleus, should measure their conduct against what the others think and be criticized for the things done badly.

That member of the Union of Young Communists (UJC) and of the Party was accumulating merits and winning prestige, gaining authority. Unfortunately, nobody discovered his mistakes in time. It all came out quite suddenly, according to everything that I have been able to prove. It was in 1985. He already had authority and had been a leader of the UJC and a member of the Council of State. He was a member of the Central Committee of the Party and worked on my team — we try to encourage young people. Every year I recruit outstanding cadres from the UJC to work in my office on important activities, which are assigned to them so they will acquire a global view of problems.

He had respect and consideration, and quite suddenly he acquired those problems. He was handling funds, resources. Nobody would have imagined it of him. Any comrade would have been hurt to imagine that he was stealing. In the beginning, it seemed that he had enjoyed some privileges, that he had made use of his position to do certain things for his own benefit. Not stealing; nobody thought of that at first. When we dug deeper, we discovered everything.

I have explained to the people, step by step, how we found everything out. I've conveyed how, step by step, I discovered and was surprised by this. That is, I have enabled every citizen to accompany me in this process of discovery. And we drew the pertinent conclusions.

This is the first time that we've had such a case — such a proven case of an individual in a high position who misappropriated funds. There are some crazy features of his conduct, because his actions — I'm not going to repeat them now — made him seem like a kleptomaniac. I had to publicly explain this episode. It was painful and hard — and not only for me. There are hundreds of thousands of young people whose UJC cards bear his signature, because he was a leader when they received their cards, and many of them are now saying that they want new membership cards, with another signature, and this problem has to be solved.

Of course, there are human problems of this kind, people who can be corrupted, but you can be sure that you won't find a more healthy atmosphere than ours. Here, corruption is the exception. It isn't extensive; it isn't like in other parts of the world, where corruption is generalized. We must fight it before it becomes generalized.

Gianni Minà: Some people interpret this event as if the new well-being that exists in Cuba brings with it the destruction of the revolution's values.

Fidel Castro: To the contrary. Certain measures of the economic management system, certain elements of that system, such as the farm markets for unrationed produce — which influenced only a small proportion of the population — and some of our laws, such as the Housing Law, made it possible for some people to make a lot of money, and money began to have more value. Many administrators and others wanted to solve problems with money rather than by improving discipline, carrying out political work and providing more effective leadership. Often, good use wasn't made of the workday, and they then paid for overtime. The norms were old and obsolete. Many activities began to change the workers' mentality and to increase the importance of money. I think that was a weakening, corrupting trend.

When we detected those negative trends toward trying to solve everything with money, with some people becoming rich, we began to combat those trends and set about establishing discipline in this regard. This case arose, and it is even more spectacular in the midst of the process of rectification in which we have been struggling — silently and in an organized way — to combat all manifestations of privilege and all tendencies toward making incorrect use of resources. We discovered this problem in the midst of this process, and it acquired a notoriety and an importance that made it necessary to discuss it publicly, because it couldn't be rectified in any other way. A person may be making a mistake and you tell them to rectify it. But if they have already committed a crime, a serious crime, then you reach a point at which there can't be any rectification, because they have passed the borderline and their activity has become a crime — and therefore it is no longer a political problem but has become a violation of the law.

Gianni Minà: With regard to those matters and to the way in which you tackled them, I ask you the following: In their congress, Cuban journalists emphasized the responsibility that the press has for the lack of a critical spirit in its work. Some of them referred to the "syndrome of mystery," by virtue of which only those who don't hurt anybody are mentioned. What measures have been taken to make the newspapers more informative, keeping in mind the clarity with which you speak when you go on television?

Fidel Castro: The press in Cuba is revolutionary, and its journalists are revolutionaries. The various organizations have their newspapers; the workers and the members of the Union of Young Communists have their own newspapers; the Party has its national-circulation newspaper, as well as papers in the provinces. The farmers have their newspaper. The Armed Forces, the Ministry of the Interior and the artists have magazines. All of the mass organizations have their own newspapers or magazines, and there are dozens of them, all revolutionary. Cuba's newspapers and magazines aren't in the hands of enemies of the revolution. They aren't in the hands of US agents. They have always been in the hands of revolutionaries, and this was one of the results of this struggle, this life-or-death struggle that we waged. All this is in a situation of struggle, or war, in which the enemy was attacking us.

At one time, there was a trend of supposing that critical comments and the denunciation of errors played into the enemy's hands, helped the enemy and helped the counter-revolution. For a while, in that situation of fierce, intensive struggle, those trends prevailed. This was until, in a period of greater peace, we began to discover that in the struggle against those negative trends or mistakes the work of the Party and the mass organizations wasn't enough. The role of the newspapers and magazines was also very important. We then came to the conclusion that we had to develop a greater critical spirit. We became convinced of the value and importance of public criticism in the press — not only self-criticism and criticism by the Party but also criticism by the newspapers, magazines and journalists. I have been greatly stimulated by that critical spirit of our newspapers and magazines, and we have come a long way along that path. I would say that is one of the main factors in this battle to improve our system, our institutions and our work.

I was the one who the coined the term, "syndrome of mystery." I am the author of that term — not the journalists. In the meeting with the journalists, I said, "We have the syndrome of mystery, the fear of informing the people about something, because we think it may serve the enemy."

We know that there are drawbacks. We want responsible criticism. The journalists make many mistakes, even in the numbers and data they provide. I criticize that; they should analyze their figures. Many people make those mistakes. The other day, there was an article about a cardboard factory, and there was a heading that said, "50 Million Tons to be Produced," when it should have said "50,000 Tons." The criticism is often superficial; the journalists don't dig deeply into the subject. But I say that whatever the consequences and no matter what mistakes may be made, this is preferable to an absence of criticism.

We have promoted criticism and it is developing. Journalists are being trained who have specialized in sports, agriculture, certain industries and specific areas. Other journalists write about general topics of national policy, ideological policy and international politics. I can tell you with satisfaction that, even though the Party, the State Inspection Department and other sources send me many reports about problems — that a certain problem occurred in such-and-such a place — my most important source of information, the one I value the most, is the newspapers.

Gianni Minà: In the 2nd Plenary Session of the Central Committee of the Communist Party of Cuba, held in the summer of 1986, you criticized those who think they are revolutionaries but don't work or produce as they should. Don't you think, as it is claimed in the Western world, that lack of access to material incentives may sometimes be the main cause of low productivity in a socialist regime?

Fidel Castro: In our experience that isn't so. Productivity is determined, first of all, by technology, and Cuban workers have increased productivity tremendously. In the past, 350,000 cane-cutters used to work in a sugar harvest; we now need only 70,000. Nearly everything is mechanized: port activities, construction activities and agriculture — it's all mechanized — and productivity has been raised considerably.

You can't talk about low productivity. We've been raising productivity year by year. Nor can you talk about a lack of incentives. I've already explained that, at some moments, we made mistakes, with an egalitarian concept of payment. The incentives exist. There aren't as many incentives as in a capitalist consumer society. Many of the workers' problems are solved. The efficiency problems in production aren't determined by the workers — by defects in the workers or in the workers' attitude. In general, the workers in our factories have an excellent attitude. The difficulties arise from the lack of organizational ability and leadership of the cadres, the cadres' failure to impose discipline. That is our weak point as I see it. When there are good cadres and good leadership, everything goes smoothly. In the meeting with representatives of the enterprises in Havana, I emphasized the importance of leadership methods and techniques.

Some of our measures and concepts have also caused difficulties for production, such as the excessive number — some 14,500 — of occupations, the narrow job descriptions for those occupations. These job classifications often made it necessary to have two or three workers where one could have carried out the work in an eight-hour workday. Also the matter of seniority lists — which often interfere with the selection of the best worker for each piece of equipment or for certain posts. Thus, concepts that stemmed somewhat from the workers' aspirations in their struggles under capitalism, led the revolution to establish certain ideas and principles that interfered with efficiency and production. We are now striving to overcome all of those obstacles and difficulties. The workers have responded wonderfully; the problems lie not in the workers, in their work spirit or in their attitude, but in the other factors I mentioned.

Gianni Minà: In the Soviet Union, the Constitution has once again recognized the possibility of there being small private enterprise. Will Cuban legislation do the same?

Fidel Castro: Historically, self-employment has existed in the countryside. There are still tens of thousands of independent farmers, each of whom owns up to 60 acres. Even though most of the farmers' land has been joined together in cooperatives, it is a gradual process that has advanced patiently as a need for the development of agriculture and for the application of the most modern, most efficient techniques. You can't use a harvester or dust crops on small landholdings, as we do on the big state farms and agricultural cooperatives. But there are still tens of thousands of small independent farmers and thousands of truck owners. And there are independent taxi owners, as well.

Many people are also self-employed as dressmakers. A large number of women go to dressmakers for their clothes. And there are self-employed hairdressers. Many years ago, we even passed laws about that. Retired people may work on their own in many traditional occupations, and people who aren't retired may do such work in certain spheres. We have analyzed the contradictions that sometimes arise: for example, labor power is needed in construction. There are people who have the resources, with relatively high incomes, to pay for buildings and compete for the work force against priority projects for the country. We must avoid those contradictions and their negative consequences. It is understood that second jobs should be done after the normal workday, but the workday is often under-utilized and there is some indiscipline. We are studying all those activities in which private jobs are opportune and those which aren't. For example, if service workers in a state workshop repairing televisions are authorized to do work on the side, they may not do their normal work correctly, so as to force people to hire them privately. We are noting where those contradictions appear and seeking solutions for those problems.

In medicine, I told you there are only 40 or 50 doctors in private practice, because we have applied a consistent policy on the training of doctors, and none of the new doctors intend to go into private practice — the idea doesn't even occur to them. In general, in the university professions we state that we aren't going to do that. Nobody in our country would think of a doctor going into private practice. We have educated and trained our doctors for social medicine. In that field, we have made great advances. There's no reason for introducing private practice.

That is, we decide whether or not to authorize private jobs on a case-by-case basis, in accord with our experience. There are laws governing that. After 10 years of experience, we are studying where it worked and where it didn't, where it helped to solve problems and where it created problems. That is the policy we're applying.

Gianni Minà: In the light of all this, you have obviously always been critical of the capitalist system, but on various occasions, you haven't been entirely opposed to it. What do you think of that economic system, with all its defects and advantages, on which we all depend, either directly or indirectly?

Fidel Castro: First of all, we should make an historical assessment. Every succeeding social regime has been more advanced than the one preceding it. In the various stages, there were the old societies in Rome and Greece, slavery and the class struggles. The old slave regime was replaced by the feudal regime, which was better, more humane, than the slave regime and signified an advance. The capitalist regime was better than the feudal regime. It appeared in a given historical stage and promoted a tremendous upsurge in the productive forces. This isn't my thesis — it is the thesis of Marx, Engels and Lenin. It gave a tremendous boost to the productive forces, until it had given everything it could of itself. The historic moment came when, inevitably, it had to be replaced by a better system that eliminated the contradiction between ownership based on private appropriation and the ever more social nature of a production process that had to be directed and controlled with a social sense and whose motor force was the satisfaction of the material and spiritual needs of all society rather than irrational consumerism and the desire to acquire individual wealth.

Historically, you have to make a positive evaluation of capitalist society and of all the advances it brought about.

I really consider — especially from the human point of view — the socialist regime to be much better in all ways. Judging from our experience, I can say that truly fabulous things can be achieved by socialism: a new technology can be extended rapidly throughout the country in any field. In agriculture, a new variety of seed or a new technique can be generalized in a very short time. In medicine, for example, every time a new technique has appeared, it has been utilized in a matter of days or months in our country. In a capitalist society, full of private clinics, it is very unlikely that will happen.

Because of my own experience, I have absolute, total preference for socialism. I don't really have any fondness for capitalism; it seems to me to be an alienating system that divides humanity, a system of inequality, of privileges and selfishness. Nonetheless, in view of the fear of social revolutions and the fear of socialism, modern capitalism has tried and has developed new forms of distribution, has tried to humanize the system. The conditions in which workers live under capitalism are not the same as those in which they lived when the system was still young, although the system hasn't managed to escape cyclical economic crises — such as we are witnessing at present — or the growing presence of unemployment, drugs, crime, violence and social inequality, which goes from the most opulent wealth to the most horrifying poverty, even in the developed capitalist countries. I don't have any admiration for the capitalist system, and I believe that the future belongs to socialism.

Yes, I admit that capitalism has provided some useful experiences, but I don't admire the mechanisms of capitalism or the laws of capitalism or the principle of blind, spontaneous development of the economy without any program or plan. The capitalist countries have considerable technological advances, important experience in the organization of production and important advances in management techniques, which they have developed as a science. I tell Cuban workers and the enterprises that, while not copying the mechanisms of the capitalist system, we should use its experience in the organization and management of production. We should do this in the conditions of socialism, which doesn't have the cruel instruments for coercing workers that exist in capitalism.

The organization and efficient management of production is still one of our weak links. The socialist system is very new, and it still has a lot to learn.

Chapter 6

The new human being

There is a striking idealism in the path that Cuba has chosen and continues to choose — seemingly against all logic — in the search for its development and of a model of life.

This idealism is an almost religious feeling.

However, I don't feel qualified — nor do I think I have the right — to judge this way of political life, keeping in mind that it has achieved results. Moreover, as Fidel has said many times, "Without a large dose of idealism, you can't be revolutionary." I think that this is a sincere feeling and has been at the heart of every action — whether correct or not — undertaken by those who, with Fidel, have tried to build the revolution throughout these years. I don't know if this feeling will be maintained with the same rigorous fervor, with the same strength and with the same romanticism in young Cubans, in the "new man" born in more recent years.

At the time of this interview I met the members of Fidel's team, those who live and work closest to him. I ate in his houses. It isn't discreet to mentions names, but it is clear that they still live in conditions of austerity, moderation, modesty and I would almost say dignified poverty, unusual in any present structure of government. It is as if the revolution had triumphed only yesterday. Naturally, this would not absolve the revolution if it were stained with all the sins of which its adversaries accuse it, but it is a sign of a morality of life not found in those who flaunt the privileges of power.

But the young people, those who were born after Fidel, Che Guevara and Camilo Cienfuegos had already changed the country's

Fidel Castro cutting cane during voluntary work *Photo: Osvaldo Salas*

image and recovered a national dignity and identity, those who know of the dictator Batista only through their school books — will they have the same faith in that model of life?

Fidel is convinced of this, and — as shown in the preceding chapter — is not worried by having to explain on television how and why Luis Orlando Domínguez, a capable, promising young man who was a former leader of the Union of Young Communists whom he himself had chosen as director of Civil Aviation, one day appeared implicated in a history of private interests that seems to have come from the consumer oriented Western world.

I have no reason or proof for doubting Fidel's confidence.

A memorable concert that the Moncada Group gave on the steps of the University of Havana comes to mind as an impression I received of Cuban young people today. I observed there that their conduct during the concert, their communal rites, of lighting matches while enchanted by a romantic song — in short, their way of consuming the entertainment — was just like that of young people in Milan, Paris, Madrid, London or New York. But there was no violence, that senseless tension that surrounds rock concerts in the West.

Perhaps this fact, which may seem simply a detail to some, marks a difference. Or perhaps not.

G.M.

Gianni Minà: President Castro, ever since the first years after the triumph of the revolution, you have maintained that it was necessary, above all else, to cultivate the political awareness of the population. It seems to me that you are convinced that, in the years that have passed, the consciousness of Cuban citizens has already been formed.

Fidel Castro: If you don't talk about political consciousness, you can't talk about socialism. You can't be a socialist if you don't think that consciousness is the main factor. How can you aspire to communism without consciousness? Can you form a society based on solidarity if you develop individualism and selfishness? Moral values have tremendous importance, even in capitalist society. If you were faced with aggression, the people would fight in Italy defending themselves against foreign aggression. What values are you defending? Your homeland, the national interest. People are capable of fighting and dying for that. When a soldier goes to a trench — you have had plenty of wars — he doesn't go because he's paid a wage; he's defending some value. Men uphold values to such an extent that, often, they have died en masse, as in World War I, in veritable massacres that could only occur because of the way men upheld certain values. In socialism, people love their homeland and national independence, and they also support social values — especially the sense of human solidarity, without which you can't even talk of socialism.

We try to emphasize those values, because we believe that men and women can live in socialism, which is an organized, conscious society with programmed development. In capitalism, everything obeys blind laws, which direct all economic and social processes. In socialism, that can't happen; the idea of a new society without a profound awareness of high ethical and human values can't even be imagined. They are of fundamental importance. In capitalism, people are under very great pressure to work, for fear of losing their jobs. Unemployment is very real. Workers depend on their wages for everything: they need money for the education of their children, for medical treatment, for old age, for seeing them through accidents and sickness. Our society gives men and women protection in all those aspects: it guarantees them protection against sickness and accidents; no children are left unprotected; all have access to medical treatment, to schools and to employment. In capitalism, people pursue jobs. In socialism, the jobs pursue the people, because everyone has possibilities of all kinds. If you don't like it here, you can go there or somewhere else. We must create a conscious discipline in the people, an attitude of conscientious work; if we don't, you can't even conceive of socialism.

We have done that, and we have advanced considerably in this sphere.

Gianni Minà: President Castro, 30 years ago Cuba was the island of pleasure for US citizens. There were prostitutes, and all the big hotels and casinos were owned by Mafia chieftains — Lucky Luciano, Frank Costello and others. Therefore, nobody can deny that your revolution has created a political consciousness among Cubans and has re-established what I might call a lost sense of national identity. How, without rhetoric, would you define this new Cuba, or as Che described him, this "new man"?

Fidel Castro: "Without rhetoric." Well, I'll try not to engage in any rhetoric.

It is true — I see that you are well-informed — that there were 100,000 prostitutes, something incredible in a population of 6.5 million. I could speak about direct and indirect prostitution; many women were taken to work in the bars, restaurants and many other places in a more subtle form of prostitution. Women were exploited terribly. Some shops or establishments selected girls on the basis of their beauty. Prostitution was nearly generalized. Matrimony was almost a form of prostitution, because of the discrimination that existed against women. In that society, there was a lot of prejudice against women who had been divorced. Women were looked on as decorations, as instruments of pleasure. That was one of the most inhuman aspects of that society.

But it wasn't the only one. There were many other problems, which I've examined.

Che spoke of the new man. It is the continuation of the other idea, that a new society has to create a new consciousness. A socialist revolutionary process has to create a new human being also. In essence, that new human being has to express much more solidarity, be much more selfless, to look on all others as brothers. Sometimes, in capitalism, not even blood brothers respect or love each other.

We postulate something to which the Christian doctrine also subscribes: the brotherhood of all people, solidarity, selflessness and generosity, to which we add a high education, advanced technical training, national dignity, and an internationalist approach. I'm not trying to define all of the values for you; I'm simply pointing out some of the aspects of the new human being of whom Che spoke. I don't think we can say that all people are new human beings in our country; we couldn't even say that all our young people are new human beings. But it is a fact that an enormous leap in the quality of human beings has been made in our homeland. We have hundreds of thousands — millions — of people, young people, both manual and intellectual workers and farmers, with such a large dose of that consciousness that we can call them new human beings.

You may ask, what is this based on? I'll give you an example: when the Sandinista revolution triumphed, the Nicaraguans asked us for 1,000 teachers. We asked the teachers how many were willing to go, and 30,000 volunteered. Later, the Sandinistas asked for 1,000 more, and we chose 2,000, most of whom were women

— many women work in education — who were assigned to the most isolated, least accessible parts of Nicaragua. It was like missionary work, the work of those nuns and priests who were practically considered saints when they used to do this, living in the same conditions. When the counter-revolutionaries killed some of those teachers, some 100,000 — practically all of the teachers in Cuba — volunteered.

Before the revolution, no teachers wanted to work in the mountains. Now, we have teachers who go to Nicaragua and Angola, and they're willing to go to any other country in the world. Before the revolution, no doctors were willing to sacrifice and provide health services in the mountains or other parts of the countryside. We now have doctors in nearly 30 countries — several hundred in Nicaragua, Ethiopia, Angola, Mozambique . . . .

Gianni Minà: More than the World Health Organization?

Fidel Castro: I think we have twice as many as the World Health Organization, working in around 30 countries as a donation. Two countries that have extensive resources proposed and wanted to pay for our doctors' services, but in more than 90 percent of the countries the host country provides food and lodging, while we pay those doctors' salaries.

Gianni Minà: Which are the two countries that pay for those services?

Fidel Castro: One of them is Algeria. For many years, after Algeria's independence, we sent doctors there. After 15 years, the Algerians improved their economic conditions and at their own initiative, stated that they would pay the doctors. We accepted.

There are doctors in Libya. The Libyans have resources and pay. Before the war, there were doctors who were paid in Iraq, but when the war broke out and the doctors there became absolutely indispensable — they treat all of the wounded, not only Iraqis who are wounded, but also the Iranians who are wounded and are in Iraqi hospitals — we suggested suspending payment of the doctors for the duration of the war.

So, to the best of my memory, two countries pay for the doctors now. They don't pay the high salaries that they would have to pay for a World Health Organization doctor, but they pay our doctors a fair salary. In all the other countries, our doctors work as a Cuban donation. We can do this because we pay their salaries, while the host country provides their food and lodging. Sometimes, several doctors live in a single house. A doctor from the World Health Organization takes his family along; that is much more expensive. The host country has to pay for the vacation of the doctor and all his family every year. It has to create living conditions that often didn't exist previously, and it has to pay high salaries — I don't know, but a World Health Organization doctor must cost between $40,000 and $60,000 a year.

We have doctors, teachers and technicians. In addition, at the time of the internationalist mission in support of Angola, when the South African racists invaded Angola, we took a poll of how many fighters, people of fighting age, were willing to carry out that mission, and 300,000 volunteered. I ask myself, does this happen in other countries? I have great affection and respect for the other Latin American peoples, but they live under another system. Could 1,000 teachers be recruited to go to work in the conditions in which our teachers went to work in Nicaragua? I don't doubt that our Latin American brothers and sisters have many potential virtues, but could 1,000, 30,000 or 100,000 have been recruited to work in those conditions or to go to any other country?

We have doctors in Vietnam; we've had doctors in Vietnam ever since the war. We also have them in Laos, Kampuchea and South Yemen. We have doctors in the poorest countries in the world, living there, separated from their families for a long time. Already, this is a mass phenomenon. It isn't a matter of our being able to recruit 100 or 200. Around 50,000 Cubans are carrying out internationalist missions right now: doctors, teachers, construction workers, military personnel and other workers. In any case, our military personnel are workers who belong to the reserves; they aren't professional soldiers, though their officers are. Thus, that new spirit is a mass phenomenon now in our country. I can't say that it includes all of society, but we have more than enough proof that that spirit is a reality.

Gianni Minà: Many people say that the Cuban soldiers who are sent to Ethiopia or Angola, where some of them lose their lives or are wounded, don't always go with their families' blessing, which causes sadness and grief . . .

Fidel Castro: There's one very important thing: every Cuban who goes to carry out an internationalist mission does so voluntarily; nobody is forced to go on an internationalist mission. Those who go consider it the highest honor — and not only they, but their families, too, consider it an honor, because it is a moral value that is greatly esteemed in our country. I wouldn't say that a family doesn't worry when one of its members goes as a soldier or as a teacher, a doctor, an agronomist, a construction worker, a sports trainer or any other kind of adviser, because there are risks. There are counter-revolutionary activities in many of those countries. There's the dirty war in Nicaragua, and quite a few of our compatriots who weren't combatants have died there. They may also die in Angola, because the counter-revolutionary bands have murdered civilians. In addition, there are many diseases in Africa, Asia and all over. That is, not only the military personnel but the civilians, too, run risks of all kinds: political risks, risks of acts of terrorism and risks to their health. Naturally, that implies sacrifices for them and their families.

Some of them may be killed — not just military personnel, but civilians, too. And that, unquestionably, is a sacrifice. It shows that it isn't easy to carry out an internationalist mission. Our internationalists are in the poorest countries, the ones with the most difficult living conditions. There are bands of mercenaries in Mozambique. In Angola, there are armed secessionist groups and bands of armed counter-revolutionaries. In Nicaragua, there are bands of armed counter-revolutionaries. Cuban doctors, teachers and construction workers were in Grenada, and the country was the victim of an invasion that cost the lives of more than two dozen of our compatriots.

Anywhere in the world today, there are risks. But we run risks here, as well. There is a permanent threat of attack against our country, of military aggression against our country, that has forced all of our citizens to be prepared. It has forced the country to make tremendous efforts in defense. Even here in Cuba, a Cuban is running risks, because you never know when a madman — in one those irresponsible, aggressive US administrations — may engage in aggression. To some extent, our people have learned to live with risks and dangers.

Now, when Cubans go on these internationalist missions and our country is threatened, we don't withdraw our men; even when our country is being threatened, we keep them there.

Gianni Minà: How many Cubans have died while carrying out internationalist missions?

Artillery gunner after return from internationalist mission to Angola

Fidel Castro: We haven't given any official figures, because they may be of interest to the enemy. In this case, it isn't a "syndrome of mystery." But I can tell you that the figure isn't large; there weren't many. This is because the conditions are well prepared, and they don't go on adventures. For example, our people's internationalist mission in Angola is to protect the country against attack by South Africa. It isn't to take any direct part in the country's internal affairs.

Around 130 were killed during the [1975] war in Angola and not so many in the war in Ethiopia. Since the Somalian invasion of Ethiopia, there has been external peace. Our people are there, but they aren't fighting; they are in position like a shield, for support. And there aren't many of them, because Ethiopia has developed a great military force.

We have more combatants in Angola. There has been an internal war, but the internal war is the task mainly of the Angolans. Our job is to defend the southern part of the country to ensure there won't be any more large-scale attacks from outside.

Gianni Minà: By South Africa.

Fidel Castro: Naturally, I'm not including deaths caused by disease — more diseases may strike there. I'm including deaths as a result of accidents and deaths as a result of ambushes set by the enemy. The puppets, supported by South Africa, set ambushes and lay mines. Those situations occur more frequently than battles. Sometimes, our fighters have been attacked and have defended themselves. They have had to support advisers who are with the Angolan forces, and there are battles, but not intensive or continuous ones.

After the war, several hundred died while on missions in Angola — not 10,000 as some people say; that is an out-and-out lie. Someday, the exact figures and names of those who died will be made known.

Gianni Minà: When?

Fidel Castro: When all of these problems have been solved — and we do hope that, in one way or another, these problems will be solved. We are ready to continue our support and solidarity. We think that apartheid is in crisis. Namibia's independence will have to come. Apartheid will have to disappear. And, even though we won't decide this unilaterally — because we are helping Angola as the result of an agreement with its government — when Angola considers that our forces aren't necessary, we will withdraw them. The Angolans have grown much stronger militarily. They have a large army, a large force, but they also have a powerful enemy — South Africa. When our fighters return home, that will be the time for taking stock. At this time, the enemy may be interested in knowing the number of those killed. In other words, that information is presently secret.

I've given you some approximate figures, and I can tell you that the real ones are less than 10 percent of what imperialism says.

Gianni Minà: That is, 10,000?

Fidel Castro: Those are the figures that imperialism gives. I've spoken to you about military and civilian deaths. More have occurred in Angola, and over a longer time, than anywhere else, and the mortality figures were highest there. In other places there may not be any fighting. There is fighting in Nicaragua, because of the dirty war and other activities, in which some of our military and civilian personnel have been killed occasionally, but very few.

Gianni Minà: Let's go back to the concept of a new human being. The 1987 Congress of the Union of Young Communists (UJC) of Cuba was sensational. The young people spoke there with much more clarity than the adults, and some people say they spoke with less formalism than in the Party Congress. Are these young Cubans more advanced than the society in which they live?

Fidel Castro: Well, there are three factors.

Our last Party Congress was very open. The First Congress was still too organized; even the speeches were prepared. The people who took part in the discussions were well prepared on the topics; the delegations from the various provinces came with their programs. That method was changed, and the discussion was opened more widely. Written speeches were suspended, as were statements prepared ahead of time, and anybody who wanted to talk was given the floor. Of course, there are always more people who want to talk than time permits, but our last Congress was very broad and open, with the delegates making free, entirely unrestricted statements. And the last Congress wasn't bad.

Now, as you say, the UJC Congress was sensational, spectacular. It pleased everyone, because we had an opportunity to see the maturity and political consciousness of our young people and their high cultural and technical level. It was very open, like the Party Congress, and I would say it had greater vitality. That Congress reflected a higher level of culture and education and a spirit among the young people that we want to see developed. That's why the Congress had such a great impact and some appreciated it even more than the previous one.

The UJC Congress should always be fresher and more open, because its participants come from a new, ever more prepared generation. It's only logical that this should happen.

Gianni Minà: And you think that . . .?

Fidel Castro: That they are more advanced now? Yes, I think so.

Gianni Minà: More advanced?

Fidel Castro: Cuban young people are more politically demanding; they're more politically conscious than the average person. The youth who have received their training since the triumph of the revolution have a higher average intellectual level than the average Cuban.

Gianni Minà: In particular, President, what are today's young Cubans like, and how do they differ from those in other countries, in terms of how they think?

Fidel Castro: I spoke to you about this before, when I said they have a much higher educational level. It's hard to find a young person today who has less than a ninth-grade education.

Gianni Minà: And in comparison with those of other countries?

Fidel Castro: Most of our young people have finished the 12th grade. The average may be above that level, depending on their age, because there are hundreds of thousands of high school and university students. If I were to compare them with the young people in other countries, I'd have to look at the statistics for an average Latin American country. Some Latin American countries have made more progress in education than others, but an average Latin American country — I don't want to mention names — probably has from 25 to 30 percent illiteracy; some have more. It is possible that the figure is lower — 20, 15 or 12 percent — for young people.

You won't find any illiterate young people in our country, because we have schools even for those who are mentally handicapped — special schools. It's hard to find a young person who hasn't completed the ninth grade. The average educational level of young people in any other Latin American country must be third or fourth grade — the average — although Latin America has good development in its universities, and a large number of university students get degrees but then can't find jobs. That's one problem. Of course, you'll find extreme situations: a high level of illiteracy and a low average educational level for the masses; with a high proportion of university students who, after graduating, are unable to find jobs. This creates truly dangerous problems, an explosive situation in society.

Gianni Minà: That's an Italian problem, too.

Fidel Castro: It's one of the situations faced in Latin America.

As I said, Cuban youth have a different attitude. It doesn't occur to any of our doctors to think about private practice; they don't even think about it. All of those doctors who go to the mountains and beyond — you may not have had a chance to meet and talk with them — are encouraging examples in our society. Cuban technicians don't have a market-oriented mentality. The teachers — all the people — work for society as a whole. They receive a decent wage, but it isn't exaggerated; and they go to carry out any internationalist mission, anywhere, en masse.

I'll give you an example. I already told you what happened with the teachers and Nicaragua. We had also sent a large number of doctors there, but more were needed. We would have had to reduce our services here. That was several years ago — I think in 1982. In that period, we were graduating 1,000 doctors a year; we didn't yet have the large graduating classes that we have now. We asked the Nicaraguans: do you want sixth-year students, who will do their last year, helped by the Cuban and Nicaraguan doctors and professors over there? They agreed. We called together the 1,000 university students in their last year, to see who was willing to go. Of the 1,000, all 1,000 volunteered.

I wouldn't say that all of them made the offer with the same enthusiasm; that wouldn't be realistic. But all were willing to go, because it was a matter of high social prestige. No individual wanted to admit that they lacked a spirit of sacrifice and the courage to go on one of those missions. All 1,000 volunteered.

I would say that one of the characteristics of Cuban youth is a lack of self-interest combined with solidarity for their own and other peoples. Their high political level and consciousness as well as their high level of training differentiate them from other Latin American young people. We want the best for all Latin American youth. I wish they had the opportunities that Cuban young people have. I don't say this boastingly or with pride. Rather, I say it with sadness.

Chapter 7

Two controversial individuals

One of the most surprising aspects of recent Cuban history is the hostility still directed at the revolution, not only among many of those who left Cuba out of fear of communism in the early '60s or later, but also among those who followed Fidel and then renounced him.

In few other events in modern history has the aversion of those who have lost a political and social battle survived for so many years and so violently — not even in Germany or in Italy, where the cruelty of the fighting and of events during the war and especially in its final stage was evident, nor in Argentina, where hatred was appeased only recently.

Obviously there are those interested in fanning the flames of an interminable confrontation, an "infinite history" of lack of understanding, beyond the painful events that divided families and friends in a cruel way. It is also possible that Fidel Castro's personality and the particular culture of his revolution contribute to this situation. Like others, Fidel has made and continues to make mistakes. But the propaganda against Cuba almost always makes even more mistakes. It diminishes the achievements of the revolution in eradicating poverty and Cuba's growing international prestige in culture, sports, medicine and Third World politics. Someone very close to Castro told me, "When the counter-revolutionaries and the CIA created the misnamed Radio Martí in Miami to hammer away at our people every day with its programs and convince them that our values are unsuitable and our way of living too simple, we were worried.

INMINENTE

INVASION YANQUI

ROA A LA ONU PARA DENUNCIAR EL ATAQUE

Vea información en la página DOS

REVOLUCION

ORGANO DEL MOVIMIENTO 26 DE JULIO

2ª EDICION Año III ● La Habana, Sábado 31 de Dic. de 1960

10 Centavos ● Director: Carlos Franqui ● No. 637

Patria o Muerte ¡Venceremos!

Revolucion, December 31, 1960

But soon our fears disappeared. Its arguments, its language, the music it broadcasts — almost always with a nostalgic aura of the '50s — and even the artists it presents have no appeal for today's Cubans (who are much better informed and much more culturally developed, accustomed to the vanguard sounds of the Cuban New Song Movement), so Radio Martí doesn't even awaken curiosity. I think it shows a lack of culture on their part."

I thought about this while Fidel gave me his version of the story of Carlos Franqui, who first was on his side as the director of Radio Rebelde in the Sierra Maestra and then became his adversary. I thought of how, in this age of advanced communication, many Western media continue to use the stories of the Cuban exiles. I understood to what extent a dimension of hatred is often born of intellectual impotence, of the inability to understand the good and the bad in what has happened during these years in Cuba and how its people have changed.

The latest episode of this kind is that of General Rafael del Pino, a hero of the Bay of Pigs for his feats as pilot. Some time ago, egged on by his young wife whom he had just married (it was his second marriage), he stole a plane and fled to Miami. From there, he now speaks often over Radio Martí. "Del Pino is renouncing his past," I was told in Cuba. "He must have received a lot of money for his statements. But when — in a couple of years — he isn't of any further propaganda use against us, he'll only be one of the many Cubans in the United States who have to struggle to survive. Here, even though he was grounded for eye problems, he would always have been one of the heroes of the Bay of Pigs."

G.M.

Gianni Minà: Now, let's talk about two much-publicized individuals. The first: in 1964, you were willing to write the history of the revolution, to be published by Feltrinelli, together with Carlos Franqui and Valerio Riva, an Italian journalist who now works for *Corriere della Sera*. Now, more than 20 years later, both of them speak ill of you. They take part in the campaign against Cuba for supposed violations of human rights, and claim that, with the help of the Soviet Union, you have imposed a personal dictatorship in Cuba. What do you think of this statement of Carlos Franqui and Valerio Riva?

Fidel Castro: I believe it would be an unfair accusation against the Soviets. First of all, because the Soviets didn't have anything to do with our revolutionary movement, our struggle and our war of liberation; we didn't know even one Soviet, and they didn't know us. When the revolution triumphed, we hadn't received any assistance at all from the Soviet Union. The Soviet Union helped at a later stage, not immediately. A few months after the triumph of the revolution we initiated trade relations with the Soviet Union — we didn't have diplomatic relations, because the United States had said Cuba could not have relations with the Soviet Union. Diplomatic relations came later. The Soviet Union became one of our sugar markets when the United States began to blockade us, and political relations were established only after a time. The first weapons that we purchased so we could defend ourselves against the threats of the United States were Western — from Belgium, in fact. The CIA sabotaged a shipload of Belgian weapons; causing the loss of nearly 100 lives. Political relations with the Soviet Union came later on, when the revolution was firmly in power.

I don't pay any attention to the adjectives Franqui uses to describe the Cuban government. But it contradicts Franqui's early enthusiastic support for the revolution. I showed you the editorial, in which he urged that captured terrorists be shot — and Valladares headed the list.

Now, you speak of a book being prepared in 1964. I don't know if it was in 1964 or not, but it was in the early years of the revolution. I don't know if Franqui was still with the revolution in 1964, but I do know that, in the early years, Franqui had relations with Feltrinelli. He knew him, and both of them were insisting that I should write or dictate a book that would be about more than the revolution itself and more than a biography; it was to be a book about the war of liberation. It was a very broad and ambitious project with the revolution still to be carried through. In view of such insistence, I agreed, even though I had an enormous amount of work. That was when I met Feltrinelli. Some efforts were even made — taking some days, some hours of work. I really tried to do it. Then I saw that the task was complex and would take a lot of time, which I didn't have, and I put it off until another time. I still haven't gotten around to it. Some 28 years have passed since the triumph of the revolution and I still haven't written that book. Many people are clamoring for it, reminding me of my responsibility to give my historic account of what happened.

There are many things that one knows, such as how the first ideas developed, that others can't know. I've seen many accounts of the war by different comrades, and each one saw it from their own perspective: they may not know the tactical or strategic concept of a battle or another event. I note the lack of these details.

The effort Franqui advocated was positive, not negative. That was the period when I met Feltrinelli, but in the end, the plan couldn't be put into effect. Carlos Franqui took some of the things I had dictated. He stole papers. *Compañera* Celia Sánchez had collected many messages, many documents, during the war. She was very concerned about that, although I wasn't. Thanks to her, countless communications, messages written by hand during the war and in battles were saved. Later on, many people were asked for their testimony. An office of historic affairs was established, and Franqui copied some materials there. He couldn't steal them, but he copied, borrowed and showed great interest. He hadn't betrayed the revolution at that time. But in a disloyal way, possibly because he was interested in gathering them, he copied and finally stole copies of some of those materials — not all of them or the most important ones. That was what Franqui did.

I remember Feltrinelli well. I don't remember that other journalist, I must honestly admit. It's possible that someone else may have come with Feltrinelli and was there. Feltrinelli may not have been able to do everything and may have delegated somebody else to do it. That man must have been a good friend of Franqui and that friendship may have been maintained when Franqui betrayed the revolution. The information to which that journalist obtained access or the attitude he harbored may have been greatly influenced by his relations with Franqui. I can't say anything good or bad about him as I really don't remember another journalist. But I do remember Franqui, and I can give you some opinions about him.

I already showed you the daily *Revolución,* the official organ which Franqui edited for a number of years. Now, why was Franqui the editor of that newspaper? It has its history.

Franqui had been a member of the Communist Party of Cuba and, at one point, left the Communist Party — he left it or they threw him out or he had conflicts with the Communist Party. And, all my life, I haven't trusted some people who take one position, adopt one ideology, and then abandon it.

The Popular Socialist Party (PSP), the Communist Party of

Cuba at that time, had many very good people, many cadres, many labor leaders who were unselfish and self-sacrificing and had been members for a long time. They were disciplined, very serious people. Our Movement also had many good people, but it was a newer movement that was supported by people from all social strata: workers, farmers, members of the petit bourgeoisie, professionals and even members of the bourgeoisie who helped our revolutionary movement. It gathered a lot of people in a short time.

We began the Movement with the attack on the Moncada military garrison. That was when we organized the first cells. I personally worked a great deal on this. We formed a small nucleus and worked to recruit the 1,200 fighters we had: their selection, organization and training — all of it clandestine but legal, disguised with other activities. Really, Batista underestimated us. He knew we didn't have any resources or money, and he was more afraid of those who had been in government and were millionaires, rich people. Then came the attack on Moncada, followed by prison. When popular pressure resulted in our release from jail we had already decided to go to Mexico, organize the expedition and return. Meanwhile, the Movement was organized throughout Cuba. It had its leadership, which consulted on some matters with those of us in exile, but they were responsible for the work of recruiting and organizing forces and the raising of funds.

The leaders of our Movement — some of whom had participated in the July 26 attack on the Moncada military barracks, and others of whom were new — recruited people during that period. They sent some people to us in Mexico while we organized the group there, training and arming it to return to Cuba and begin the guerrilla struggle in the Sierra Maestra. This had been our idea when we attacked Moncada if we couldn't cause the collapse of the regime by seizing the fortress, triggering an uprising in Oriente province and the calling of a revolutionary general strike, counting on the public hatred of the dictatorship. The plan couldn't be carried out, and we failed to seize the fortress. I'm not going to go into details now, because that would be another story.

I returned with 81 others. We were scattered; only a few of us were left, and we regrouped. We began the struggle with around seven guns, and we kept fighting until victory was won, when we had around 3,000 men under arms. I won't go into that long chapter. But during that period, the Movement developed inside the country, recruiting many people. It recruited some of those who had been in the Communist Party and had some theoretical education, but they weren't good recruits. I wouldn't advise that such people be recruited; those who renounce one idea aren't usually good supporters of another cause. But one day Carlos Franqui arrived in the Sierra. The Movement had a small underground newspaper called *Revolución,* and Franqui worked on it.

After the April strike, a few months before the triumph of the revolution — I think it was more or less in that period; some of the comrades should know exactly when it was — Franqui arrived in the Sierra Maestra, sent by the Movement to help us at the Radio Rebelde station.

When I saw him in the Sierra Maestra for the first time, I welcomed him with pleasure. Radio Rebelde was very important, and Franqui was placed in charge of Radio Rebelde. I remember that those were the days of the last powerful offensive against us when Batista's army threw 10,000 men against our forces. We had fewer than 300, but we decided to defend the territory and waged a very hard-fought battle. It lasted around 70 days; we had to move in many directions. So, Carlos Franqui was in charge of Radio Rebelde. He had to provide daily news reports and commentaries. I remember that we had set up telephone communications throughout a section of the Sierra to keep in touch with far-flung positions of our front and also Radio Rebelde.

The first thing I discovered — and I tell you this frankly — was that Carlos Franqui didn't know how to write or edit. I had to direct operations and take care of all the activities related to the fighting and the war, and I also had to constantly edit war communiques and commentaries for the station. Sometimes they were sent by telephone. My first harsh awakening was to the fact that Franqui didn't know how to edit. Therefore, I was amazed later on when Franqui appeared as a writer, poet and chronicler, meeting with intellectuals such as Jean-Paul Sartre. The man I had known, didn't know how to edit. And I know that because I had the experience of having to take on the enormous work of writing many communiques.

But he remained there. Our relations were good, normal, and he tried to contribute something. There are other comrades who worked on the team, but he was in charge as he had been the editor of an underground newspaper.

When the revolution triumphed, Franqui was very enthusiastic about it — a great admirer of the feats of the Rebel Army. He had witnessed many of our victories and therefore felt great admiration. He came to the capital. One of Batista's newspapers was confiscated and renamed *Revolución.* Carlos Franqui was appointed editor. He supported all of the revolutionary laws, all of the measures for punishing the war criminals. He supported the revolutionary courts and their sentences. Some of them were executed — not all, but some were executed, carrying out the sentences that the courts imposed on Batista's butchers. He also supported all of the sentences given to CIA agents and known counter-revolutionaries. That was up to the Bay of Pigs invasion and even a little after. I recall that he was still editor of the newspaper in 1961.

Problems arose at that time. We were trying to unite the people, but he, who had been in the Communist Party, bore grudges and was always promoting criticism and splits, waging campaigns against members of the Communist Party while the revolution was trying to unite all the revolutionary forces. I think that one of the problems that contributed most to his later attitude was the fact that Carlos Franqui brought out a cultural weekly called *Lunes de Revolución.* He wanted to become the czar of culture in Cuba. No one knows why, because Franqui never was someone of great culture. Nevertheless, he had those dreams. He began to promote a coterie of friends, giving them publicity and publishing their work. Some of them were writers; others were artists. It was a small group that rejected and even scorned many of the artistic and cultural values in our country. That attitude aroused conflicts.

I don't remember how long he continued to edit *Revolución.* In that same period he tried to get me to write the book, showing great admiration and saying that he didn't want lost what he described as "feats." He insisted on that.

I don't know when he left the newspaper. There were some small problems — they weren't significant or numerous.

At that time Franqui had a son who had some problems with his sight. That situation led him to ask to travel, and he took his son to see a doctor in Geneva several times. We assisted him, paying his expenses. We would have done the same for anyone else, but we did it for him out of personal considerations, as well — which is

Fidel Castro and Raúl Castro in Sierra Maestra prior to revolution

logical — and our relations were excellent. He came and went many times. But there is no question that, for some reason, his resentment and frustration increased throughout that period, although he never expressed any differences with the revolution.

Franqui was no longer a Marxist. I had known that ever since his time in the Sierra Maestra. I remember, during that campaign, he had with him some books which attacked dialectical materialism. He was an anti-Marxist on philosophical questions even then. He tried to exert subtle influences, something I didn't like. I would observe him and smile at his attempt to influence others with anti-Marxist literature. On those long, hard treks, any other literature was better reading than heavy philosophical problems. I had observed him and had my reservations. I spoke with him, because I spoke with many very different social strata, in an effort to unite them. They were very heterogeneous. I said that the July 26 Movement was like a small river in the Amazon of the masses, because its structure and organization were very small.

I was never sectarian. Franqui was. I was aware of the Movement's role in the war, and I always had a policy of uniting and bringing people together. Franqui drove them apart. We wound up uniting all of the revolutionary forces. In the end he was to have great ambitions — he couldn't be the czar of culture, so he dedicated himself to matters of a personal nature.

We always assisted him and treated him well. Moreover, on one of his trips to Geneva with his son — in the end, the doctor's visits turned into a pretext — he sent for his wife's parents. He said that he hadn't seen them for some time, and his son . . . And his in-laws traveled. That's when it emerged that Franqui was opposed to the revolution, and he began to attack it.

Franqui's mother, who was an old woman, stayed here in Cuba. He took the rest of the family and his in-laws but abandoned his mother, leaving her in Cuba. The revolution had to take care of Franqui's mother, who wasn't to blame. He abandoned her, and the revolution took care of her for the rest of her life. This shows you what kind of person he was.

He left. Then, over there, he tried to come out smelling of roses. That man, whose intellectual faculties are really very limited, keeps appearing at congresses of intellectuals and writes books. I think he's even a poet. Most recently, in the farce that was organized in Valencia at the anti-fascist congress — a farce that didn't have anything to do with the real, history-making congress of anti-fascist writers — there was Franqui, presenting a major speech.

He is a very resentful, ambitious, embittered individual. I always saw those characteristics and tolerated them. Really, I didn't think he was going to wind up in that role. I would say that Franqui isn't a big traitor — he is a little traitor to the revolution, and he's not of any great importance, but since we were speaking of this and it was necessary to speak of Mr. Franqui, I told you what I knew about him.

Gianni Minà: President Castro, let's talk about the second much-publicized individual. You have appeared on Cuban television in a live broadcast to present the Cuban people with the facts about the case of General Rafael del Pino, a hero of the Bay of Pigs, who, 25 years later, stole a plane and took his family to the United States. It is possible that he, too, had frustrations in his daily life, but some people consider that episode to be a crack in the system — that is, a symptom of discontent within the revolution.

Fidel Castro: There have been traitors in all epochs, ever since the Christian era began. Not for nothing did the Bible dedicate whole paragraphs to Judas. Even before the betrayal of Christ, in the battle of Thermopylae, someone showed the Persians a path that enabled them to dislodge the Spartans from that nearly inaccessible pass.

I went into the great betrayals that took place in our revolutionary struggle. We had some traitors; the more minor up to the major — who have assisted us, forcing us to perfect our underground work. I remember the case of one who betrayed us in Mexico, who sold our secrets for $25,000. Later, we were betrayed by a farmer who had been with us. Those who took him prisoner offered him his life, money and more.

That man you mentioned spent years with the revolution. He always seemed contented; he enjoyed the honors and distinctions of the revolution. He fought at the Bay of Pigs and was an outstanding combatant. Many people were outstanding. Around 150 lost their lives, including those who later died of their wounds. Hundreds were wounded. There are many monuments along the road that leads to the Bay of Pigs, bearing the names of those who were killed.

The people who fought at the Bay of Pigs received a lot of publicity. The air pilots played an important role, and he was one of the few we had. Others were also very outstanding. And many pilots have carried out excellent work over the years and are unsung heroes.

I went into that case at length in my presentation. I don't think it is necessary to repeat that explanation here. A thorough investigation was made of all the factors that led to his treason — his moral weakening, which led him to pass over to the enemy. And I have said that even if, one day, one thought that our cause for which we have struggled was utopian, it surely is the fairest and most inspiring of all utopias, one that I would remain with until the end. I wouldn't go over to the enemy: to that enemy which attacked us, sent the mercenaries, killed so many *compañeros*, caused the loss of life of so many brothers at the Bay of Pigs, killed the pilots — pilots who were the traitor's *compañeros* — and which has threatened us for so many years. That will never have any justification.

Moreover, he didn't change sides during the Kennedy administration. He did so during the Reagan administration, the most reactionary, the sponsor of the Star Wars weapons program, promoting the arms race and the dirty war in Nicaragua, invading Grenada and responsible for the dirty war in Angola and other countries — the worst, most deceitful, most immoral of all. That's when he changed sides, selling out to the enemy.

Our people don't take kindly to treason. They feel a deep loathing for all those things. I presented a detailed explanation, examined the factors, but I don't really think that I should go into this now. I've spoken enough of him. There are some moral elements that I didn't want to set forth, and I'm not going into them now. Some weren't made known; others were — enough for a better understanding of the political weakness of that man who turned traitor.

Anyway, I've spoken at length about this.

The revolution may have difficulties and run risks, but the revolution has carried out an unsurpassable feat. It has developed a strength in these years when Reagan was in power in the United States. It has made such a great effort in defense, mobilizing and organizing all the people, and we really have become a very hard nut for the United States to crack and impossible for it to swallow. We have achieved a high degree of security, thanks to that effort.

Then, when the people had carried out that feat he went over to the enemy and became a tool against the revolution. At that same time the US administration with the least prestige of all was nearing the end of its term following the Irangate scandal, which brought it out into the open and showed the real character of that administration, with its lack of morals. He went over to the enemy. But I don't think that he's very important — we've talked about other things that are much more worthwhile.

Gianni Minà: We consider it exceptional and unprecedented for a head of state to go on television to explain the details of a much-publicized case such as this. It's unusual, and we think it worthy of consideration.

Fidel Castro: We have always followed this practice and style of tackling problems, for it makes the revolution stronger and increases its moral fortitude. It even gives to revolutionaries the arguments to use against the enemy's campaigns and slander. That's why we do it.

Fidel Castro and Gabriel García Márquez

Chapter 8

Culture

The day that the International Cinema and Television School was inaugurated in San Antonio de los Baños, 40 kilometers from Havana, the four founders of the School called Rome to speak to their first teacher, Césare Zavattini, now in his 90s, as a gesture of gratitude for a never-forgotten nor interrupted cultural link.

The four — who are also central figures in the Foundation that seeks to promote Latin American cinema — are Gabriel García Márquez, Colombian writer and winner of the Nobel Prize for Literature, who, in addition to teaching playwriting, is also president of the Foundation; Fernando Birri, noted Argentinian movie director, who is also director of the School; Tomás Gutiérrez Alea, an esteemed Cuban movie director; and Julio García Espinosa, Cuban deputy minister of culture, a former movie director. All had studied together in Rome's Experimental Cinematography Center in the '50s.

With festivals and seminars, Havana's cultural activity is more intensive than all the other Latin American capitals. Francis Coppola, Harry Belafonte and Sydney Pollack give classes or talks at the Cinema School. The most representative personalities of world cinema and culture, from Jorge Amado to Carlos Saura, from Gregory Peck to Robert De Niro, from Julie Christie to Jack Lemmon and from Chico Buarque de Hollanda to Héctor Babenco, meet every year at the Latin American Film Festival.

The cultural prominence of Cuba is not well-known in Europe or the United States. To accept all this would mean giving up preconceived ideas which are skilfully nurtured by those who have to sell a certain product on the entertainment market and can't allow access to new ideas and a cultural world that affirms different values and is free of the economic control exercised by the communication corporations.

Exactly the same thing happens in the world of popular music as in the world of cinematography, unless that music serves at a given time to save a market that always needs new styles and new products to sell, as in the case of Latin sounds and rhythms.

Cuban music — in the opinion of Harry Belafonte — is now more advanced than the music in the United States. There are even better soloists. But Cuban music is not widely known outside of Latin America.

The cultural fervor that characterizes Cuba today, like the battle won in its time against illiteracy, doesn't free Fidel's government of responsibility or remove the contradictions that are often attributed to it in this sphere. Why, then, do people fear to make it known? Instead, a false impression of this Cuban reality is created.

G.M.

Gianni Minà: Let's talk about culture, President Castro. I have some data on education in Cuba, which I obtained from international agencies, that confirm that there were 100,000 literacy teachers in 1961 who, in a few months, taught close to a million illiterates how to read and write. Now, with a population of 10 million, there are close to 3.5 million students. Moreover, 22,000 foreigners are studying in Cuba on scholarships. Why was this priority given to education? Was it simply a moral commitment, or as your enemies say, was it for political — or rather, propaganda — purposes?

Fidel Castro: It is true that we have 22,000 foreign scholarship students, which I think is the highest number of foreign scholarship students per capita in the world. This is because of our close relations with other Third World countries.

Why do we have such close relations with the rest of the Third World? The United States blockaded us and tried to isolate us, and we responded by developing extensive relations with that world. They are our friends. In that process, close ties were established — commitments — and when they have had needs, we have helped them, even support against attack from abroad, as occurred in Angola and Ethiopia.

We also have a wide knowledge and awareness of the problems

of the Third World. Those ties have given rise to a demand for scholarships. As I said, there is no country in the world with more foreign scholarships per inhabitant. In Cuba, we have scholarship students from more than 80 countries, and they return to their own countries when they finish studying. They are not like those who go to London, Paris and other parts of Europe or the United States and then want to stay there, drawn by the consumer societies. They receive a different kind of education here, and we don't promote a brain drain. Very valuable people are trained.

We have been doing this for many years, and we are pleased with the work results of the technicians who are trained in our country.

There have been cases of African countries in which different tribes live, and the government has selected students from each of the regions to send them to these schools, which helps to stimulate a sense of national identity. They maintain their culture and are taught the history of their own country. Representatives of their government give them their political education. We don't teach political theory in those schools; their own governments provide that.

Gianni Minà: Those schools are on the Isle of Youth?

Fidel Castro: On the Isle of Youth — you were there. It's a big effort, and I repeat, they come from at least 80 countries.

Now, according to the theory that everything is for propaganda purposes, you could say that the revolution itself was carried out for propaganda purposes and that every one of the dozens of programs we've implemented was for propaganda purposes — health programs, programs to reduce infant mortality and programs to increase life expectancy (which we are hoping to increase to over 80 within the next ten years). They will also say that we ended unemployment, begging, prostitution, drugs and gambling for propaganda purposes. But I'll tell you something more: we're fighting against smoking, and Cuba is one of the main tobacco-exporting countries. Tobacco is one of our most important export lines. And we not only launched an anti-smoking campaign inside the country but also support the World Health Organization's campaign against smoking, which goes against our interests. That can only be done as a matter of principle.

So, everything that we have done in all fields, all the work of the revolution, could be presented as a propaganda stunt. If that were so, I would say, "How magnificent propaganda is! What an inspiring source of so many good things! It saves lives, protects people and solves all social problems."

If all the propaganda in the world were like that, a monument to propaganda should be built. And, if we engage in propaganda, why don't the other countries, the other governments, do it, too? Why don't the capitalist societies do it? Why don't they solve all of their problems through "propaganda"? What is real propaganda? Lies about all this, the negation of all this. That's where the real propaganda is. That is my opinion.

Gianni Minà: Right now, Cuba is a veritable cultural laboratory. There is a bienniale of art; a film festival in which such figures of US cinema as Gregory Peck, Francis Coppola and Robert De Niro participate; the Casa de las Américas literary contest; a pop music festival in Varadero; seminars in medicine, science and literature; and recently, the creation of a Latin American film school and foundation. Do you intend to make Cuba the cultural capital of Latin America, a little like Paris in Europe?

Fidel Castro: No, no one was thinking of that. This has come about through the accumulation of activities over the years. Twenty eight years have passed since the triumph of the revolution. No one developed a program to create all those institutions. As I recall it, the first one was the Casa de las Américas, virtually at the beginning. Haydée Santamaría worked there for a long time, and the institution gained prestige. Latin American writers participated and it created awards in various literary genres. It gained prestige. I myself was surprised by the fact that, year after year, that institution was the one most esteemed by Latin Americans. It was the only one of its kind in the beginning; others were later created.

I don't remember when the Varadero Festival began, but it was years ago, too. Then came the bienniales of art; they are more recent. The New Latin American Film Festival was begun after Salvador Allende was overthrown in Chile, because the film makers who created that movement had a first meeting in Viña del Mar. At the time of Pinochet's coup many went into exile. Many of those who had attended that meeting created something like a Latin American films makers' committee of solidarity with Chile.

And they decided to hold a first festival here, because they had Cuba's cooperation for doing so. Thus, the first festival was held around nine years ago. I have to admit that I didn't even know about it when the first one was held. I've helped in some ways, as people have come up with ideas and presented them to me. I came to appreciate the value of the film festival when around four of them had already been held.

I like the cinema, and when those festivals began I had an opportunity to see some good movies. I liked the Latin American movies and their diversity, from scenic panoramas to portrayals of social problems. I discovered movies that I liked. Frankly, I appreciated them more than European and US cinema, with excesses of violence, the Mafia, sex, car chases and all that. Then, suddenly, I discovered movies with other aspects — human, social, cultural. I appreciated them, as I said, even for their scenery, the architecture, the people's customs and their way of living. It was like traveling through Latin America. I benefited during those festivals, because I saw many of the films that were submitted.

Then I suggested to the members of the festival that we ought to make a video copy of each film to keep as a historic record, with permission to use them in schools — not for commercial purposes. We would buy those we wanted to use for commercial purposes, and we do buy a large number of those movies every year: feature films, documentaries, etc.

I discovered in practice the value of that new film movement. I realized that we could promote the movement more. The festival films were being shown in only a few theaters. The people went to those theaters, and so I asked, "Why don't we extend it and use more theaters, so everyone can participate?" And, it was extended.

Not all of them had suitable equipment. We improved the technical conditions for showing films. I had taken part in a closing session, and I noticed that it was a little disorganized. It seemed to me that everything was confused, and I made a suggestion. I said, "Why don't we have a better program, in a bigger theater? Why don't we show excerpts of the award-winning movies so the people will remember and be stimulated to see them — clips with the best actors?" I discussed this with the organizers and they took a series of measures, also increasing the number of awards. Thus, the festival became better and better. It was held in a large theater —

the Karl Marx Theater — that can seat around 5,000 people. Everything was better organized.

When I suggested that, somebody from Cuba said, "Well, it's like that — disorderly — at the Academy Awards." I was a little miffed that they brought up the Oscars, even if they are so famous, and I said, "So what, if it's that way there?"

It really is very well-organized, with a ceremony for presenting the awards. And new ideas kept emerging: to encourage international cooperation and opening the film markets in the socialist countries. I had spoken to them about the socialist countries and the need to work those markets.

Then, two years ago, someone proposed the idea of the Foundation, a foundation to raise funds and support new films. We became more and more enthusiastic because of the high quality of the new film movement. Especially after the democratic openings in Brazil and Argentina, excellent movies began to be made. The Mexican films, whose quality had begun to decline, at this time began to improve. The Colombians and Venezuelans also began to make better movies. That's how this movement, which is now a great one, was created.

My participation was only to give support when I saw how important it was.

The Foundation was created. But the most important thing isn't the fact of the creation of the Foundation, which led to this movement. What is most important is that exactly the right president was found for that Foundation. It occurred to somebody to propose Gabriel García Márquez. Then they had to convince García Márquez, but they succeeded.

Gianni Minà: You convinced him?

Fidel Castro: No, I did not intervene in this. They told me they were going to write in order to convince him, and they did. He accepted. That was the key to the Foundation's success.

I never even imagined that García Márquez was so enthusiastic about the cinema — you could say it is his passion, even though he's a great writer. His literature is associated with scripts. The success of the Foundation was guaranteed by the fact that García Márquez became its president. That opened doors all over.

Together with the Foundation, the idea arose — and this wasn't my idea — of creating a new film school. I agreed, and in doing so I had to pledge that the government assign resources for the school's construction and for its first equipment and laboratories. I accepted the idea and worked to provide the required conditions. We did it in record time. We modified a senior high school in the countryside, remodeling it. A brigade was created, and it carried out excellent work. Within a year we had the School. In all, it will have 300 or so students. This year it had its first group. It offers not only regular courses but also workshops, seminars and talks. Gabriel García Márquez contributed a lot to it, on developing the idea of the School's organization and programs.

We were also very lucky in finding a director, exactly the right person: Fernando Birri. Two outstanding people have contributed to the success of the Foundation and School. I have spoken at length about this, but I wanted to explain how those institutions arose.

We hold many scientific conferences, especially as medical and research centers are developed. We learn from them, they are very useful, as scientists from all over attend. This is the result of work, not a program. Now, they are solid institutions: the new film movement is a great institution, and the Foundation is something spectacular.

I think I forgot to tell you that I never imagined the tremendous talent García Márquez has for organizing. You always tend to think of intellectuals, writers, as being not very good at organizing. I am amazed by his executive ability. He's been here for several months and done an excellent job.

That was the origin. People may say that it is propaganda, but we're pleased. If only all propaganda were as fruitful as this!

Gianni Minà: The four founders of the movie school in Cuba were Nobel Prize-winner Gabriel García Márquez; Julio García Espinosa, deputy minister of culture of Cuba; Fernando Birri, Argentinian movie director; and Tomás Gutiérrez Alea, Cuban movie director. The four are alumni of Rome's Experimental Cinematography Center and are former students of Italy's Césare Zavattini.

Fidel Castro: This school is really the spiritual child of the school in Rome, because they were trained there. They also worked in the new film movement. They continue to reminisce of that period in Rome.

The former Latin American Film School is now the International Cinema and Television School. It now includes all the Third World. We even call the building in which the school was inaugurated the "old school," because it was modified. Now, with two years of experience and work behind us, we're planning to design a new, larger one. It will have students from all over the Third World, and a capacity for 300 isn't enough. It needs a capacity for around 800 students. Nobody had any idea of what a school of this kind would be like or what difficulties it would confront. But it has been a success.

Gianni Minà: Is it true that you want to buy a chain of theaters in Europe so that Latin American films can be distributed, as are US and European movies?

Fidel Castro: The problem with films is distribution. Latin Americans make excellent movies, but they can't distribute them because of the monopoly — the transnational corporations control the distribution network. One of the Foundation's purposes is to open up markets and make it possible to distribute Latin American films. It has obtained the cooperation of several countries, and theaters are being obtained — as donations, as cooperation in various Latin American countries. I understand that they are to do the same in Europe.

I think the Foundation is going to have funds, because interest is growing. García Márquez is very active in this. It doesn't yet have much money, but I think it will receive the funds. The idea of breaking the blockade imposed on Latin American cinema will gain ground. Yes, they are blockaded now.

Showings are being guaranteed in Japan, India, China and other socialist countries. García Márquez is active in all this, in addition to writing a book, I understand. No, I *know* he's writing a book. I don't know if he's talked about it, which is why I don't want to give it a lot of publicity. He was here for several months, working on the book in the mornings and teaching in the School in the afternoon. In giving classes — he calls them workshops — he gathers together a group of people with some experience, some preparation. His courses are on scriptwriting, how to prepare stories. He has created a very original workshop, with many hours of discussion. I was telling him that it would be extremely valuable to one day transcribe it as they are master classes on how to write.

In the end, they wound up writing a story, all of them together.

It seems he found his vocation as a teacher in that work. I know that, by the end, the book was half-forgotten — that is, he was giving all his attention to the cinema.

He's in Europe now — he's quite dedicated to promoting movies. And that is the key to the Foundation's success.

Gianni Minà: Do all the movie greats who give classes at the School — such as Francis Coppola — do so because of their relations with García Márquez?

Fidel Castro: García Márquez's relations have been decisive in this. Many of them already had relations with Cuban cinematography and with the new film movement, but the presence of García Márquez strengthened those relations.

You spoke of US movie personalities, but very important figures in Latin American and European cinema have also come. The phenomenon is quite universal. People have also come from Africa and the other socialist countries. It is a very strong movement, and it's still growing.

Gianni Minà: My last question on this theme may seem out of sequence, but has a cultural aspect. People recall that some 20 years ago you expressed interest in ecological problems. You wanted to replant the forest destroyed by mining activities in the eastern part of the country, and you warned about the dangers inherent in the use of chemical products in agriculture. Now, evidently for economic reasons, a nuclear power plant is being built in Cienfuegos. I've seen it, and it's an enormous project. Aren't you afraid that dangers that are much more serious to nature and human health may arise because of this?

Fidel Castro: It is true that I have been very concerned about ecological matters, and we've done a lot of work and devoted considerable effort to protecting the natural environment, the forests and the sea. We've carried out an ambitious program of reforestation, as our forests had been destroyed. If they had not been replaced, they would not have regenerated themselves. We've made great efforts and enormous investments to protect the water, the rivers. In the past, there wasn't any environmental protection in Cuba. The sugar mills, for example, used to dump their waste water into the rivers and the sea.

We're even trying to salvage some of that waste, using oxidation lakes to cleanse the water and turn that waste into animal feed. We've made a great effort in that direction, and we intend to continue. It's expensive, and we're earmarking a relatively high percentage of all investments for environmental protection. We haven't renounced that policy at all, and we are aware of the problem.

I remember many years ago I read a book with a very suggestive title — *Silent Spring* — by Rachel Carson, a US writer. She is now dead. She wrote an excellent, very illustrative book about the effects which chemical products — such as pesticides, that are used in the struggle against insects and other pests — could have on human health. She favored biological methods for controlling diseases. I distributed many copies of the book. She stated which of those products could cause cancer, and many of them appear in the origins of cancer — not only cigarettes and carbon dioxide, but also many of the chemical products that are used in agriculture, including fertilizers.

André Voisin, a French scientist I knew, also wrote some very interesting books on this subject. One, titled *Grass, Soil and Cancer*, explained what influence the soil and even fertilizers — different kinds of fertilizers — have on human health. They were very interesting books. We are aware of those problems in our country.

Now, you raise the question of the nuclear power plant. My reply is this: In today's world, countries such as Cuba don't have any alternative. If we had great water resources, we could exploit them, but we don't have any. If we had extensive coal deposits, we might be able to postpone the decision, but we don't have any. If we had large oil reserves, we could put off the decision — even though it's a crime to burn oil to produce electricity, as even the latest technology makes relatively poor use of the energy value of a ton of oil. We don't have any of those resources. We don't even have what the Eastern European socialist countries have, and they can hook their energy networks up with that of the USSR or hook up among themselves. We don't have large reserves of gas — just some oil deposits which, although growing, aren't large. No large oil deposits have yet been discovered.

You can't have development without energy. As I've told you, we don't aspire to a consumer society, and we don't want every family to have a car — which is a waste of energy. What we do want is to have all the energy we need for our schools, hospitals and textile industry; the energy we need for irrigation and agriculture; the energy we need to refrigerate products in our tropical climate; the energy we need to provide all of the citizens in this country with electricity. To renounce energy is to renounce development and progress. We need a growing amount of energy. During the 28 years since the triumph of the revolution, the consumption of energy in Cuba has grown by nearly 10 percent per year — 10 percent! In the last few years, we have reduced the growth rate in the consumption of electric power by trying harder to reduce wastage. We've raised the rates and done everything else we could to hold back excessive consumption of electricity, but the growth is still tremendous. And, if our energy system were not developed, we would not have any light here, and the temperature wouldn't even be bearable. You and I would be perspiring profusely, and there wouldn't be any cameras or television — there wouldn't be anything.

We have no energy alternative. The use of solar energy is being developed. We already have more information, more knowledge, and we're undertaking research, but it requires enormous investments. I have heard that you need around 200 hectares covered with cells that can assimilate sufficient solar energy to produce 30,000 kilowatts, at an enormous investment cost. It isn't developed enough at this time and it requires physical space. Some countries don't have much physical space. For its part, wind power can be harnessed to light a house or to raise water from a well — things such as that.

No alternative to nuclear energy has appeared for a country such as ours — and many are in this situation. Even countries that have great deposits of coal, oil and gas — such as the United States — are using nuclear energy. France, with enormous coal deposits, is using it — almost 30 percent of all its electric power comes from nuclear power plants. Thus, it is a reality that has been imposed. We have no alternative. What we have to do is increase the training of our personnel and the safety measures in the construction and functioning of those plants.

You are the first person who has filmed there. Perhaps due to the "syndrome of mystery" journalists haven't gone there. You are the first who has gone, except for those who have accompanied foreign visitors.

Ten thousand men are working there with great dedication, carrying out high-quality work. We're building that plant with many more safety measures than are included in those built in the United States. It will have many more engineers and other skilled workers than work in the nuclear power plants in the United States. We are faced with a situation in which we have no other option.

Gianni Minà: Is the Cienfuegos plant enclosed — not open, as at Chernobyl?

Fidel Castro: Yes, it's enclosed, and water cooled. It doesn't use graphite, as did Chernobyl. Its technology is more widely used throughout the world, and the safest nuclear power plant in the world is the one we're building here.

We trust in the quality of our work and in the alternative of using nuclear energy. We need it not only for electric power but also in medicine; it has many peaceful uses. We trust that humanity is capable of mastering the atom, which is such a dangerous demon when unleashed.

Chapter 9

Religion

The Catholic faith is a part of daily life in Cuba. It couldn't be otherwise, since Fidel himself studied with the Jesuits. Just as many of the revolutionary leaders have brothers, sisters or other relatives who left for the United States, they also — as they themselves tell you — have mothers, grandmothers and other relatives who still go to Mass on Sunday.

Nevertheless, for some time the vilest propaganda against the revolution hammered away at its alleged religious persecution. The facts were simpler: a certain sector of the church hierarchy allied itself with the most conservative part of society, and the Cuban revolution was involved in a confrontation with some prelates accused of having engaged in counter-revolutionary activities.

Something similar has occurred in many other revolutions and in all of the processes of social change. Even now, 70 years after the Mexican revolution, priests in Mexico are not allowed to wear long habits, because many of them did not support Emiliano Zapata, Pancho Villa and General Carranza.

With time, Vatican and Cuban diplomats have smoothed over their differences. Monsignor Césare Zacchi, a cultured and concerned Apostolic Nuncio who was later named director of the institute in charge of training the Vatican's diplomats, established such open, direct relations with the revolutionary government at the beginning of his stay in Cuba that the most reactionary anti-Castro groups accused him of conniving with Marxism. That so-called connivance has paved the way for a dialogue which at any time could lead John Paul II to come to Cuba.

Proof of this possibility can be read between the lines in the pages that follow. Even though I led him to that point, Fidel never made any criticisms of the Pope, not even the manifest contradiction between his policy on Poland and the one he is applying in Latin America.

"The Pope plays the role of Pope; he can't do anything else," I was told by a Cuban friend who is up on the policies of the Holy See.

G.M.

Gianni Minà: President Castro, let's talk about religion. The Jesuits at the Belén School, where you studied, were the first to recognize that you would become an important man. In your final evaluation for the school year when you were 18 years of age, they wrote, "He will make a brilliant name for himself. Fidel has what it takes and will make something of his life." What do you think of the Jesuits' teaching and of their moral values?

Fidel Castro: First, I'm going to explain that comment in the year-book.

Those Jesuits were Spaniards. I'm not going to tell you that their ideas were very progressive; actually, they were nationalist, rightist, anti-communist ideas. They had lived through the war in Spain. Some of them told me about everything that happened, including the mass executions they saw after the war. They served as health officers and told many stories of it all. I noted the cruelty of the Spanish Civil War — cruelty on both sides. It was a merciless war.

Those Spaniards were on Franco's side. They didn't support progressive thought, but they had a lot character, discipline, dedication and talent. Since they were Spaniards — Spaniards have always been quixotic to a certain extent, with that eminently Spanish ability to hold certain values in esteem — some of my activities at school in sports, on excursions and in explorations undoubtedly pleased them in some way.

I also had a lot of conflicts and contradictions with them because of my character. But they were respectful and didn't stop admiring certain of my qualities — especially those of character — as an individual.

Since I had been outstanding in many of those activities and they had to write something, they finally came up with a text, and that was it. Later events made it seem a profound premonition, but I could have died on several occasions, and the comment would not have had any greater value.

But there is a chance relationship between what they wrote in the year-book and those events that involved myself. They said that I would make something of my life. I didn't have anyone to do it for me. I wish I had, but I had no alternative to doing it myself. There is no way of knowing how much easier it would have been to have someone do it for me, because I had to make my way in practically everything. Luck was a kind of preceptor that assisted me.

Now, what do I think about the training they provided? It was a good education. They were demanding, not tolerant. They imposed discipline, and their scientific teaching was of good quality. If you take away the dogmatic aspect of the religious teaching — the obligation to go to Mass every day and many other formal aspects of religion and their dogmatic way of thinking, which I didn't agree with — I would say that it was an education of a high standard, one that influenced us.

I always went to boarding school, because my family lived in the countryside. I went to the La Salle School up to the fifth grade. I clashed a great deal with my teachers there, as well, because of my character and some obvious injustices that I witnessed. I'm not going into it now. Then I went to study with the Jesuits, at the Dolores School, in Santiago de Cuba. When I was about to enter my junior year I asked my family to transfer me to the Belén School because of what I had heard of it. I studied for many years, and I experienced two kinds of schooling. There was a great difference between the La Salle Brothers, which was a French order, and the Jesuits, although both were in general good schools.

Throughout history, the Jesuits have been very rebellious. They have played an important, frequently progressive role in some countries and certain circumstances. I think well of their work. In general, I respect that order and that institution.

Gianni Minà: A recent film, *Mission*, portrayed the Jesuits' progressive spirit in past centuries.

Fidel Castro: The King of Spain even expelled them from Cuba. The Spaniards expelled them from more than one place.

Gianni Minà: What do you think of the Jesuits' military or "militant spirit," as Frei Betto of Brazil has described it?

Fidel Castro: The Jesuits had a quite militant spirit which had something of the military about it. It wasn't formal discipline. They didn't teach us to march or to stand to attention, although they did teach some formal military formations for the parades. But there was strict discipline in punctuality, work expectations. It wasn't like our schools today. It was a boys' school, for boys who had few contacts outside, and the more they repressed the individual, the more the boys thought of girls and women. There wasn't any of the co-education that exists today. It was a hard life.

I think that our schools are better, with their freer, more natural relations between people. The schools that we have created are good schools. We have some excellent schools, such as the high schools of exact sciences and the schools in the countryside, where work is combined with study.

We have taken the ideas of Marxism, Martí and our own and combined them with our experience. Our schools are entirely different. Even though I am not sorry I went to those schools, I think it isn't right to subject children and adolescents to that kind of teaching. I don't think it is right to waste the best years of young people's lives without giving them more rational, more scientific teaching — without teaching them how to think, which is one of the most important skills to learn.

That was a very weak aspect in the teaching of that period. Naturally, we've had to change those concepts, but I don't have unpleasant memories of those years.

Gianni Minà: A formal dialogue with the Catholic Church on the relations between the Church and state was begun not long ago. How has the work schedule been programmed, and how far advanced are the negotiations on the visit to Cuba of the Pope?

Fidel Castro: In response to your first question, there is mention of a dialogue, but I don't believe it's correct to call it a dialogue, since there hasn't been any conflict. Contacts were made with the Catholic Church and some other churches. The visit made by some US bishops helped in this, because our relations aren't bad — they are relations of respect. There are some religious orders that work in old people's homes, hospitals and some other institutions — I cite them as an example. I've even said in Party meetings that the nuns who carry out all those activities are setting an example for us communists. We have excellent relations with them. Practically everything they ask from the state is given to them, because they are austere, they aren't wasteful, and they ask for little. We consider them a model. There isn't any conflict. Therefore, there is no need to negotiate or have a dialogue. I would say that what we have is contact, exchanges of opinions and channels for solving certain problems.

A state of expectancy has been created around this — too much expectancy and publicity. It's as if there had been a conflict and we were seeking solution for the conflict by means of dialogue. People have spoken of dialogue when it was a matter of contact or exchange of opinions, that should be normal and shouldn't be viewed as anything sensational or spectacular.

Some time ago, such contacts didn't exist, but there isn't any problem. The Church has made some historical analyses. We don't entirely agree with those historical analyses. They met, invited many guests and engaged in a kind of self-criticism. It was a step forward, an effort that should be valued, but this doesn't mean that we entirely agree with or coincide with the historical assessments they made.

However, they have had complete freedom to work and meet. There is complete religious freedom in our country, and there really isn't conflict. One of the cadres of the Party and state, *compañero* Felipe Carneado, has dedicated a lot of attention to relations with the churches. That is the present situation.

Gianni Minà: But how far advanced are the negotiations on the Pope's visit to Cuba?

Fidel Castro: Negotiations on the Pope's visiting Cuba were never established. When we talked, we had those exchanges, and I believe — this is what we think — that that policy should be preceded by greater understanding, or greater rapprochement between the positions of the Party and the Church.

If a visit is to be useful, positive, and not be turned into a source of conflict — I'm telling you this frankly — certain conditions are required. We have relations with the Vatican — diplomatic, official relations. We've always had them; they are relations of friendship and respect. We have always informed the Holy See and the Pope about our point of view on the foreign debt, on the economic crisis. We read with great interest everything he says, his statements on the economic crisis and the foreign debt. We have those relations, and there will surely be more topics that could be the subject of exchanges.

However, before contemplating a visit of that kind, we would need to have the conditions that would allow for a successful, positive, and useful visit. There is no reason for running any risk, if such conditions don't exist. A visit is a visit, with many speeches and statements. I don't believe we should allow even the least discrepancy or discord over ideas to arise. Inasmuch as we don't have the same points of view on all international problems, we do have points in common on peace and disarmament and a shared concern over the international economic crisis, the debt, etc.

Gianni Minà: The Pope will make a visit to Miami, however.

Fidel Castro: Yes, the Pope is going to pay a visit to the United States, and Miami is one of the cities he'll visit.

I don't have any complaints about the Pope or problems of any kind. I've expressed my admiration for the efforts he is making, for his ability to move and act. He has been a real leader of the Church. I've noted and said that. I've also read with great interest the statements he has made about the poor, because he has met with workers in South America, with South American Indians and with slum dwellers. He has made statements that, if I had made them, would be called subversive. He has talked about employment for heads of families, medicine for the sick, land for the farmers and housing for those who live in slums. He can get away with saying those things, which are often the same as our own declarations on those problems. There have been points of coincidence that have been of great interest to us, because of the role the Church can play concerning those problems.

Gianni Minà: President Castro, excuse me if I insist. Some time ago, it was said that a schism could be noted in Latin America, caused by the popular priests of the Church, or by those who follow liberation theology — who represent the majority. The militant Catholics who live alongside the oppressed feel deceived by the Catholic Church's policy in Latin America, which is different, for example, from the policy the Church applied in Poland. What political consequences could a schism of that kind cause?

Fidel Castro: I think that the age of schisms is past. There were schisms within the international communist movement, as I told you, but the Church has 2,000 years of experience and has learned how to handle difficult situations. In the period when I went to the Jesuit schools, there were many differences, many prejudices and much sectarianism: a Protestant was the enemy, the worst in the world; a Jew was the enemy, the worst in the world. There was a lot of sectarianism within the Church.

What I have noted in this period is an ecumenical feeling of rapprochement among the churches, a different feeling, one of exchange — things that were inconceivable in the past. Progress is being made toward a rapprochement and an improvement in the relations among all churches. I don't think there is any room for schisms.

I know some of those priests, some of the most prestigious figures in the liberation theology movement. I've read their books, and I've never noted even the least symptom of schism. To the contrary, they obey Church discipline. Boff showed this. If Cardinal Ratzinger — I think that's his name — of the tribunal . . . What's that tribunal called? You should know that better than I; it was the old Inquisition, but I think it has another name now. If he makes a declaration and even if some measures are decreed, they obey them. I've noted a lack of pretense, much humility and great discipline. They have their criteria and social ideas, because they have lived alongside the people and have seen misery, poverty and injustice.

Some very powerful movements have developed, such as the one in Brazil. The Church has almost 300 bishops in Brazil. They have a very progressive position in favor of the farmers, the workers, the poor people in Brazil. The movement has developed in many places in this way.

I've had an opportunity to be in correspondence with Cardinal Arns and others, and I really don't think there is even the least possibility of there being a schism in the Catholic Church, because the Church is very mature. The upper echelons in the Church are mature, and so are the champions of liberation theology. They understand that there is no sense in having divisions or schisms, for they wouldn't benefit anybody. Therefore, the idea of a schism hadn't even occurred to me.

Gianni Minà: Do you understand the disillusionment of those Latin American priests who sometimes feel at a great distance from the words of the Pope?

Fidel Castro: Well, not on religious matters. There may be some differences with the Church's official position on political matters. The position of those priests is obviously different from that of many bishops, as they are in closer contact with the people. I think the Pope discovered many of the problems and spoke out about those problems when he traveled to Latin America. The living conditions in Rome, Paris, London and New York aren't the same as those in Latin America. The Pope came into contact with those realities and in my opinion was impressed by them.

Those priests are in constant contact with those realities and have more defined political positions in favor of all the exploited, low-income sectors of society.

Chapter 10

Health

The filmed interview that gave me the opportunity to prepare this book began in the Center of Genetic Engineering and Biotechnology. The preceding night, I had made what seemed to be an unprecedented request for an interview with Fidel Castro: to begin our dialogue in a place that was representative of Cuba's new reality. Medicine is unquestionably one of those realities, and the Center of Genetic Engineering is an exceptional — if not unthinkable — project in a Third World country.

In this chapter, Fidel tells of how the project was born and carried out. I am sure that he accepted my proposal that evening, breaking a custom — interviews are usually held in places prepared for television — because, from the political point of view, for those who may harbor reservations about the revolution, there is no more convincing image in present-day Cuba than the one offered by its achievements in medicine and health care.

"I can't do it in the morning," Fidel told me, "but, if you wait for me, I'll be there at 2:00pm. And, five minutes before the hour, his car arrived at the Center's plaza. Doctors and researchers who had helped that morning with filming in the various laboratories had heard rumors, and the result was that dozens of scientific workers, friends and students had gathered in the hallway. A visit from the Comandante, *even when not official — and when few should know of it — is always an event.*

The doctors and researchers were very young, of which Fidel was clearly proud, as he was of the Center itself.

The precise knowledge that Fidel showed — not only of the equipment and its functioning but also of the present state of scientific research in the sector and its vocabulary — was quite surprising.

In the pages of this chapter, where at times ethical and moral aspects of medicine are discussed — social problems of the economy or the topic of aesthetics — Fidel's intellectual approach toward the quality of life is evident.

For a journalist, this was a quite unusual experience within the norms of modern politics.

G.M.

Gianni Minà: President Castro, when did you begin this Center of Genetic Engineering and Biotechnology?

Fidel Castro: It began with a small laboratory that was created to produce interferon.

I knew of research that was being carried out in the United States through a doctor from Texas, a cancer specialist who is a friend of mine. On one of his visits to Cuba, I asked him what hopes they had of developing techniques for fighting cancer, and he told me about interferon.

He asked us to send one of our doctors to see him. We sent two doctors. At that stage, a lot of hope was placed in interferon — perhaps a little more than was really justified, though it has produced some results. It is a medicine that is very important in modern medicine and new research can be carried out, as there are several variants.

But the fact is, it was very difficult to obtain interferon for undertaking research. Through that friend, I heard of a Finnish scientist, Cantell, who had developed the technology for producing interferon from white corpuscles. Cantell also invited us to send two doctors to see him. We sent six. They were there for a short time and, in an intensive course, learned how to produce interferon.

While they were there, a small laboratory was set up in a protocol house, following their instructions. On returning, they immediately set to work. Barely four months went by between the time we first heard about interferon and the moment when we began to produce it in Cuba. It was a record.

That laboratory made us very enthusiastic. We quickly began doing studies, both on viral diseases and on various kinds of cancer, and it may well be that no other country has carried out as many studies on that product in the fight against cancer, with some positive results for certain kinds of cancer. When we already had that laboratory, those there began to work on genetic engineering, with the idea of producing interferon through genetic engineering techniques.

That was how we were introduced to the world of genetic engineering. We became very enthusiastic, and the results obtained have been good. Then we heard that the United Nations was promoting a center of genetic engineering and biotechnology.

Since we have given a lot of attention to these activities — and to scientific research in general and to medical studies — we hoped that we would be granted that UN center, and we began to struggle and work toward that goal. We requested it and a committee of experts visited, but many countries had made similar applications.

Gianni Minà: Italy, too.

Fidel Castro: Italy, Spain, Belgium and I think Sweden also wanted the center. Italy even offered $40 million as a contribution. We couldn't offer that much. The Indians wanted it as well, but they were really supporting us.

When we saw that the discussion there was prolonged, we decided to create the center by ourselves. We took the United Nations' program, gathered information in other similar centers in more advanced countries, and drew up our own program. Our initial laboratory group, headed by *compañero* Limonta, drafted the center's program.

Gianni Minà: Had Dr. Limonta studied in Houston with Clark?

Fidel Castro: He had been to several places, including Clark's hospital in Houston, and he had studied it all. Once the program was drawn up, work began on the plans, and we began to build the center, even before the plans were completed.

We built it in two years, although most of the project was built in the second year. It was intensive work. That was how we created this center, which places us among the top eight countries in the world in this branch of scientific research, in a vanguard technology. Biotechnology and genetic engineering — together with robotics and electronics — play a very important role in development prospects. This influences the production not only of medicines and vaccines but also of varieties of new plants that are disease-resistant and more productive; it is developing the technology for turning straw into fuel, for example, or, even more important, for turning agricultural waste into proteins by using various fermentation processes. It also promotes the struggle to protect the environment. There are many fields.

Biotechnology is just as old as civilization itself, since the Chaldeans and Sumerians used biotechnology for making beer. I understand that they made 30 different kinds of beer, and beer production is a biotechnological process. Of course, genetic engineering is very modern and offers great hopes for the solution of many problems, especially in the field of medicine. So, we have this center.

But I was going to say that the scientists who work here, the workers of this center, are more important than the center itself. I don't know if they've told you about the way they work, without any time limits. I think they work 14 or 15 hours a day.

How did that come about? When they started out in the small laboratory, an ethical question arose: How should scientists work in a branch of this kind? If we are struggling to find a medicine that can solve the problem of cancer, and if many lives may depend on the effort they make, they couldn't have the same attitude toward work as that of those employed in material production. Keeping that idea in mind, they had to speed up the development of those products as much as possible. That is the spirit with which they work here.

We're setting up a small gym nearby, and we want to have them work one hour less each day and spend it in systematic physical exercise as something obligatory — well, not to force them to exercise, for they'll have that hour off as it is, to do what they want, but we've had to set some kind of a limit on the intensity with which they work.

They have good food in this center. They have breakfast, lunch, snacks and dinner here. Some even sleep here, and we're putting up some buildings nearby where they will live.

Gianni Minà: How can an underdeveloped country afford to have a center such as this? Where does the money come from for a project of this size? How is that money saved? Where does it come from?

Fidel Castro: I'll tell you. Really, this center wasn't in the plan.

Gianni Minà: How could you do it?

Fidel Castro: We have a small fund for meeting new needs that may arise, and we drew on that reserve of money that wasn't pledged to other plans in order to make this center. I was quite active, doing everything possible to encourage the Ministry of Construction to support it. I talked with the workers, asking that they make a big effort, and the resources were taken from that small fund. Since the center was built in two years, I would say that it used nearly 50 percent of the money in that reserve in each of those years. We hope the fund will grow, because even though planning is very good, it shouldn't become something rigid, like a straitjacket. You can make a five-year plan, but new possibilities, new ideas, keep emerging, and you shouldn't have all your resources tied up. This is why I say that the ideal thing in centralized planning is to set aside a reserve fund so you can respond to new contingencies.

Gianni Minà: There's something that I would like clarified. A minute ago, you said something that I think is interesting as regards the future of humanity: a Cuban doctor went to receive some training in Houston.

Fidel Castro: He was there for only a short time. He went to learn about the cancer studies that are being carried out with interferon.

Gianni Minà: How was that possible? The US government is very hostile toward you. Are some US scientists friends of yours?

Fidel Castro: That was in 1981, and Reagan was in the White House. Professor Clark is a very noble, very unselfish man. There are many scientists like him in the United States and many other noble, unselfish people who are always ready to help in an activity of this kind that may be useful to human beings. The government doesn't like it at all, but it can't stop them completely. The government puts obstacles in the way of all such exchanges and visits. Sometimes those visits are made through the Pan American

Health Organization. The US authorities don't like it, and they try to block our medical and other scientific studies. The blockade includes a total ban on exporting medical equipment to Cuba — not even an aspirin can be exported to us. That government, which talks so much about human rights, applies a blockade that prohibits exports of medicine, and sometimes we have to use indirect means to purchase what we need.

Gianni Minà: But I see that something can be done, independently of the political ideas of Professor Clark and other scientists.

Fidel Castro: I think that Clark is a humanist. Naturally, I've never asked him what he thinks of capitalism, socialism or anything like that. But he is a very noble man. He spoke here when the center was inaugurated. He is an independent, courageous man — a truly magnificent person.

Gianni Minà: I would like to move on to some questions on medicine. What are the present statistics on infant mortality in Cuba and the rest of Latin America?

Fidel Castro: Infant mortality in 1986 was 13.6 for every 1000 live births. In 1987 and coming years we will be struggling to reduce it. Within five years, with the programs we're applying, we hope to lower it to less than 10. Practically the only ones who die are those who have very few possibilities of survival, some with congenital malformations that are incompatible with life, as the doctors say.

We even have a team in the Children's Cardiovascular Surgery Center — it's another new, very important center — that can detect in the first few weeks of development if an embryo has a congenital malformation that is incompatible with life. If that is discovered and pregnancy in those cases is interrupted, a family tragedy is averted. We also have a program for detecting congenital malformations in general, especially those of the neural tube, which is what gives rise to the birth of those greatly malformed — which may well be the most traumatic tragedy that can happen to a family. In those cases, an examination is made very early on so that, under the laws of our country, pregnancy can be interrupted voluntarily. It isn't obligatory. Any woman can choose not to interrupt her pregnancy — either because she doesn't believe in the research or because she wants to have the child anyway — and her decision is respected. But those cases are included in the infant mortality statistics.

There's another factor that influences those statistics: pregnancy at an early age that may lead to premature births. The possibilities of death are much greater for premature babies. We try to avoid pregnancies at an early age and have launched a campaign aimed at avoiding it. But that requires much more sophisticated medicine.

With the programs we're applying, we should bring the infant mortality rate down to less than 10 within five years. It can be reduced to 9.8. I don't know how far we will lower it in the end, because climatic factors here militate against lowering it much more. I've wondered if it can be reduced to under 10 in a tropical climate. There may also be genetic factors. And I've wondered if our people's genetic potential for survival would make it possible to lower it to less than 10. There are a few countries whose infant mortality rates are less than 10. I understand that it's less than 10 in Japan, and it's under 10 in Sweden. There are others, but they are countries where the birth rate is very low and much better living conditions. We are already sure that we will reduce it to less than 10. This is a very good index, in the sense that it implies a great struggle to improve the quality of medical services.

What was the situation prior to the triumph of the revolution? There aren't any statistics, because many cases weren't recorded, especially babies born in the countryside. We estimate that the infant mortality rate must have been around 60 or 70 for every 1,000 live births. We reduced the rate to 45, then to 30, and so on, in the past years, and now we're about to achieve one of the lowest infant mortality rates in the world. We already have a better rate than many of the developed countries; it's more or less the same as in the United States. The infant mortality rate in the United States is a little lower than here, but there are areas in the United States, in the Hispanic and black communities, where the rate is much higher than in Cuba. We have entire provinces that have lower rates than Washington and than many states in the United States. In addition, the rates for the various provinces here are more or less the same; there aren't any great differences among them.

In Latin America, taking a conservative estimate, the average is somewhere between 60 and 70. Some countries have rates of under 60, and others have rates of over 60 — of 70 or 80. You would have to ask the Brazilians about this, but I understand that their rate is high. There are some regions in Brazil where the rate is high, up to 150. It's very high in Peru, as well — around 100. There are some regions in Peru and Bolivia where the infant mortality rate is over 200 for every 1,000 live births. That is more or less the comparison that can be made.

The infant mortality rate here must be only a fifth or a sixth of the average for Latin America. I think there is just one country whose rate is around 20 — according to the statistics, which aren't always reliable. Our statistics are extremely rigorous. I think there is one — it may be Costa Rica — that has a rate of 19. The rates in all others are much higher.

Gianni Minà: President Castro, before going on, I would like to go into an aspect that is a delicate one for Catholics, especially in Italy. You mentioned the cases of births of grossly deformed children. You know that, for Catholics, any human being, even if it is so deformed, is a child of God. Could we go into the problem of human beings who are born in conditions that are, shall we say, not normal?

Fidel Castro: The point is, the fathers and mothers are also children of God, and I've never seen anything comparable to the tragedy a family confronts when such a child — one so deformed — is born. I know of cases, because some are born in our hospitals, and although many of them die, some survive, and they live for years. There have been cases of parents who haven't wanted to take them home, and the state has taken care of them. Our hospitals have some of those cases who survive, who are given excellent care. We uphold the ethical principle of giving the best possible attention to any human being in any condition, but I know of families who haven't wanted to take them home, because they have another child who is 4 or 5 years old.

Naturally, I respect the criteria of the Church. I don't want to get involved in matters of religious doctrine. I'm not saying they should be killed. I don't know how people's ideas will evolve in the future. Perhaps someday the principle of euthanasia will be applied. But that is more delicate. Some countries already accept it and don't prohibit it, but that's something else again.

Here, we aren't even talking about babies who have been born.

We're talking about embryos a few weeks after conception whose situation is incompatible with life — even with minimally conscious life. This is Cuba's position and that of many countries. Note that it isn't a matter of interrupting a normal pregnancy. We're talking about interrupting pregnancy in one of those exceptional cases in which a child will be born who cannot live.

At some point, I think the Church will make its policy more flexible. I've discussed this with religious figures at times. I've even discussed it with some bishops. Several years ago, a cardinal from Benin visited Cuba and I talked at length with him. I asked him when the Church's position on some of these problems would be made more flexible. It wasn't about this kind of case. I had spoken of the Church's policy on contraceptives, on birth control. I explained the situation of the Third World countries, with billions of people whose socio-economic conditions didn't allow them to feed — much less, care for — their children properly. I said, "This is a great tragedy. They are born and then starve to death or die of diseases. You can't say they are born on earth. They are born in hell, for life is hell for them, and their social conditions condemn them to that tragedy."

I've discussed this a great deal, and I even told him, "I hope you will make that position more flexible someday, because the Third World has very tragic problems that are related to the population explosion." It isn't that I'm against ethical principles or the preaching of certain virtues, such as abstinence. I'm not criticizing that, and I don't want to get involved in that problem. What I am saying is that billions of human beings are faced with a tragic reality — in which, of course, there's a contradiction between the needs of the states, the governments and the people and the criteria and concepts of the Church. This is the case precisely in the Catholic countries — and the vast majority of Latin Americans are Catholics. Others aren't Catholics: the Africans aren't Catholics, and they don't have that kind of problem; the Indians and Chinese aren't Catholics. But this concept has a very great influence. That is, I'm not against ethical principles in general or against upholding ethical values. I am simply speaking about realities.

I told the cardinal on that occasion that the Church has always been very flexible and has always adapted to successive stages of human history and I expressed the hope that, someday, it would have a more flexible position on that problem.

When Frei Betto talked with me, he spoke of the principle of responsible paternity — I think that was what he said — and explained what the Church accepted in this sphere, which was a step forward compared to what it had accepted 20 or 30 years ago.

Was that what you wanted to know?

Gianni Minà: Yes, that was what I wanted to know, because everyone has their own way of tackling certain problems. Let's return to Cuban medicine, on which you have given me data. How many doctors left the country after the triumph of the revolution in 1959, how did you face that flight of talent, and how did you change that situation in the following three decades?

Fidel Castro: If you allow me, before answering you directly, I think there is an important figure on health that's missing. Life expectancy in our country is already over 74 years. In that regard, we are level with the United States. In matters of health, our emulation is with the United States, not with other Third World countries. I think that our historic response to its policy of hostility and its blockade, even in the field of medicine, is to achieve better health indices than the United States.

You ask me how many doctors there were. There were 6,000 when the revolution triumphed. Many of them were in the capital, and many were unemployed. We began to build hospitals and develop medical services throughout the countryside. But, in response to the revolution's laws — especially the Agrarian Reform Law, which was one of the first — the United States began its hostility toward Cuba and tried to leave us without any skilled workers. Before that, it had a quota for those wanting to go to the United States, just as it now has for other countries, but at that time it opened its doors wide to everybody who wanted to leave to Cuba.

There was a surplus of doctors who wanted to work in the United States but couldn't obtain visas. They had possibilities of finding employment and better pay. Not all of them were moved by patriotic sentiments; many had reservations about the revolution. We opened our doors for them. What did we do? We let everybody leave who wanted to, and at the same time began the expansion of the School of Medicine. Three thousand of the 6,000 left, including the professors of the School of Medicine. With the 3,000 loyal doctors, the ones who remained in the country, we began to carry out our health program to achieve the results we have today.

Now, we have over 25,000 doctors. In the next three months, around 3,000 more will join them. We will have 28,000 doctors.

Gianni Minà: Out of a population of 10.5 million inhabitants.

Fidel Castro: Three thousand two hundred will be graduated in 1988, and 3,600 in 1989. By 1990, we'll be graduating around 4,000 doctors a year. Some 5,500 students enrol in the School of Medicine each year, selected for their good grades and vocational interest. We have 21 schools of medicine. Doctors are trained in all the provinces. The capital has six such schools, and we even have a number of scholarships for students from other Third World countries to study medicine in Cuba.

As for the future, we estimate that we'll have around 65,000 doctors by the year 2000, which isn't all that far away. Of those 65,000, some 30,000 will work in the hospital network, and 20,000 will work in the community as family doctors. This is a very new program that other countries haven't yet developed but which is yielding some truly extraordinary results. Each family doctor cares for a given community as the main element of primary medicine. We will have 20,000 doctors participating in that. We will have around 5,000 in factories and schools, for we believe that there should be a doctor wherever there is a citizen: in each work place, neighborhood, school and hospital. That's the concept.

Of those 65,000, we will have 10,000 working abroad, according to our estimates, because there is a great demand for our doctors. This will be in cooperation with the other Third World countries. Then we will graduate another 10,000 so we can give our doctors a sabbatical year for study once every seven years.

I could go on at length about this. It would take all our time if I were to talk about the programs we're applying in medicine.

Gianni Minà: How were those results obtained? How did you manage to change a situation which I imagine was tragic? Who helped you?

Fidel Castro: We received very little help from abroad in the field of medicine. We applied ideas, some ideas that turned out to be correct: to emphasize preventive medicine, that was very important. It's more economical, as well. The Third World countries can do a lot with small expenditure through preventive medicine. That's what produces the most immediate results.

We extended medical services all over the country, to all the towns and the countryside. We applied a program of building hospitals and sent doctors to work in the countryside. It wasn't like things are now, with family doctors in the mountains, but we started that way. We were determined to do it. It was a promise, a program, an ardent desire and one of the areas of most suffering. It was one of the aspects in which our society was most backward.

Medicine had some technical development, but it was limited to an elite of rich people in a few hospitals — not for the masses. A large part of the population didn't have any medical services.

I would say that the main factor was our determination to carry it out, as well as some correct criteria and concepts about the development of medicine. We didn't prohibit private practice; there has never been a decree prohibiting it. What did we do? Basing ourselves on the students' revolutionary fervor, starting in the first year after the triumph of the revolution, we asked them in a political movement to renounce the exercise of private medicine. Ever since, all of the graduates have renounced it. They not only take the Hippocratic oath but also pledge not to engage in private practice. Nobody thinks twice about it. Nevertheless, there are some 40 doctors who were trained prior to the triumph of the revolution who do have private practice. It was never prohibited. This was achieved by means of a political movement among the students and has had tremendous results, for as a rule, our doctors dedicate themselves to their work with great fervor.

Gianni Minà: Now, I'd like to give our readers some data on the state of medicine in Cuba: more than 800 kidney transplants; many heart operations; an institute of genetic engineering and biotechnology; and a leading position in traumatology, tropical medicine and even aesthetic surgery for those who want to become more beautiful. All this is free for Cubans. Is this why people in Western Europe don't want to hear about Cuban medicine?

Fidel Castro: Let me first clarify one thing: we develop aesthetic surgery not so much to make people more beautiful — I think people should be content with what nature gave them, and it isn't bad to be slightly different from others — but mainly because there are accidents and burns. People have accidents that disfigure their faces or their hands. For example, one of the specialties is hand surgery, reconstruction of hands after serious accidents. Of course, this doesn't mean that there are not also people who aren't content with their age and want some improvement, some remodeling. This is also justified in people who have manifest natural defects.

Gianni Minà: Can it be done?

Fidel Castro: It can be done. But the main purpose was to meet that need, and we're promoting aesthetic surgery. It's important.

All those things, as you say, are true. We even have a national system of kidney transplants. We have what we might call an inventory — a list of everybody who has problems and needs, with their blood group and other characteristics. We've launched a campaign for voluntary organ donations. Nearly all the people have pledged to donate their organs when they die; the pledge is in their ID cards.

We created that movement, which had a great response, and some organs are available, but not all kinds. It's always a problem, because hundreds of people are waiting. When there's an accident the computers determine which person should receive the organ, because that person is most compatible with the victim of the accident.

Heart transplant surgery is something recent; we did the first such operation just two years ago. Two neurological transplants to combat Parkinson's disease have been carried out in the Institute of Neurology. I think Cuba is one of only four countries where that kind of operation has been performed. This is very promising. It may solve some problems of medullary accidents that condemn people to be invalids for the rest of their lives. We have great hopes for this transplant technique, and it is free.

A heart transplant in the United States costs $120,000, and sometimes it has to be repeated. To receive one, you have to be rich or the object of a big charity drive.

Here, every citizen gets all the medical care they need, no matter what it costs. In the cases of children who had congenital heart trouble and needed operations, we used to send them abroad. Now, we have inaugurated a children's cardiovascular surgery center, which is functioning excellently, with very highly trained personnel, and we are preparing for operating on children

— even newborn babies. The important thing in this is the diagnosis.

Cuba has never hesitated to make any sacrifice if it could save a life or if it could save somebody's eyesight. In the past, we sent patients abroad — even to capitalist countries — to have very expensive operations.

Gianni Minà: On the plane, I met a US engineer who was coming to have an operation in Cuba — where, he said, ophthalmology was very advanced.

Fidel Castro: It's possible. The operation is even less expensive here.

But we haven't yet exported medical services on a large scale.

Foreigners pay. The members of the diplomatic corps, who have the resources to do so, pay for the medical services they receive. Tourists should pay for medical services, as well. Many of those who ask to come as paying patients, asking for an operation or other medical treatment, are needy, with low incomes. In those cases, we offer them the care they need. I would say that most of those who come to have operations here cannot pay the expenses.

If these facts aren't known abroad it's because the information is blocked. No transnational wire service — especially of the United States — is going to use even one line to publicize Cuba's successes. Rather, they use all their space to publicize the problems that Cuba may have: if there's a shortage of some product, if there's some difficulty, if there's a dissident or some other problem. That's what they send on their wire services. The tens of thousands of lives that are saved and the benefits that everybody receives in our country — there's never even one line about any of that.

It isn't because we charge $48 for fitting someone with contact lenses. I don't know the prices, but there's a clinic that takes care of diplomats.

Gianni Minà: Really, $6,000 dollars for a transplant or $48 for some contact lenses is very little . . . .

Fidel Castro: That's little?

Gianni Minà: Extremely little. It costs much more in Europe.

Fidel Castro: OK, but don't go around drumming up business for us. For contact lenses, OK. But for kidney operations we have a lot of people waiting for a transplant, for a donor, and if we dedicate ourselves to getting hard currency from kidney transplants — since kidneys can't be imported or produced at will — we would adversely affect a Cuban citizen, a fellow citizen who would have to wait, and it might even cost a life. The same goes for heart transplants, even if they paid us a million dollars. We don't have many donors, because a donor appears only when there's an accident. You should remember that there are fewer car accidents in Cuba than in Italy or France, because there are many more cars there, and they're worse speed demons than we are — at least, it seems that way from what I see in the movies. So, we have fewer donors, and if we bring in a transplant case in order to obtain a million dollars, we would be sacrificing a Cuban life. It isn't easy, and you can't make a business out of those things. Naturally, some people come for kidney transplants and bring their own donors.

Now, if you're talking about extracorporeal lithotrity — the destruction of kidney stones by means of ultrasound — which also costs a lot, you can do anything you want about that, because we have that technique here and it's just a matter of buying the equipment. There are many medical services that can be exported without entailing sacrifices for the population, and we may start exporting those services or offering those services here someday.

For example, we have a technique for curing vitiligo. One of our doctors developed it. There isn't any other medicine for this. As a result, a lot of people come every month, hundreds of people come to get treatment, and they buy the medicine periodically afterwards and they receive a cure. There are millions of people with vitiligo in the world, and some come here for that treatment.

We're developing other things, as well, such as a vaccine against type B meningococcic meningitis. We have already developed a vaccine that has great prospects; it's in the mass-testing phase. We can't yet say the final word on this, but it will unquestionably be good news internationally when we've proved the vaccine's efficacy. I'm very optimistic; I don't like to talk about things before we've gotten the last word, but since we're talking about this subject . . . .

Gianni Minà: Does homeopathic medicine exist in Cuba?

Fidel Castro: We practice modern, scientific medicine. But we don't rule anything out. To the contrary, we're trying to discover and know more. For example, traditional medicine is also being developed a lot. We're studying the medicinal plants and their possible application to many diseases; we're paying a lot of attention to that. There are even many countries that have discovered medicines through empirical methods. That is one of the reasons why it is so important to protect plant species. Industrialization and deforestation destroy them in many places. They may be of great medicinal value, and we're studying and developing them. We're setting up small nurseries or gardens of medicinal plants in each province. We even consider this a part of the country's defense, because in a situation of total military blockade, in which we couldn't receive any raw materials, that medicine would be useful.

We're also studying acupuncture and applying it whenever possible. We don't rule out any school of medicine.

When did homeopathic medicine begin? Back in antiquity, in the age of Greece. It dates from distant times; I think Galen applied it, and maybe Hippocrates, too. We haven't worked a great deal in that field, but we haven't ruled it out.

Gianni Minà: They say that cancer studies are very advanced in Cuba, based on a plant that grows here: *Petiveria alliacea.*

Fidel Castro: Yes, it's possible that some studies have been made, because when news of a certain plant arrives, we don't rule it out. Instead, we study all its possibilities in this regard. Cancer seems to have very different forms, and very different techniques will be needed in the fight against cancer.

Interferon, for example, solves some problems. Sometimes it's used in combination with radiation; at other times, we combine it with cytostatic serum. Intensive efforts are being made to seek solutions, and people are working on this all over the world. Preventive measures are very important in the fight against cancer. If the mental energy and creativity working to produce weapons in the world had been dedicated to the struggle against this disease, I think we would have advanced a very long way, and a solution might have been found.

Gianni Minà: This is my last question on medicine. It's on something that's quite alarming. I'll read my notes. Medicines that have been banned in the United States because they are still in the experimental stage, are being sold all over Latin America. Thus, the people in the Latin American countries are being turned into defenseless guinea pigs for the chemical industry and its corporations. What measures has Cuba taken in this regard?

Fidel Castro: Unfortunately, this happens quite frequently. I see that you are well-informed about some of the problems in our area.

News is published frequently about medicines banned by the US authorities that the transnational corporations have kept on selling for years in all of these countries, at really high prices. Some medicines have been found to be harmful to pregnant women and to those with tumors, for they can cause cancer or mental problems. Some medicines that are launched on the market before all of their possible consequences have been tested can cause many problems.

When they are discovered in the United States, they are banned, but the transnational corporations keep on selling those products as a commercial venture. In this regard, our countries are turned not only into laboratories but also into tools of immoral commerce. And people are protesting against this.

It may be that the most expensive things imported by the Latin American and other Third World countries are medicines. The terms of trade are unequal when we buy a machine, a lathe or an industrial machine. They are even more unequal when we buy medicine. I say this because an aspirin may cost a fraction of a cent to produce — I'm talking about a fraction of a cent three years ago; nobody knows what a cent is worth, if anything, now — and it is usually sold to the population for 10 cents. Thus, its price is 10 or 12 times its production cost. This price includes the advertising, because those corporations present the same product in 10 different forms, with 10 different colors, 10 designs and 10 different packages. The same product with a different name, but it's the same product. You pay for all that, and they also make high profits. It's very expensive and affects an aspect of the utmost importance, which is human health. They make a business out of that.

What did we do? As part of our policy of recovering our national resources, we nationalized all of the pharmaceutical companies, both domestic and foreign — not the head offices, but in some cases the laboratories they had here — and developed the production of medicines in Cuba. It isn't all that difficult or expensive, because as I was saying, it is relatively inexpensive to import or produce the raw materials. Thus, we now produce more than 80 percent of the medicines we use; it may be 85 percent — I don't guarantee the exact figure, but it's more than 80 percent. We import some processed medicines, either because we don't have the patents for producing them or because they are small quantities that we bring from the other socialist countries or from some capitalist countries. We also import raw materials; we don't have all of the raw materials here.

We're developing our pharmaceutical industry. We have advanced our work with blood products, because we developed an awareness of the need to make blood donations, right from the beginning. The Cuban people have been educated to give blood, and hundreds of thousands of people give blood every year. Before, people used to buy blood donations and made a business of it. Some people made a living out of "giving" blood, and there were laboratories that mixed blood with water and dye — we discovered all those things. Now, we have plenty of blood donations. We use them in hospitals and produce medicines, blood derivatives, from the excess.

Gianni Minà: Maybe right here, in this laboratory.

Fidel Castro: Yes. Work will be completed soon on a plant that's going to produce a large amount of blood derivatives. The blood of Cubans is very healthy. We have very few cases of AIDS, and they are strictly controlled. All blood donations are examined, and there is great safety regarding all those products. It was one of the branches that was developed. We're continuing to promote it, and the pharmaceutical industry may provide some of Cuba's most important lines for export in the future.

All of this has helped to make medicines much less expensive. Medicines in Cuba are sold at about half the price they were sold at in 1959. If we had to buy from the transnational corporations the medicines that the people now consume, we would have to pay $1.2 or $1.5 billion dollars. But the population spend only around 200 million pesos on medicines — what they buy for family use, because the medicines that are used in the hospitals are free — and it costs the country a few dozen million dollars in foreign currency to buy the imported components of processed medicines. The state has laboratories in which it produces the medicines and distributes them without it becoming a money-making venture. Naturally, the people have to pay something for the medicines they buy, but as I said, they pay around half as much as the medicines cost prior to the revolution.

I've often talked with the leaders of other Third World countries and explained what we have done in the field of medicine, saying that they can do a lot in this field with preventive medicine and with a minimal development of the pharmaceutical industry. Our experience has had excellent results.

Fidel Castro pitching, 1964 *Photo: Osvaldo Salas*

Chapter 11

Sport

Cuba is among the leading sporting countries in the world, as measured by the number of victories or medals won in international competitions, the number of times its athletes have participated in the finals in important competitions in all disciplines, and the organization of its sporting activities. This is inconceivable for any other Third World country, including such large nations as Argentina, Brazil and Mexico.

The sensational victory of Cuban heavyweight Teófilo Stevenson over Bobbick of the United States — who had been described as "the great white hope of boxing" — in the 1972 Munich Olympic Games, unquestionably went beyond the bounds of sports while consolidating Cuban boxing's number-one position in the world arena. Later, Cuba set the world back on its heels again, in the 1976 Montreal Games. With his two incredible victories in the 400 and 800-meter races, Alberto Juantorena was the hero of those Olympics. He is now vice-president of the National Institute of Sports, Physical Education and Recreation (INDER), practically a deputy minister of sports.

In the socialist countries, sports have frequently been a means for reaffirming the positive aspects of an ideology. But when it becomes a tradition and establishes a firm place in the world sports arena, then it is probable that it has become a tangible conquest in the life of a country. Among other things, you can't produce champions in so many disciplines in modern sports if you can't provide the masses of athletes with an adequate diet. In Cuba, 3 million people engage in sports — out of a total population of a little more than 10 million

inhabitants. Certainly, sports are a way to distinguish yourself, to stand out from the masses and to affirm your individuality in a socialist country more than in the capitalist world. But such an extended success cannot be explained only by those motivations.
G.M.

Gianni Minà: Shall we talk about sport?

Fidel Castro: All right.

Gianni Minà: I know you like sport, and they were a part of my journalistic career. Like medicine and culture, sport has been one of the priorities in the revolution. Was this out of conviction, or for reasons of . . . ?

Fidel Castro: Propaganda?

Gianni Minà: That's right: propaganda.

Fidel Castro: It's true that a lot of attention has been given to sport. It also formed part of our program and of our policy of developing all activities that could be useful to the population, promoting their health.

Sport has two meanings for us: it is related to people's health and recreation. Some sports activities provide entertainment for hundreds of thousands of people and those who don't see them live can watch them on television. Sports were promoted almost right from the start — out of conviction, even though everything is propaganda. We've already agreed that propaganda is good if it takes the shape of all these results. So that is my reply.

What else did you want to know about sport?

Gianni Minà: In Cuba, 3 million of the 10 million inhabitants participate in sport. Everybody knows that you have to be well-nourished to engage in sport. How is this possible in an under-developed country?

Fidel Castro: As I already told you, no child or anyone else is undernourished in Cuba. Every child gets a quart of milk a day until they are seven years old; it is subsidized and sold at a low price. I already told you about the average consumption of calories, more than are required, and of proteins. The people have a good diet.

We've graduated around 20,000 physical education and sports teachers. When the revolution triumphed there were only a few dozen of them, so we built schools to train more. Now, we have all the ones we need to teach physical education and sports, in all the schools and work places.

We have massive programs to get people to do physical exercises — especially older people. They do exercises on a mass scale and have scored tremendous results. This is done in conjunction with the family doctors, and it's one of the factors on which we base our goal of raising life expectancy to more than 80 years within the next 10 years. I'm really enthusiastic about the effort that's being made. Of course, as regards diet, this is possible because the country's wealth is better distributed and the economy is being developed. I think that other countries could do it, as well — they have the land and other resources, but they come up against the capitalist system. We've already talked about that.

We talked about capitalism earlier, but you were thinking about the Italian, French, Spanish and German capitalist systems. There are two capitalisms: capitalism in the highly industrialized countries and capitalism in the underdeveloped countries. Capitalism produces some fruits for you, but capitalism in the underdeveloped world is a complete disaster: vast inequality, an horrendous amount of unemployment and no social security — all of which creates a truly chaotic situation.

It may be that Italy doesn't need thorough-going social changes, because some problems have been solved; that's your business. But our countries do need thoroughgoing social changes, because of the number of undernourished, illiterate and sick people, the number of children who die each year, and the enormous number of people who die of curable diseases. That is part of this capitalism. Perhaps I should have spoken of this when we were talking about capitalism and what I think of it. I know this capitalism of the underdeveloped world, and I tell you frankly that I have a very poor opinion of that system.

Gianni Minà: Is this why, for example, of all the Latin American countries, only Cuba wins victories in the Olympic Games or in the other major sports competitions?

Fidel Castro: There are two reasons: first, we've given attention to sport, training teachers and developing techniques. Second, sports are practised on a mass scale here.

I think that if sports had been given more attention in the other countries they could have won many more medals, even with their present levels of malnutrition. Even in their social situations and with the problems of malnutrition, a part of their population (that is much larger than the entire population of Cuba) does have a good diet. And if they discover an athlete — even in the low-income sectors of the population — and train and feed them well, good results can be achieved. Two factors are involved here: they haven't given enough attention to sport and haven't promoted it on a mass scale. In Cuba, we've given attention to sport and have promoted mass participation. Those are the factors that are responsible for the large number of medals we win in international competitions and the fact that we can challenge the United States in many sports.

Gianni Minà: Now for some questions that are a little less profound but which help people to understand a nation and its president. You are known to like swimming and spear fishing, and you also played basketball. What is the position and kind of play you prefer in basketball?

Fidel Castro: I usually played near the basket, but in the last few years — I played in basketball championships even after the triumph of the revolution — I played forward in the defense and farther back in the attack.

There are two techniques I always favored. One is pressure guarding, player to player. I made a specialty of that kind of guarding, which is quite psychological. When you become your adversary's shadow, the shadow of the player you have to guard, guarding becomes a psychological tool. The player feels desperate and your responsibility is clearly defined. It isn't so clear in zone guarding. I always favored that policy of player-to-player guarding on our team.

In the attack, I liked going in close to the basket, playing on the offensive, trying not to commit any fouls on the offensive and forcing my opponent to commit fouls.

I wasn't against distance shots. I was a good long-distance shot, but it seemed safer to me to go in closer through various ways. I liked combinations and passes. Others prefer distance shots. That depends on controlling rebounds, what results you have and your average in making baskets, but I always favored that kind of offensive game as a basic principle.

Basketball has been revolutionized, and new rules keep appearing. Now it's not two but three free shots; a long distance basket is worth more than one closer in. I think that it will keep on improving and being enriched. It's been some time since I've played basketball and baseball. I'm talking about more than 10 years ago.

Gianni Minà: Cuba's national sport is baseball. You are closely linked to the United States in that, at least.

Fidel Castro: Yes.

Gianni Minà: Can you explain where the passion for that game comes from and what the special attraction of that sport is? It hasn't caught on in Europe.

Fidel Castro: Actually, we should have been soccer enthusiasts, because Cuba was a Spanish colony, and the Spaniards play soccer, not baseball. I think it's the result of the US influence and the prestige of the Major Leagues, with all their publicity.

Great interest and fanaticism was developed starting at the turn of the century. I don't think it was a positive thing, even though our team is the world champion and we participate very successfully in all the international competitions.

I think the Italians are learning how to play baseball now and are improving.

Gianni Minà: A little.

Fidel Castro: It isn't a very complete sport. Some players have very active positions, requiring a lot of movement, but others have very passive positions. I think soccer is a more complete sport, in terms of exercise. The great liking for baseball has kept soccer from developing. We're trying to publicize and promote soccer. We broadcast the world championships, but we haven't had much success. It's advancing, but not enough. Baseball has that predominance, that hegemony, which has held back other, more complete sports.

Gianni Minà: Do you like soccer?

Fidel Castro: Well, I played soccer on the Belén School team when I was in high school. And I had played at the Dolores School before that.

Gianni Minà: What position?

Fidel Castro: Right forward. I was usually right forward.

Gianni Minà: What do you think of this game, which is almost a religion in Europe and Latin America?

Fidel Castro: Soccer?

Gianni Minà: Yes.

Fidel Castro: I remember that I liked soccer when I was a boy. I even went to see games, starting when I was in the fourth or fifth grade. I was quite a fanatic. I played it then in competitions. Later, I gradually dropped out of soccer.

Gianni Minà: You played on the right. That may well have been the only time in your life that you were on the right.

Fidel Castro: Maybe. I'm right-handed, though I also practised with my left. That's why. You may have to be left-handed to play on the other side. I played a lot at school. I went in for practically all of the sports when I was at school.

Gianni Minà: What do you think of the fact that, in Europe and Latin America . . . ?

Fidel Castro: You said it was a religion, and that's true. I'm amazed by the fanaticism it triggers, which even leads to violence and death. You have to understand it well, because there aren't very many goals and you don't see the same plays repeated. It isn't like basketball, in which there are many baskets and a lot of points; volleyball, which is very fast, with lots of action; or baseball, that has hits, home runs and other spectacular things. In soccer, a bunch of people run this way and that, and it may be that no goals are scored. They are scored at very few times, which are the most interesting moments in the game. Nevertheless, for some reason, in Latin America and in Europe — in the world — people are very enthusiastic, crazy about soccer. Personally, I find other sports more entertaining, with more action.

Gianni Minà: It may be, as some say, that soccer is the opiate of the people.

Fidel Castro: Perhaps. That's something that you who have the European experience can say.

Gianni Minà: You love boxing. I, too, have loved boxing and am a fan of Cuban boxers, from Kid Chocolate to Teófilo Stevenson. They were always great champions. Have you ever, metaphorically or in practice, boxed with anyone?

Fidel Castro: Without metaphors. When I was in the seventh grade, the first year of junior high school, we boarded at school, and one time I bought some boxing gloves and took them home to the countryside. It was summer vacation. We set up a ring in a cockfight pit — which is round — and we roped off a square. I put on the gloves and spent many hours boxing that summer.

Gianni Minà: Were you ever knocked down?

Fidel Castro: Well, I almost was. I was boxing with the young son of a sugar-cane worker, a kid who I think was a potential Stevenson, and I remember that once he hit me real hard. I didn't fall down, but I was half-dazed; that's a fact. Then I reacted: I was a little mad because of the punch. That was the hardest punch I got in that period, and I remember it very clearly. He connected with my head.

Gianni Minà: Your country is also the homeland of great chess players. Did you ever play chess with Camilo or Che? If so, who won?

Fidel Castro: Not with Camilo, but I played chess with Che. It so happened that Che . . . Several of us were arrested in Mexico, and Che and I were held longer than the others. Che was imprisoned because he was Argentinian and had quite an argument on theoretical questions with the police, and I, because I was the main leader. We were there by ourselves for several weeks, mixed in with other immigration prisoners, and books and chess were our only means of entertainment. Che and I played chess there, killing time that way.

Gianni Minà: Who won?

Fidel Castro: Well, Che knew more about it than I did, because he had studied something of chess. I played more on the basis of intuition. I was a little like a guerrilla and I won some games from him, but he won most of the time, because he knew more about chess than I did. He really liked it.

Even after the triumph of the revolution he kept on studying chess. He was crazy about it. After the revolution I played chess occasionally. I didn't want to study it and I deliberately stopped playing. It was so absorbing that you could spend six, eight or ten hours playing, and I couldn't afford the time. If you want to master it, you really should study it, but I decided neither to study it nor to play it as a sport.

Gianni Minà: Mao Zedong used to say that real revolutionaries were more like pingpong players than chess players. What do you think?

Fidel Castro: He probably drew that conclusion based on his political experience in diplomacy, because they say that relations with the United States were begun during a pingpong game. I haven't had that experience, but I think that the work of a political figure — of a statesman, if not of a revolutionary — resembles chess more than pingpong.

Chapter 12

Memories of Che

I had never imagined that Fidel would share with me his innermost thoughts on Ernesto Che Guevara.

Fidel had never spoken of Che Guevara in this way with any other journalist and I believe that he did so on this occasion not so much for political motivations, but instead as an opportunity to defend a friendship which was both wonderful as well as tragic.

Perhaps for this reason, these two men and their ideas have been so villified, even attempting to denigrate the image of their friendship.

The recollection offered by Fidel in this chapter of his Argentinian friend, Che, is exceptional. This is so not only because of the historical revelations about the presence of Che in Africa and his clandestine return to Cuba in order to prepare for the expedition to Bolivia, the location of the tragic and final adventure. This recollection also provides an intimate glimpse of the friendship between Fidel and Che. We are able to observe the moral quality of this friendship.

Others could have perhaps presented these questions in another form to Fidel Castro. What is important is that this unique testimony has been presented.

G.M.

Gianni Minà: President Castro, you are a witness to contemporary history like few others in our time. This interview is proof of that. I would like to move on to your most intimate recollections of some comrades in struggle, in particular Che Guevara and Camilo Cienfuegos. For example, Che represents a symbol, an

Che Guevara during voluntary work

ideal, for at least three generations in Europe and the world. When you think of your friend Che, what is the first thought that comes to your mind?

Fidel Castro: For me, as well, it has been hard to accept the thought that Che is dead. I have dreamed many times — you sometimes tell people the things you dream — I dreamed I spoke with him, that he was alive. It's a very special thing, a person whose death it is hard to resign yourself to. What's the reason? In my opinion, it is because he has a permanent presence in everything.

His death occurred far away, many kilometers from our country. I tell you, the idea that Che was dead was something very difficult to get used to. It hit me differently from the death of other *compañeros*, for we have lost many *compañeros* in the struggle. We have seen many *compañeros* die. One has the impression Che is still present because of what he symbolizes, because of his character, his conduct, his principles. He had a great number of truly exceptional qualities. I knew him very well, from the time he made contact with us in Mexico until he left Cuba for the last time.

I really believe, with sorrow, that with Che's death a great mind was lost. He was a person who still had much to contribute to the theory and practice of building socialism.

Gianni Minà: In the letter to you written by Che before leaving, he seems almost bitter for not having earlier recognized your quality as a leader.

Fidel Castro: What might be the reason for that? First, Che was a very quiet man. He was not expressive. He didn't communicate these things. He felt things but he did not say them. By the way, some very warm-hearted verses he wrote about me have come to light; someone saved them.

He was naturally a little sceptical about Latin America, about Latin American politicians. He may have thought our revolution might end the way other revolutions have ended. But in reality he never gave me the slightest impression of having such doubts. He was always extraordinarily fraternal and respectful with me. He may have been a little mistrustful of the Movement. He may have observed that our movement was heterogeneous, that it included people from many different sectors.

He already had an excellent revolutionary education, a Marxist education. He was very studious. He had graduated from medical school, conducted research, and was very rigorous in studying the questions of Marxism. So for this reason he was a little sceptical.

I think if he wrote that it must have been from an excess of integrity. Because in reality I had to act, to coordinate many factors, and I had to promote unity over the reservations demonstrated by one or another *compañero*; I had to have patience in my relations with them.

For Che, who was impulsive, very courageous, very daring, at times even reckless, I always had special regard. On more than one occasion he would step forward as a volunteer. Whatever the mission, the first volunteer was always Che. He volunteered for the most difficult actions and suggested them in the midst of combat. He was totally selfless and altruistic. Cuba wasn't his homeland. Yet he had joined us, and every day he was ready to give his life for the revolution.

I would, of course, use cadres according to the importance of a mission. When a cadre had acquired more skills, more experience, we would send out new cadres so they too could learn and develop. In war you can't continually use a cadre in dangerous situations, because at one moment or another you will lose them. We really had to protect the cadres, preserve them, because they wanted to do things. And I took on the task of preserving them as much as possible and using them in the most important missions.

I often rotated the men in these types of responsibilities, but as for him . . . Well, I truly believe if we hadn't followed this policy, Che — because of his character traits — would not have come out of the war alive. But Che was exceedingly straightforward. If at any moment he thought there was some doubt about something, he felt obligated to speak up about it. That's the way he was.

Gianni Minà: The Cuban revolution is incredible. It united an intellectual like Che, an intellectual like yourself, and a simple man of the people like Camilo — men of different backgrounds and educational levels, who functioned together in harmony. There was clearly a common dream.

Fidel Castro: They were three people of three different origins, different characteristics.

What is extraordinary about Che is that he wasn't Cuban, he was Argentinian. When we met in Mexico, he had been working in Guatemala as a doctor. He was filled with enthusiasm by the political process in Guatemala, by the agrarian reform. He witnessed the intervention of the United States and suffered very much over all that. It was something he carried within him. He joined us right away. As he relates, he joined us the first time we had a conversation.

He envisioned an anti-imperialist revolution, a revolution of national liberation. He did not yet see the socialist revolution — he envisioned that to be a little bit down the road — but he committed himself totally.

Moreover, Che was our doctor. No one thought of Che as being a great soldier. He liked sports. He tried to climb Popocatépetl almost every week; he never reached the top, but tried every week. He suffered from asthma; but despite that handicap, he made a heroic effort to climb that volcano. Although he never made it to the top, he never stopped trying to climb it once more. That also shows what kind of character he had. He was our doctor, he went as our doctor because he had that handicap. No one imagined him as a soldier. But he wasn't only an intellectual; he was also a great soldier.

Camilo was a man of the people. At first no one could have guessed his qualities. Later he really distinguished himself. I am sure many more would have done so, because in our group of 82 men — I later gave this quite a bit of thought — there were some 40 who were suited to become leaders. Out of those few who survived, several brilliant leaders emerged: Camilo, Che, and other *compañeros*, including one outstanding leader not mentioned so much — Raúl.

Gianni Minà: How were Camilo and Che different?

Fidel Castro: They had two different personalities, even though they loved and respected each other a great deal. Camilo liked to joke a lot, he always had a sense of humor.

Gianni Minà: Cuban.

Fidel Castro: He had a Cuban sense of humor, always laughing, very daring, very intelligent, less intellectual than Che but also an excellent leader, one who never gave the enemy an opportunity. He was very courageous, but wasn't as reckless as Che. Che seemed to be a man who sought death. Camilo defied death; he wasn't afraid of it, but he wasn't reckless. Those are two differences between them.

They had great affection for each other.

Gianni Minà: And your brother Raúl?

Fidel Castro: Another leader who, as I said, is not mentioned so much in this connection. Raúl is capable, responsible and brilliant. He also played a very important role.

Of the group that survived, several very good leaders emerged. That's why I think there were many young men who, had they survived the initial expedition, were well-suited to become leaders. At least 15 or 20 outstanding leaders could have emerged from our group — because someone needs both the opportunity and responsibilities to distinguish themselves.

Gianni Minà: More than 20 years ago Che left Cuba to fight in Bolivia. Can you tell me where he went from the time he left Havana until he arrived in Bolivia?

Fidel Castro: Che very much wanted to go to South America. This was an old idea of his, because when he joined us in Mexico — although it is not that he made it a condition — he did ask: "The only thing I want after the victory of the revolution is to go fight in Argentina" — his country — "that you don't keep me from doing so, that no reasons of state will stand in the way." And I promised him that. It was a long way off, after all. Firstly, no one knew if we would win the war or who was going to be alive at the end — and he surely, because of his impetuousness, had little chance of coming out alive — but this is what he asked. Once in a while, in the Sierra and afterward, he would remind me of this plan and promise. He was certainly farsighted.

After gaining experience in the Sierra Maestra, he grew more enthusiastic about the idea of making a revolution in South America, in his own country. Che knew firsthand our exceptional experience, beginning with the difficult conditions in which we rebuilt our army and carried through the struggle, and he developed a great faith in the possibilities of the revolutionary movement in South America. When I speak of South America, I am actually speaking of the southern part of South America. The promise had been given and I always told him, "Don't worry, we will keep our word." He raised it perhaps two or three times.

With the triumph of the revolution there were many tasks to carry out and problems of all kinds to be solved. We had political problems, problems with the unification of our forces, state problems, economic problems, and so on. Of course, no one knew what

Che Guevara and Fidel Castro *Photo: Osvaldo Salas*

a great soldier Che would turn out to be. He was, as I said, our doctor, who began to distinguish himself in the first battles and was to become a great military leader. Both he and Camilo carried out a very important task in the war — the invasion of the central part of the country, under difficult conditions. Much more could be said about that, but this is not the time.

We had to confront all the tasks of a victorious revolution, where nothing remained of the former state, the old armed forces, or the administrative apparatus. The various revolutionary organizations — although ours carried the principal weight — had the support of the immense majority of the population, and we used our influence to bring about unity. We always fought sectarianism. We experienced a process of uniting of the revolutionary forces. Camilo took part in all this but his death was very premature, in October [1959], in connection with the events in Camagüey and the problem of Hubert Matos.

Che was later assigned to head the Ministry of Industry. He worked very methodically. He also had several other responsibilities. Every time a serious comrade was needed for an important post, Che would volunteer. He was named president of the National Bank in the days when technicians, specialists in banking but politically inconsistent, were abandoning the country. Jokes and anecdotes followed. People would say that we had asked for an economist and Che volunteered. And we asked him, "You're an economist?" "No," he answered, "I'm a communist." Because the struggle inside the country was just beginning, and right-wing elements were accusing Che of being a communist and all kinds of things like that.

But Che always had great authority. Every assignment he was given he would fulfill strictly and brilliantly. He worked hard and acquired his first experiences in building socialism in the sector of nationalized industry. He worked hard in organizing production, in checking production, in voluntary work. He was one of the pioneers of voluntary work. He participated in almost every activity. He was very consistent in everything he did; he set an example in everything he did.

That is how he spent the first years of the revolution. Evidently, he later began to feel impatient about carrying out his old plans and ideas. I believe he was influenced in part by the fact that time was passing. He knew that special physical conditions were required for this. He felt he was capable of doing it and, in reality, he was at the peak of his mental and physical capacities. He had many ideas, based on the experience he had gained in Cuba, of what could be done in his native country. He was thinking of his country, but not only of his own country. He thought of all the Americas.

He was impatient. From our own experience, I knew the difficulty of the initial phase of a process like the one he wanted to carry out. I thought better conditions could be created for what he was thinking of doing. We attempted to persuade him not to be impatient, to convince him that more time was needed. He wanted to start out from the very first day and do it all, while we wanted other, less well-known cadres to carry out the initial steps.

Che was also very interested in international questions, in the problems faced by Africa. At the time, mercenaries had intervened in the former Belgian Congo, now Zaire. Lumumba had been killed, a neocolonial regime was established, and a movement of armed struggle emerged in Zaire. We never made this public. But the revolutionary movement asked us for help, so we sent instructors and combatants on an internationalist mission.

Gianni Minà: And the movement of Lumumba?

Fidel Castro: At that time Soumialot was its leader. It was the same movement, but Lumumba was dead.

I myself suggested the idea to Che. He had time on his hands, he had to wait. At the same time he wanted to train cadres, to develop their experience. So we put him in charge of the group that was going to help the revolutionaries in what is today Zaire. They went in by way of Tanzania, crossing Lake Tanganyika. In all, about 100 Cubans went, and stayed there several months.

He followed the approach of teaching Zairians how to fight. Cubans and Zairian patriots fought white mercenaries and forces sent by the government. They fought many battles against the mercenaries. The idea was not to fight the war in place of the Zairians but rather to help them, to teach them how to fight.

But that movement was just beginning. It didn't have sufficient strength or unity. In the end the revolutionary leaders of the former Belgian colony decided to halt the struggle, and our personnel were withdrawn. That decision was quite correct. It had become clear that conditions did not exist at the time for developing the struggle. The Zairians analyzed the situation along with the Cuban contingent, and we were in agreement with their assessment. Consequently the unit was withdrawn, and the Cuban personnel returned home.

Having now spent about six months in Zaire, Che stayed for a while in Tanzania, assessing the experience he had just lived through. His conduct on the mission was, as always, exemplary to the highest degree. His stay in Africa was temporary, awaiting creation of conditions for traveling to South America.

During this whole period the situation became highly awkward for us as Che had already said good-bye. He had written the letter before he left, and he left quietly of course — you might even say clandestinely. We kept the letter quiet and this gave rise to many rumors as well as some genuine slanders. Some said that Che had been made to disappear, others that Che was dead, or that there were differences — all sorts of stories. We took that downpour of rumors and intrigues silently, so as not to endanger the mission he wanted to accomplish and the personnel he intended to take to his final destination — South America.

So after finishing the phase in Zaire he went to Tanzania, marking time. He spent some months in Tanzania and then went to a socialist country in Eastern Europe. In fact . . . Well, I'm not going to say more, because I haven't checked with the country in question to see if it can be told. He stayed there. He didn't want to return to Cuba because it would have been an embarrassment to come back after the publication of the letter.

Eventually, publication of the letter became unavoidable. It was becoming very harmful to allow the campaign of slander to continue without an answer, an explanation to world public opinion. The only alternative was to publish the letter. The letter, of course, said nothing specific about his mission. He spoke only of fighting in other parts of the world.

Once the letter had been made public — politically, it had become unavoidable to publish it — Che, with his particular character, felt very awkward about returning to Cuba after having said farewell. But in the end I persuaded him to return, because it was the best move given all the practical matters he wanted to take care of. So he secretly returned to Cuba. He stayed several months, training in a remote mountainous region. He spent months in training with those who were to accompany him.

He asked for the collaboration of a group of *compañeros* — some were veteran guerrilla fighters, some were new men who had been in Zaire with him. He selected the group and spoke with each one of them. We authorized the selection of a group of highly experienced *compañeros* to accompany him, because the task he intended to carry out really required a group of experienced volunteers. He trained with them for several months while groundwork was undertaken to arrange for transporting him and his group to Bolivia.

Che chose the territory and worked out the plan of struggle. We gave him cooperation and support in carrying out the project, although naturally we were concerned about the inherent risks. We would have preferred a movement that was already much more developed, a movement Che could join; but he wanted to get there almost at the very beginning. We managed to hold him until at least some preliminary work had been carried out, so he could go there with a little more safety. The initial stages are the most difficult.

In fact, all this was organized perfectly, down to the last detail. Che and the other *compañeros* were transported to a camp in the area selected. They had to overcome difficult obstacles, pass through complicated places. It wasn't easy, but it was accomplished thanks to the methods used. They managed to join with a group of *compañeros* in the area of Ñancahuazú, I believe it's called, in the part of Bolivia he chose.

That was more or less the itinerary: a stay in Africa, leaving via Tanzania; eastern Zaire; a return to Tanzania; a socialist country in Europe; Cuba again and, finally, the trip to the area he had selected in Bolivia.

Gianni Minà: Was it a mistake to have chosen Bolivia, where the people were probably not yet ready for a revolution? Was it a romantic error determined by a geographic choice that was neither tactically nor strategically justified?

Fidel Castro: I wouldn't say that. He was interested in Argentina, he was genuinely inspired by the idea of making a revolution in Argentina. But at that time we had no relations with any country in South America — all those governments had joined with the United States against Cuba. In the early days Che had recruited a

Che Guevara in the Congo, 1965

group of Argentinians, including Jorge Ricardo Massetti, who worked with us in the Sierra Maestra as a journalist and who later founded Prensa Latina. Che had recruited him to his ideas of struggle in Argentina. Massetti, in agreement with Che, attempted to establish a front in northern Argentina, in the Salta area. Massetti died on that mission.

Che was always a very sensitive man, highly committed to his *compañeros*. The mere fact that he had initiated the effort, the struggle, in which some *compañeros* had already given their lives was without doubt a factor that greatly influenced his impatience to carry out his plans. He had already studied the area in question. And the importance of the area he selected seems to have been its proximity to the Argentinian border.

Che knew the Bolivian peasants were very quiet, reserved, and mistrustful. He knew they were very different from Cuban peasants. After graduating from medical school, he had traveled through South America on a motorbike. He visited a number of places, even as far as the Amazon. He had extensive contact with the people there and knew the tragedy of the Indians, their characteristics. He knew this very well and felt it deeply. More than once he explained to me, told me what they were like, how you had to work with them, how this took time, that it wasn't easy. He was conscious of the difficulties of the task ahead.

So what happened? He had witnessed our experience, our almost incredible experience. After the initial set-backs, he saw how a very small group could reorganize and carry out a struggle under very difficult conditions. He had blind faith in this type of struggle and its possibilities, even more so now that he had enormous experience in it.

So Che chose the territory, the place. And essentially, in my opinion, he made no mistake in his choice. No mistake was made. He tried to gain the support of organized political forces. He assumed he could count on the support of the Bolivian Communist Party and other forces. It turned out that other forces joined him, because there were divisions at that time within the left, within the communist movement.

Gianni Minà: In this regard, Che's father has said publicly that the Bolivian Communist Party is responsible for Che's death: that if they did not betray him, they surely left him to die. And is it true, as Régis Debray has said, that Che could have been saved if an expedition of young Bolivian Communists had set out from Cochabamba?

Fidel Castro: I share none of those views. And I believe I am very well-informed on these questions.

The Communist Party had various leaders. The general secretary, Mario Monje, had already been spoken with, and an agreement of sorts had been reached. But other leaders were involved as well. That was what really led to the conflict with Monje. That is well known, it's part of history. A conflict arose between Che and Monje over certain of Monje's positions, perhaps over his pretensions concerning leadership, pretensions Che did not accept.

I believe that formal factors prevailed in Monje's thinking, along the lines that it was his country where action was to begin, that he was the general secretary of the party. But in reality there was no one, no cadre, better prepared than Che to lead an action that transcended the borders of Bolivia. This gave rise to misunderstandings, and they were not able to reach agreement. Monje withdrew his support.

We received this information and immediately arranged meetings here with other important and prestigious leaders of the party, Kolle and Simón Reyes, a well-known and very good workers' leader. I asked them to come to Cuba, spoke with them, and told them: "A crisis has emerged, and it's a very delicate situation. I have asked you to come meet with us because it is essential that you give Che some help."

They promised to help, they were ready to provide assistance and collaboration. They did everything possible, although in disagreement with the party secretary. What happened is that the pace of events quickened, and there was no chance for them to help. But they had an excellent attitude and understood everything in the meeting I had with them. Kolle later became leader of the party, replacing Monje. Simón Reyes also took on important responsibilities in the party leadership. They were part of the Communist Party and they made a commitment.

When we received information about this situation, that is the kind of solution we sought. We managed to gain the support of other movements and also of a few Latin Americans. This was the stage the work was at when events became complicated and, in fact, their presence was discovered. For one reason or another, a combination of factors, the detachment was spotted while it was still in the stage of organization. I believe they needed a little bit more time.

Monje bears a certain responsibility, but historically it would be unjust to blame the Communist Party as a whole. A number of Communists joined Che. These included the Peredo brothers, excellent people who proved to be very fine cadres. They joined and supported Che, gave him a great deal of help. And important cadres in the party leadership differed with Monje and wanted to help Che. So, when responsibility is assigned, it should be given to Monje; but you cannot accuse the entire Communist Party or blame it for the way events developed.

Gianni Minà: In Europe it is also said . . .

Fidel Castro: As for Debray, I didn't even respond to that because it belongs to the realm of fantasy. Yes, it is only fantasy, because not even the most minimal conditions existed to organize a column that could have helped Che. There were no weapons, no trained combatants, and no trainees. It's a theory, it can only be spoken of as a theory; it's a fantasy. You have to understand this is not regular war, it's guerrilla war, irregular war, and this kind of war has its own laws. It wasn't that way. You can't solve things so easily.

Gianni Minà: In Europe it's also said the publisher Feltrinelli contributed — without intending to, of course — to leading the CIA to the tracks of Che's little group in the woods near Vallegrande. Is there any truth in that?

Fidel Castro: This is the first time, in fact, I have heard that rumor, that version. There isn't the slightest possibility Feltrinelli did anything that affected the situation. Today the whole history of the matter is known. Many books have been written about it, and I have read them. First of all, there is Che's diary, which have I studied carefully, very carefully. I knew Che very well, and through the diary I was able to see his state of mind, everything, because I knew him so well.

Then there are all the documents written by the Bolivian army, detailing the information they were receiving: when, at what point, how they interpreted it, what they did. This whole story has been written, and not just by revolutionaries. In addition there are the diaries of other *compañeros* who survived, of those who were with Che until the final moments, diaries that fell into the hands of the Bolivian army. We know the testimony, we know step by step what occurred. There were a few lapses in discipline, some acts of poor judgment that gave the enemy indications something was going on, although they didn't know the magnitude. But this, in fact, had nothing to do with Feltrinelli or with anybody. These facts are known in minute detail.

There is one factor. They already had camps set up, they had created all the conditions; these are facts that have been told before. The army managed to determine there was something strange going on, but this coincided with other circumstances. Che began an incursion with a large detachment to explore the terrain and make a broad sweep through the area. They left the newest people in camp, those who had just arrived. But the trip lasted several weeks; it turned into a veritable odyssey. Che's diary describes in detail how they confronted high mountains, harsh terrain, swollen rivers. They also suffered some losses on the trip — some drownings, one or two casualties.

The troops returned completely exhausted after several weeks on the march. When they returned to the camp they discovered there had been some problems in Che's absence — some infractions of discipline, some difficulties. But the worst was that although the troops were worn out, with a few men ill, they had no time to recover. In a few short days the army began to carry out some explorations and the first fighting took place. Because of their experience, Che's men suffered no losses. In fact they captured weapons with ambushes of a few men and dealt the adversary a hard blow.

But I would say all this happened prematurely. They made another incursion, again leaving a force behind in the camp. This produced a division into two groups that were never to make contact with one another again. Moreover, Che didn't have enough medicine for his asthma. It was the same thing that had happened on the *Granma*, where there was no medicine. In the Sierra Maestra we really had to make an exceptional effort to get Che medicine at any cost, because the terrible asthma attacks paralyzed him. He was in great need of the medicine, but during this whole period he went without it.

All this is described in Che's diary with great rigor, precision,

Camilo Cienfuegos, 1959

and narrative quality. Each event is described very clearly and with great precision. This was quite a feat, because they spent months evading and fighting the army. These were not the circumstances for discussing the idea of a support column. Nobody knew where they were. All communications had been cut by the enemy. In the cities the contact points were under constant observation.

At that moment the fate of the guerrilla unit depended on what they themselves did. Che believed his guerrilla unit of 20 men could survive if they relocated, as he proposed, to a place with a social base, where Inti and Coco Peredo were known. That is where they were headed in this final stage. Che knew this was their best chance and was headed in that direction.

From the description of everything that took place — not only from his diary but also the accounts of the Bolivian army — the feat they did accomplish is impressive, including the number of battles they waged against the army. What they accomplished was of epic proportions. All this is well known.

What could have influenced him? I have an opinion. I think he was deeply affected by the death of the other group. We had news of their death from wire service dispatches. They described how it happened. From our own experience we concluded at once that the news was exact, correct, and the truth. Tamara, Joaquín, the whole unit had been killed. But Che resisted believing it. You can see from his diary he resisted believing it for months. He thought it was another lie by the army, because they had put out a number of false reports. For our part, however, when we saw the dispatches we were immediately convinced it was true.

When he was really convinced — because nearly all his efforts and many of their marches were aimed at trying to make contact with the other unit — when he was really persuaded they no longer existed and he was not going to meet up with them, that is when he began the march toward an area with a social base. By this time he already had some good Bolivian cadres who had distinguished themselves. It was the correct decision; he did have a chance to survive.

How much did the death of the other *compañeros* affect his state of mind? I believe at the end he acted with a certain recklessness. They were walking along a road and at one point he stopped on high ground and observed: "Radio Bemba has been here ahead of us, everyone is expecting us." That's more or less what he said.

You can read it in his diary. They were walking along a road toward the area, a public road, when he reached a ridge and wrote in his diary: "Our arrival is being announced by Radio Bemba." That is, everyone was waiting for them.

I think the certainty that Joaquín's unit had been killed influenced his state of mind. I knew him well, I knew how strongly he felt things, and I think in that moment he was acting in conformity with his nature, with a certain degree of recklessness.

He continued to advance, entered the town in daylight, and found it empty. An empty town is a sign that something is up. The people sense a battle is going to take place. Any army — any in the world! — under those circumstances has only to wait somewhere along the road and set an ambush. And on one of those barren hills, in full light of day, the advance guard began to march as though the army didn't exist. It fell into an ambush in broad daylight, and several men were killed. It was a very serious blow.

The group was also carrying some sick men, including a sick doctor. Che insisted on carrying them even though it held up their movement. Sometimes we ourselves, in similar situations, sought a place where we could leave a sick person — someone who could no longer march — with someone who could take care of them. Che must have been looking for such a possibility. But he had already lost his advance guard. They had been spotted and trapped in a valley, and the dead included some of the good people among the Bolivians. Among the dead was one of the two Peredo brothers who had distinguished themselves so greatly as Bolivian cadres.

The attack left Che in a very difficult situation in difficult terrain. He had managed to evade the army for months while fighting constantly. He had carried out a feat of epic proportions. But he now found himself in an extremely critical situation. He had been spotted, attacked, and wounded. His rifle had been destroyed. He was taken prisoner and moved to a nearby place.

I would say that even when marching along the road and with 20 men, including a few Bolivian cadres, that had they made it to the area they sought, they would have had possibilities not just of surviving but of developing the guerrilla movement. Up until that time, to judge by all Che knew and the experience we had, that possibility existed. The moment in which things really changed was when they advanced in broad daylight along a public road in those barren hills where the advance guard was ambushed.

So he must have been greatly influenced by something: his scorn for death — sometimes it seemed as though he went looking for death, at least at certain moments. In such circumstances he should have advanced more cautiously, gotten off the road, looked for other places. And they should have traveled by night. The ambush, had it been carried out at night, would not have inflicted such great damage. The enemy would have been shooting in the dark, and they might have been spotted by a light or some other indication. I believe that at that moment certain elements in Che's character influenced events.

I knew him very well, and I have read his diary carefully more than once.

Gianni Minà: At this stage was there anything you could have done to assist him? I mean, in this final stage of his epic struggle?

Fidel Castro: It was impossible. What could we have done? Sent a battalion, a company, a regular army? The laws of guerrilla warfare are different; everything depends on what the guerrilla unit itself does. They really did carry out an epic struggle. Some day their accomplishments will be recounted more objectively. The Bolivian army itself in its descriptions . . . There was one general, General Gary Prado, I read his book [*How I Captured Che*]. It reflects the official point of view, but he doesn't conceal his admiration for his adversary.

Clashes with the army occurred a number of times. He knew what to do just as we did. When we arrived in the Sierra we too were dispersed, we managed to gather together seven rifles. We began the struggle again in the Sierra Maestra, where we knew no one, with seven rifles. When we had reached 20 men, we were a force to be reckoned with. Che had confidence in the possibilities of irregular struggle, he knew how to do it.

In such circumstances the guerrilla unit depends on itself. It can neither expect nor receive help from abroad; such assistance is practically impossible. It wasn't possible, and secret assistance wasn't possible either: the entire network of support had been broken up. At that moment everything depended on their own actions. That's why formulas of conventional warfare, speculation about columns that set out, that come and go, don't apply here. All that belongs to the realm of fantasy.

Gianni Minà: President Castro, at the dramatic moment of Che's death a story about you circulated in Europe. It is speculated that after the 1967 summit meeting in Glassboro, New Jersey between Soviet Premier Kosygin and US President Johnson, that the United States and the Soviet Union decided to reach a truce in Asia and Latin America. And that is why Cuba was unable to do anything more to help Che in Bolivia.

Fidel Castro: I am astounded at the number of rumors and fantasies that circulate in Europe. I'm going to start believing Europe is the least informed area of the world.

Gianni Minà: That may be.

Fidel Castro: I really don't even remember that meeting. The war in Vietnam was at its peak, and Che's action was under way. Neither had anything to do with the other. There was no Soviet participation in this, there was no question of strategy that was being discussed. In fact we gave Che — with great loyalty — the assistance he asked for, the *compañeros* he asked for, the collaboration he asked for, everything. We stood by our word.

What is it that we would have preferred? That Che wait. We would have preferred that he wait until a developed guerrilla front had been established, but we couldn't impose such a decision on him.

We knew we might face political problems, state problems, denunciations, everything of that sort. But we accepted that type of inconvenience so as to fulfill our pledge to him. We respected that commitment. Not only did we respect it, we believed in what he was doing, and we believed he could carry out what he proposed.

I have always said that success or failure is not what indicates whether a line is correct. We all could have died during our struggle; we were on the verge of death many times. If we had died, many people would have said we were wrong. But I think if we had died, it would not have proved we were wrong. I think our road was correct. A series of elements, of imponderables, intervened — including luck — and we almost miraculously survived those difficult days. That would be another long story. But in such circumstances you can't say success is the measure of whether or not a line is correct. Certain factors led to an adverse result, but

Che Guevara in disguise before leaving Cuba in 1966 for Bolivia

I don't question the correctness of Che's line. What I say is that I would have preferred he avoid the initial highly dangerous stage, that he join the group as political and military leader, as strategist in a movement that had passed the early stage.

In our war we gave Che the most important missions because of his courage, his qualities, and his importance. We didn't give him this mission. The idea, the plan, everything, was his. We shared in it with him because we thought his ideas were correct. He could have done it. He could have done it!

I am not going to conclude that because certain factors exerted influence, resulting in the elimination of the guerrilla unit and the death of Che — I am not going to conclude that therefore his course was wrong. You cannot measure the correctness of a line by success or failure. That, in my opinion, would be a mistaken criterion.

That's not the only example. We have seen another case, that of Caamaño, also a man of the highest courage, who could not overcome his impatience to return to his country and did so. I talked with him a great deal, I knew him well.

I know then of two cases of great cadres whose impatience led them to their deaths. It's not simply death that is at issue here, the sadness death brings. It is rather that two great cadres, two great revolutionaries, died in this way. And Caamaño with fewer possibilities than Che. Caamaño was a good soldier and well trained. But conditions were also difficult and the group was very small. We would have preferred that these valued cadres be preserved for a more opportune moment.

We did not impose on them our point of view, nor did we prohibit their courageous actions. We had excellent relations of friendship and of trust. Che gave great attention to my point of view and to the opinions I expressed, because we maintained a deep and trusting friendship up until the end. It was his idea. Forbidding him to carry it out was outside the realm of our relationship. Not even for reasons of state would I impose an opinion on him.

What we did was help him. We helped something we thought was possible. We would not have been able to help what we thought was impossible, something in which we did not believe, because it would have been our duty to tell him: It's not possible, we can't do that, we can't sacrifice *compañeros* on this mission. But he did what he did. I shared in it and I believed in it.

There is only one thing I would have done differently. He should have waited until a strong movement had developed, before a cadre of his quality and strategic importance joined the struggle. He should not have gone through the initial stage. This is the most difficult and the most dangerous phase, as the facts showed, and it resulted in his death.

Gianni Minà: Why didn't the Bolivian authorities ever return Che's body? Did he still scare them even after his death?

Fidel Castro: They wanted to get rid of Che's body to prevent the establishment of a site that would be venerated and visited by people.

We still don't know what they did with Che's body, or where it is. This has never been clarified. Many of his belongings have turned up. We know everything that happened, from the accounts of both sides, which agree on most points. What we still don't know is where Che was buried. They wanted him to disappear. The Yankees also wanted him to disappear.

Nonetheless, Che has become a great symbol for the entire world, the perfect example of the heroic and revolutionary man. He became, I would add, one of the most outstanding examples of the combatant and revolutionary in the Third World, and perhaps in the industrialized world as well. And this idea, this image of Che, is not without justification.

Gianni Minà: There's a striking coincidence linked to Che's death. Sixteen or 17 persons directly or indirectly responsible for his murder in Bolivia have died, not always in the clearest of circumstances.

Fidel Castro: It does seem there have been people who played a part in his murder who have died this way. The likelihood is that no one organized it, that it's simply the people's spontaneous action, bringing to justice those who acted in a contemptible way. I'm not referring to the soldiers who fought against him, but rather to people who served as informers, traitors, and henchmen.

Gianni Minà: Down to the peasant who . . .

Fidel Castro: I think his name was Honorato.

Gianni Minà: Honorato Rojas.

Fidel Castro: I read about that in the book written by the Bolivian general, Gary Prado, a man who has become something of an invalid. I understand he is now in Washington as military attaché. He wrote a very objective and respectful book, although of course it also has high praise for the Bolivian army. But I'm not going to deny him, a Bolivian soldier, this sentiment toward his institution. The Bolivian army was poorly trained. It was acquiring more experience during that period, that is indisputable. The Yankees made a considerable effort, they intensified their training plans, because they wanted to destroy Che.

Gianni Minà: Two people as reserved as you and Che, how did you greet each other the last time you saw each other? With the hug of old friends, or with a handshake?

Fidel Castro: We saw each other many times. Very warmly and with much affection. No, a hug, without much effusiveness, because we are not very effusive. He wasn't, I'm not. But we feel things deeply. And with great trust. We talked many times. I went to see him several times while he was training the group. They spent months in the province of Pinar del Río.

Gianni Minà: And the day he left?

Fidel Castro: The day he left I went so far as to play a joke. The day he left for good I invited a number of members of the party leadership, the most trusted *compañeros,* to lunch with a visitor. The visitor was Che, disguised. Absolutely no one recognized him in the disguise that had been created. Che had lunch with a few others at a house here in Havana the day before he left — and none of those *compañeros* recognized him either. We had to tell the *compañeros* who came for lunch that it was Che. So as you can see he was very well prepared when he left. It was really perfect. Nobody recognized him, not even his closest *compañeros,* who were talking with him the way they would talk with a guest. So we went so far as to make jokes such as this on the *compañeros* the day before he left.

Gianni Minà: I thank you for all you have told me. I believe I had the pleasure of hearing in your words some of the history of our times, of what we are living, thinking, or have hoped. I want to thank you for this.

Fidel Castro: We have the obligation to be just. There is no reason to make accusations. We all have things we're sufficiently responsible for, but Monje's responsibility, the other . . . Well, that's why I explained the story to you in detail.

And that is why I wrote the introduction, what I called "a necessary introduction," which we published in the diary of Che. I explained everything, with many more details and the role of everyone involved. I wrote the introduction to explain a series of matters, and we published it widely. Later the diary circulated throughout the world. We have this duty to be objective.

I believe I understand quite well everything that happened. I have thought a great deal about it, analyzed all the documents, and I think I knew Che quite well; I knew him very, very, very well. I am very sure as to the facts, how they occurred, and what factors may have influenced the course of events.

This is something I have never spoken of before — a few of the things I told you. There are still many chapters of history to be written. What is missing is someone to write them, because those who can write them don't have the time to do so.

Chapter 13

Recollections and predictions

I had spent nearly an entire day throwing questions at Fidel Castro and found it difficult to formulate opinions or issue judgments about this man, who is already a part of history.

With all due modesty, I state that I do not agree with some of his statements or principles. Nor his approach toward several topics and some of his ideological dogmas. In many questions, I expressed that doubt. In some of the more delicate moments related to domestic and foreign policy, especially human rights, I tried to be provocative, perhaps revealing the arrogance and prejudices characteristic of Europeans.

However, I always tried to keep in mind the Western world's barrage of misinformation about Latin America and Cuba in particular.

Like those who have studied people's traditions through oral testimony, I tried to gather a unique heritage of the experiences of a special life that led a young Cuban lawyer, between successes and contradictions, to guide the destinies of a nation that for almost three decades has managed to confront the enmity of the most powerful and developed country on earth: the United States of America.

How then, could I harbor the vain presumption of passing judgment on Fidel?

Very simply, with the instinct — but perhaps also with the superficiality — of an old reporter, I will say only that he appeared to me to be an idealist, a person who, rightly or wrongly, always acted out of profound conviction. Perhaps even the unbending discipline of which the revolution has been accused — the real discipline, not the

one that is manufactured by clumsy, stupid misinformation — is due to that unquestioning idealism.

This final chapter is filled with that sentiment. Anyone who wishes to challenge it needs to come armed with facts, with precise data. In these hundreds of pages, Fidel has supplied them. I have verified many of them with international agencies. Anyone who wishes to disprove them will have to offer equivalent data.

Fidel Castro has stated his truth. I have gathered it, not as an act of faith, but as testimony. That was what I sought to do, and that is what I have achieved.

G.M.

Fidel Castro: We will soon have been at this for 15 hours straight. You should explain this to your viewers, because I think we're going to appear to be four different groups of people: those of the first three hours, those of the second block of three hours, those of the third block of three hours and lastly some guys who are slogging along in the last part of the race, as you put it.

Gianni Minà: Let's try to sum up: in spite of everything you have told us, and with all the annotations and all the replies that you have given us clearly, a very interesting philosophy underlies these 15 hours of talk. I am very grateful to you, not only for myself, but also for all those others who want to know and are not held back by prejudices.

Several times you have said that politics is an ugly animal, or something such as that. What led you to such bitter reflection about an activity — politics — that has formed a part of your whole life?

Fidel Castro: Did I say that? Are you sure it wasn't my double? Really, I have such a good opinion of politics that I can't have said that. I think that politics is one of the most marvelous, most fabulous, most stimulating activities to which a person can dedicate themselves — at least, as I understand politics. For me, politics is revolution. I'm speaking about pure politics, noble politics. So many things have been done in politics, and so many mistakes have been made, that politics has been given a bad name. But I hold politics in esteem. It surprises me that I should have said such a thing. I would have to see in what sense, in what context, I may have said that.

Gianni Minà: President Castro, will your brother Raúl be your successor? What qualities does he have that you lack, and at the same time, what defects does he have that you don't?

Fidel Castro: You want me to make a comparative analysis between two brothers. I don't think it would be correct for me to do that.

What happened is that immediately following the triumph of the revolution we learned of the CIA's plans to assassinate me — something that they've tried to do for a long time. Logically, we had to take some preventive measures. In that period, there was a lot of talk to the effect that Raúl was more radical — all those things. I came to the conclusion that, at that time, in those circumstances, we had to explain to the people that my death would not mean the death of the revolution and that there would immediately be another revolutionary leader. And in my opinion, the comrade who was the best equipped for carrying out that task was someone I knew very well: *compañero* Raúl. That precedent was established, and the post of Second Secretary of the Party was created.

I think that we should have not only a First Secretary, but also a Second, Third and Fourth Secretary, if we want to be really careful. As a precautionary measure we don't go anywhere in the same plane or travel in the same car; otherwise, there wouldn't be a solution for the problem of continuity. If one leader were to disappear for any reason, another leader must immediately appear. In the conditions in our country, faced with the threats and hostility of the United States, it's a very good idea to guarantee continuity of leadership.

Naturally, that wasn't my decision alone. It is a decision that the Party and state always have to make. Raúl's prestige and authority are very great within the Party, among the people and in the National Assembly, and I think that he is the most logical person at this time. What would happen if something happened to me? Undoubtedly, the Central Committee of the Party and the National Assembly would ratify his taking my place as the most appropriate person at this time. Ask any citizen. Without any doubt, that's what they would say.

This need arose because of the enemy's plans to kill me. The enemy has also made plans for killing Raúl, but I have been the main target.

Gianni Minà: What saint is protecting you, since all those plans have failed?

Fidel Castro: It must be St. Fidel of Sigmaringa, because I remember that, when I was a boy, my parents told me April 24 was my saint's day, and the almanac gives that as the day of St. Fidel of Sigmaringa.

If you ask me why I was named Fidel, it wasn't a decision made because there was any special devotion to that saint or because the family liked that name. What happened is that my father had a very rich friend, a millionaire, who was close to the family. He and my father were very close, and he also lent my father money, charging interest — and it wasn't very low interest, either, up to 6 percent at one time. That rich man, the millionaire, was going to be my godfather, and his name was Fidel. That's why I was given that name. In the end, I wasn't baptized, but people always called me Fidel. Those were the social circumstances that dictated the choice of that name. I like it, really. I've never felt unhappy about having that name.

They taught me that there was a saint — I don't know the story of the saint; he may have been Italian, but I don't know. Perhaps you can find out what his merits were and what the story was of that saint, my patron saint, who has protected me against all those plans of the CIA and has kept me alive thus far.

Gianni Minà: Hasn't living this way — knowing that somebody wants to assassinate you and also living through some moments of Cuban history as if in a besieged fortress — forced you to be too much on the defensive and distrustful? Isn't it time to open the windows and relax a little?

Fidel Castro: Actually, I don't think about personal problems and dangers; I put them out of my mind. We take institutional security measures. There are experiences in this, showing what measures the guards should take. Nevertheless, it has never kept me from mixing with people.

In general, I don't tell people ahead of time what places I'm going to visit. I don't usually tell anyone very much ahead of time, unless it's a meeting or ceremony. I go to many places — factories and other work places — on the spur of the moment; I visit them and talk with the people. I've never been worried. This is also due to the confidence I have in our security bodies, to the cooperation of the people, and the fact that it's very difficult for the CIA to organize an assassination attempt here, as it would have to look for a house in which to store the weapons and count on a number of people, and our security bodies have a lot of experience.

Now that we're talking about this, I should add that the fact that we have been very strict — and the police have never employed violence against prisoners — has had an important result: the police have developed their ability much more. The police you see in countries such as Chile and others who try to repress the revolutionary opposition use mainly violence, torture and the collaboration of a few paid informers.

Our situation is different. It is based on the cooperation of the people and on intelligent police — since they don't use violent methods, they instead have to develop investigatory techniques. Our main weapon has been penetration.

I already told you that at one time there were 300 counter-revolutionary organizations. In the end, our people headed nearly all of them. Because of that penetration we knew everything. It even got so that when an individual was arrested, we knew more about him than he himself knew. We would ask, "What did you do on January 17? With whom did you meet?" He wouldn't remember exactly, but we knew whom he had met with on January 17 and what he had done.

What happened with those counter-revolutionaries when they were arrested? Faced with the precise, exact information that the security bodies had, they would frequently become demoralized and subsequently inform. A prisoner always enters into a game: to deny one thing but admit another, and in the end, he finds himself faced with irrefutable facts and winds up explaining everything. The great success of our security bodies was to develop the techniques of investigation and of penetration in enemy organizations. That was the key. They are very efficient and work with the cooperation of all the people.

I have trust in those bodies and those measures, but it is also a matter of character. Who is going to live always fearing that somebody is hunting you or is after you? And I have traveled. When I went to Chile and visited Salvador Allende, I drove in an open car for kilometers and kilometers, with a million people around me. That was undoubtedly dangerous. Even though we didn't announce the trip until the last minute, word got out, and different armed men, CIA agents with journalists' passports and journalists' credentials, were speedily mobilized. Weapons were placed in cameras such as yours. There was even one moment, in a press conference, when I was in front of cameras that had weapons in them. They didn't shoot, because they aren't fanatics; they aren't suicidal. They are mercenaries, and before they act they always make sure they can escape. In conditions such as those, of real risk, they don't act. Later, they kept trying to track me down all over Chile. That was a very dangerous trip, because that kind of tour, in an open car, in a situation where many people were coming and going . . . The trip to Chile may well have been one of the most dangerous times.

I've gone to many places. I have been twice to the United Nations. The last time was just after the Sixth Summit Conference of Nonaligned Countries, in which Cuba was elected president of the Movement; there's a tradition of going to the UN to present a report. In those cases, you can't do anything. Naturally, some precautionary measures were taken, but I was in the hands of the US police. Perhaps there's no safer place than New York as they are responsible for security. In the other places, they are the ones who organize the assassination plans — but there they are forced to provide security. There is always a risk, but it hasn't been a problem for me.

Of course, security does entail certain inconveniences. I always argue with the *compañeros* and ask them to let people come close to talk. I think we should have that policy and refrain from doing anything discourteous. You're always accompanied by a group of *compañeros*, and you adapt to it. In short, you have to resign yourself and get used to the security measures. This doesn't constitute any great problem for me.

Gianni Minà: What will the future of Cuba be like when Fidel retires?

Fidel Castro: Haven't we talked about the young people? Haven't we talked about the Congress of the Union of the Young Communists and its impact? We have thousands of young people, hundreds of thousands of young people who have studied, who have been trained and who are developing with technical and political levels that are much higher than those of my generation. I already told you that several brilliant leaders emerged from a group of 15 and that our group of 82 from the *Granma* has produced between 30 and 40 comrades with brilliant leadership qualities. Just calculate it: out of millions of people, hundreds of thousands of young people have a higher level of training. There must be many people who are better than we are, with more possibilities than we have. I'm sure that they will do well when they have the responsibility.

We talked about that. I talked about it with you and analyzed a series of factors: experience and the authority of the leaders. I believed in the triumph of the revolution when there were just a handful of us. When there were just a few of us we believed in our cause and believed that we would triumph. How can I possibly not believe in it now, when there are millions of us? What could possibly stop this process? What could possibly stop this movement? Nothing. It would be terrible to think that you've devoted your life to something that will be defeated in the end.

If the revolution were built on individuals, it would be very sad, but it is built on the people, on the collective, on the Party. That is its guarantee. It's built on a series of values that have been created, and they give me a lot of confidence.

Gianni Minà: Because you live with this daily moral rigor, you have probably forsaken many things in your private life. Don't you ever feel nostalgic or have moments of saying, "My life could have been otherwise?"

Fidel Castro: No, my life is really quite a normal one. I don't have much occasion for nostalgia. I change from one activity to another, for I do many things. It's true that the need for security imposes certain conditions, but I have adapted to it. I can relax, exercise, rest, be alone and have my private life. Really, it hasn't been hindered.

Gianni Minà: This is the last act of provocation . . .

Fidel Castro: "The last act of provocation"?

Gianni Minà: Yes. It's 4:50. I was recalling that my friend Saverio Tutino, who was *L'Unitá*'s Havana correspondent for many years, said that Ernest Hemingway was one of your favorite authors. Therefore, he suggested a question. You surely are familiar with *The Old Man and the Sea.* I think that Italians have also read *The Old Man and the Sea.* The old fisherman catches a swordfish, and then other fish eat it, little by little. Now, imagine that the swordfish is the revolution and you are the old fisherman. Aren't you afraid you'll wind up like Ernest Hemingway's fisherman?

Fidel Castro: What I think is that the one we have to fish for is Tutino, who hasn't come back here and now goes around sending questions of that kind.

I imagine that what he wants to say is, aren't I afraid that there won't be anything left of the revolution in the end.

Gianni Minà: No . . .

Fidel Castro: It must be that, that there won't be anything but the skeleton of the revolution left.

Gianni Minà: No, he believes in the revolution.

Fidel Castro: But, if we're going to use an image of that kind, we should think that there isn't just one fisherman here — alone — because all the people are upholding the rod of the revolution, which is their work. And it isn't a whole lot of little fish that want to gobble up the revolution; it is one big shark that has wanted to snap it up, and it hasn't been able to do so yet. Moreover, it can't do it. That has been shown. So, I think that we have evaded those dangers: the revolution is a reality, and I think it will grow ever stronger.

I have great confidence in the future. As I said the other day, I believe in the people, in men and women, in values and in principles. How could I think otherwise, when we didn't have anything when we began? When the political struggle and the revolutionary struggle began we didn't have a cent, we didn't have any guns, we didn't have an organization, we didn't even have a name or any prestige. We started from scratch, from nothing. We couldn't even have made an attempt if we hadn't had faith in our principles, in the people and in humankind.

We've gained some experience. I remember when I used to walk near the symbols of power, without a cent in my pockets. I remember something that happened to me after Batista's coup. One day I was engaged in revolutionary activities, and the finance company took my car away — I was buying it on credit and was behind on the payments. I went to a cafe I used to visit to have a cup of coffee and smoke a cigar in peace, and in that situation I had the honesty to tell the man, who had always been friendly, "I don't have any money on me," and he replied, "Then you can't have anything." He didn't let me have the cup of coffee or the cigar. I walked along the Prado, passing close by the Presidential Palace, which was guarded by the military police, until I got to the corner of Prado and Neptuno streets, where newspapers were sold and were on display. I didn't even have enough money to buy a newspaper that day, so I started to read the headlines. A little kid who was there wouldn't let me. He said, "Move on, move on!" and made me leave. I didn't have enough money for the streetcar or bus, and I walked three kilometers to my room near the University. When I got there, I lay down and went to sleep. It was very hot. I slept for around three or four hours. It was a sad day for me, but even in those moments, I wasn't at all discouraged.

If I weren't an optimist, how could I have held on to those ideas, goals and plans? Now, it isn't just one individual or a group of individuals who have a doctrine, an idea and a set of values. Millions of people now have them. Who could destroy that? I believe in man, and I believe that new men and women and new generations will appear. I thoroughly expect that men who are more capable than I, better than I, will come from among them.

When we began to build socialism, how many doctors, engineers, technicians or economists were there? There wasn't anything. Nothing. Now, there are thousands of agronomists in sugar-cane and other branches of agriculture and thousands of veterinarians, technicians and engineers of all kinds — electrical, civil, industrial, mechanical . . . Cuba has 260,000 teachers. Over the years, we have built up an enormous technical reserve, and the people have a high cultural level. At the time of the triumph of the revolution, there wasn't any of this. I already told you that people with a fifth or sixth-grade education were running large factories. The coming generations can set themselves even higher goals.

This morning we were at that scientific research center. What kind of men and women did you see there? Young people dedicated to research. They are like monks, working 14 or 15 hours a day on scientific research; they are marvelous people. The people at the Immunology Center work the same way. More and more are working like that.

What did we have similar to that when we began? Nothing. And now we have all this. I'm an optimist.

Think of the topics we've discussed, of the campaigns and the lies. Why is the United States so anxious to hide all that? It must have some reason, because it doesn't want the revolution to exert an influence on other countries and other societies. It can't do anything but try to run down the revolution and deny its achievements. I would say that it's one of imperialism's defense mechanisms.

Gianni Minà: Would you like to say anything special to our television audience and to Italian and other European readers at the end of this long marathon, something that will give them a better understanding of your efforts and help them to evaluate what has happened in Cuba?

Fidel Castro: I think we have already discussed that. I have talked and I think they can draw their own conclusions. I don't like making comparisons, because people in other countries are our brothers, our friends. I try to speak as objectively as possible about problems, and I think that those who have had the patience to listen to this interview, or what you use of it, have enough elements for drawing their own conclusions.

What can I say to your Italian listeners? Cubans have always felt close to Italy and the Italians. We even resemble each other in many aspects of our character, in our sense of humor and happy approach to life. You are Mediterranean, and we are Caribbean. It has been a great pleasure to spend these hours trying to answer all your questions and trying to inform Italian public opinion, your listeners.

In closing, I should also say that, as of now, we two are also Olympic champions, because how many journalists and how many political figures have gotten together to work for 15 hours straight and tackle these tasks? I thought this interview was going to be held over two or three days. Due to pressures of work and time, we have had to do it in one day, and we have persevered to the end. I ask the pardon of your listeners and readers if I failed to answer all of your questions with sufficient clarity and if, at the end, after so many hours, we appeared to be a little tired. I have done this with great pleasure, and now somebody will have to give me a title for having set a new record — a Caribbean one, if not a world or Olympic record.

Appendix 1

Interview with CNN

The following excerpts are taken from an interview with Fidel Castro conducted by Ted Turner of the Cable News Network on June 25, 1990.

Ted Turner: President Castro, how do you feel about the changes in the Soviet Union and have they affected Cuba's relations with the Soviets?

Fidel Castro: These issues are highly sensitive at any time. I would like to very calmly speak about these matters.

We do not have any right to question any changes that the Soviets may wish to introduce. They considered that certain mistakes had been made throughout history, in the 70 years since the revolution triumphed in their country. They then decided to take several measures to streamline socialism. I believe that no-one can oppose that at all.

In our case, we at a given moment became aware of certain errors and began a process of rectification. This process began in 1986, before changes were mentioned in the Soviet Union.

We must therefore respect as a sovereign right of all countries and of all parties the decision to make any changes that they deem pertinent to improve their political processes and to improve socialism.

Based on this principle we must respect the sovereign right of the Soviet Union to carry out all the changes that they have introduced, in the same way they respect our sovereignty. Throughout these years we have had a good personal relationship with the leadership of the Soviet Union, with comrade Gorbachev — relations of friendship, high esteem, and of respect.

I have no doubt whatsoever that comrade Gorbachev is moved by the purpose of improving socialism.

They are unquestionably facing difficulties. They have met even greater difficulties than they perhaps would have imagined.

These historical tasks are very complex, very complicated. Naturally, this has not been an easy road for the Soviet Union to follow. Many problems have arisen and everybody knows of them: economical and political problems and conflicts of nationalities.

Logically, all of those things that affect the Soviet economy — independent of the will of the Soviet leadership — may affect our economic relations. But not our political relations.

Even if the Soviet Union wanted to adopt the US Constitution, we would respect that.

Ted Turner: How do you feel about the events that have transpired recently in Eastern Europe? Were you happy to see the Berlin Wall come down?

Fidel Castro: In the socialist countries of Eastern Europe several changes have taken place. Changes that began — in some of them, not all — as a project of reforms, to improve socialism.

The situation is not exactly the same in each country. Difficulties arose in Poland with strikes and discontent which began at least eight years ago and that brought about certain changes. In other countries such as the German Democratic Republic, Czechoslovakia, Hungary and Rumania there were sudden changes at the end of last year. But in each of them, the situation is not the same.

We do note a strong tendency toward changes that are contrary to socialism. What was initially put forward as a reform to socialism has become a movement toward the building of capitalism. They are becoming distant from the construction of socialism and moving toward capitalism, following capitalist methods and capitalist mechanisms.

In that sense, as a socialist — and someone fully convinced of the meaning of socialism and what it has meant for our country — I cannot agree with that movement in the socialist countries toward capitalism.

Nevertheless, we must respect the right of all countries to build the economic, social and political system that they deem necessary.

Socialism in Cuba was not imported. It was not brought by anyone to Cuba. It did not come with any foreign troops. Our socialism in Cuba was built by us. It was introduced, supported and developed by our people and therefore it is an autonomous and genuinely popular revolution.

You ask me about the Berlin Wall. I recall that the Berlin Wall was built as a result of the Cold War, at a time of great international tension when US and Soviet tanks were facing one another. We could say that the wall served to divide Soviet troops from US troops.

At a moment of international detente and when there is a change in the economic and political situation in the German Democratic Republic, a wall like that in Berlin is simply meaningless. It is therefore only logical and natural for the wall to disappear. There is no reason for it to exist in the present circumstances.

The wall in Berlin is not the only wall — there are several walls. For instance, there is the wall the United States is building on the border with Mexico. The United States is building a sophisticated, electronic wall of 3,000 kilometers' length to prevent the migration of Mexicans.

So the United States has its own experience with walls. I would ask the United States: when will that wall disappear?

In Korea there is another wall, dividing both countries. The People's Democratic Republic of Korea [North Korea] has protested about this wall and the presence of US troops there and has put forward its proposal for reunification.

There are many walls. Another is the wall built by the United States [around its base in Cuba] at Guantánamo Bay. I ask myself when will that wall come down? When will they return this territory to us?

There is another wall which has been built in the Caribbean by the United States between our two countries, to prevent trade and relations between our countries.

I would be happy to see all walls disappear.

Ted Turner: How do you feel about recent events in Central America, in particular, the elections in Nicaragua?

Fidel Castro: I believe that the elections in Nicaragua developed under very difficult circumstances for the Sandinista Front, in the midst of a serious economic crisis increased by the US blockade, worsened by this blockade, also in the midst of a dirty war which resulted in the loss of tens of thousands of lives. Those elections were unfavorable for revolutionaries. The revolutionaries became a minority. However, that does not mean the disappearance of the Nicaraguan revolution, but rather that revolutionaries now face the historic task of recovering that majority. They accepted the rules of the game, the agreements with the opposition and they must abide by those rules.

I believe that what they're doing is correct, that is, to respect the rules of the game, to respect the results of the elections — although they were held under very abnormal conditions — and to struggle so as to once again have the majority in the country.

So I do not think that the Sandinista revolution has disappeared, but rather that it is undergoing a different experience, a stage through which I hope, through their efforts, they are able to recover the majority of support of the people of Nicaragua.

Naturally, the situation in the country is not clear, the situation is complex. We cannot say that peace has been achieved. Counter-revolutionary organizations do not want to disarm themselves. They have not abided by the disarmament agreements. They have kept the best weapons and there are thousands and thousands of armed counter-revolutionaries in an area the government has granted them of 20,000 square kilometers where they will even have their own police force. They will undoubtedly preserve their organization and retain thousands of weapons.

This creates a duality of powers. It means the existence of two armed forces. I believe that it is a situation in which one does not know what the consequences will be. So we can not say, as of yet, that peace has been achieved in Nicaragua.

Ted Turner: President Castro, from your standpoint, what do you see as the major stumbling block to normalizing relations with the United States?

Fidel Castro: Well, those stumbling blocks do not depend on Cuba. They depend on the United States. First of all, I believe there is a lot of misinformation about Cuba, total misinformation, as a result of 30 years of negative campaign and publicity about Cuba. As a result, tens of millions of people in the United States simply do not know what is happening in Cuba.

On the other hand, the government in the United States has banned the visit of people from the US to Cuba. It is not possible to have greater contact between people of the US and Cuba because of this.

So there is a lot of prejudice towards Cuba and that does not allow the emergence of forces capable of defending a more realistic policy with respect to relations with Cuba and the US.

On the other hand, the US had all sorts of slogans when we were helping the Angolans to struggle against South Africa. They said that relations could not be improved as long as there were Cuban troops in Angola. Naturally, we could not negotiate our relations with the US based on Angola and Ethiopia.

All these problems evolved, the situation in Southern Africa changed, and Cuba was able to withdraw its troops. The situation in the African Horn improved and Cuba was able to withdraw its troops.

The situation in Latin America has changed and Cuba has improved its relations with most Latin American nations.

The United States is always inventing a new condition. Now the conditions are of a domestic nature for relations to improve. But I must say, very categorically, that our country will never accept any conditions that have to do with the internal policy of the country in order to improve our relations with the United States.

It is as if we were to tell the United States that in order to improve relations with Cuba that they would have to change something in their economic system, in their political system, or that they must adopt certain domestic policies. We could elaborate a long list of things that we could demand from the United States. We could demand the disappearance of drug consumption, aged people without homes, unemployment and so on. We could demand the disappearance of poverty, homelessness, racial discrimination — discrimination against Blacks and Hispanics. We could demand many things from the United States. But anyone can understand it is absurd for us to require changes in the US domestic policy to improve relations.

So there would have to be a change in the mentality of the US administration, the opinion would have to change. The possibility would have to emerge for the US people to have a better image — it's not really a question of image, but rather to have better information, true information about Cuba.

But I believe that time will have to pass until the problems that hinder the improvement of relations are overcome.

I'm not very optimistic about this.

Ted Turner: Mr President, would you please tell us your perspective of the US government's attempt to block the televising of the Pan American Games in the US?

Fidel Castro: Well, there is an attempt on a sustained basis to impede the televising of the Pan American Games to the United States. There is a goal in this. The purpose is to deprive the country of resources for the Pan American Games. Probably the US government knows that the rights received for the TV broadcasts are very small if compared to the expenditures that must be made for the Pan American Games.

It is also possible that the US would like to boycott the games. However, there would be no legal nor moral grounds for this. It would be totally unethical because Cuba had reached agreement with the US sports authorities. When the Indianapolis games took place we participated and contributed to making those games more successful. I say this because there have been rumors. But I don't think the US will make the political and ethical mistake of boycotting the Pan American Games.

Appendix 2

US hardens stand against Cuba

The following is excerpted from a speech by Fidel Castro to a rally of more than one million Cubans on July 26, 1990. The rally was held on the 37th anniversary of the attack led by Castro on the Moncada military garrison in 1953, seen as the beginning of a new revolutionary struggle that overthrew the Batista dictatorship on January 1, 1959.

We are celebrating this anniversary at a very special time in the life of the country and the revolution. We feel that now our entire population is making a special effort in all fields, and that our people are responding to this difficult time as they should . . .

We have also undertaken a profound analysis and debate on the call for the Fourth Congress of the [Communist] Party in which we try to probe and discover all possible measures that can be applied to improve our socialism.

I repeat that the country with less than ever is now doing more than ever. But fate wills that this tremendous effort should have coincided with exceptional and unexpected international events. Who could have imagined that the socialist camp would fall like a house of cards? Who could have imagined that the Soviet Union would have the difficulties and problems it now has?

We must be realistic. I can't come here today on this 37th anniversary to say everything is fine, that there are no risks or problems. We can't say such a thing!

It is sad that this extraordinary effort for the development of the country and the consolidation of socialism in our homeland should coincide with the disaster in the socialist camp and the imperialist blockade which has already lasted more than 30 years. We don't want to think about how long it will last, and we make no allowances for the imperialists in our plans. With our economy chiefly based on the solid pillars of economic relations with the socialist camp and especially the Soviet Union, all these events take place, leading to uncertainty about resources available to the country in coming years.

Thanks to the extraordinary efforts made by the revolution, to the efforts we make every day so that children won't be without milk, so that there won't be a shortage of medicine or key foodstuffs, so that there won't be a lack of transportation to keep everything going, to carry on with our development programs, the people have barely noticed the real problems. But we are working under very tense conditions — very tense — concerning the availability of essential resources, problems which we have never had before.

The situation is difficult with regards to fuel, and this is an essential product. We are receiving less than the agreed upon quantity. There is a tense situation with regards to many raw materials which I won't list . . .

Trade with a few of the countries of the former socialist community has virtually disappeared while it continues with others. We aren't complaining about the Soviets. I say so in all honesty and sincerity, we aren't complaining. Why aren't we complaining although deliveries of some products have been reduced by 50 per cent? Because we know the Soviet government is doing all it can to fulfil its commitments. It's just that its own problems and objective difficulties go beyond the desire to do the most and supply the agreed upon amounts, to continue the traditional levels of economic cooperation with Cuba.

Last year in Camaguey province I discussed some of these issues and explained our position . . . I said something that may have seemed strange or exaggerated to some people. I said: if the socialist camp disintegrates we will continue building socialism in our country. I said that although I didn't expect it to happen and I didn't think it would, if the USSR split up or disintegrated, if the USSR disappeared, we would continue building socialism in our country.

Socialism isn't a temporary choice, a passing diversion. It isn't nor can it be a transitory decision. Socialism was an unavoidable historical need, socialism was the result of the political and ideological development of our society, the greatest and best fruit of our history.

If we really want to be a free and independent country, one which masters its own destiny, controls its own resources and economy, with the right to build its future with true social justice, a country which was first a colony for centuries and then a US neocolony for many years; if we wanted to do away with all that injustice and garbage, we had to sweep away the capitalist system. We have swept that system from our country and it will never return, at least as long as there is a communist, a patriot and revolutionary in this country.

Now the enemy is no longer the socialist camp, no longer the USSR. We are the enemy of the empire. Cuba is the only enemy they have left. Well, there are a few other countries and there is the revolutionary movement, but Cuba is just 90 miles away, a few inches from the US base and it is the main enemy. For the imperialists, Cuba is the enemy and they have focused all their force and attention on Cuba, all of their propaganda.

They have been aggressive and in just a few months have carried out nearly half a dozen very hostile acts against us. One was the TV station which they named after Martí to insult our people. The things we have had to tolerate! The TV station which no one can see and now there is the radio station which can hardly be heard and will be heard less and less and we still haven't broadcast our music there with the means available. We could have everybody there, including the White House, dancing the lambada because our stations can reach there with no trouble. We have acted moderately and have silenced them but there are still many things we can do.

The TV broadcasting was really an act of aggression, a violation of international laws and codes.

A few weeks later they organized clandestine maneuvers with powerful military forces — in silence. Amidst the sugar harvest and amidst the agricultural programs we had to mobilize tens of thousands, hundreds of thousands of people without sacrificing the harvest and other fundamental tasks. The Cuban Shield maneuvers demonstrated the level of organization and training of the Revolutionary Armed Forces and our armed people.

We were obliged to put tremendous energy into this but I will tell you more, they obliged us to spend more resources on defense. I was talking to a group of those who are building fortifications and told them that this was one of the most noble and useful tasks which they are undertaking for the country. It will help us preserve everything we have created, it will demonstrate our willingness to struggle to the imperialists and that they will have to pay a high price for any adventure.

That's why we shouldn't express regret over the steel, cement and other materials, the machines and the many thousands of men who, rather than building day-care centers, schools, homes and other things, must build fortifications.

That was the second incident.

The third was the scandalous and repugnant incident whereby they released Orlando Bosch, a killer responsible for one of the most repugnant crimes ever committed in the world. It brought tears to hundreds of thousands of people who gathered in this square. They have the incredible gall and shame to release a well-known and proven gangster and terrorist, even though he had admitted his guilt. This country which talks about terrorism and other things has committed an unforgivable offense.

But that isn't all: you have surely read the news reports about the Houston meeting of the seven major richest countries in the world. Some of the those countries — in particular, France and the Federal Republic of Germany — wanted to enter into economic cooperation with the USSR. You know what the United States wanted? At a difficult period for the Soviet Union, the government of the United States said it would not provide any economic aid to the Soviet Union as long as that country did not suspend its economic and military cooperation with Cuba.

Just look at how shameless, how far the sick obsession of Mr Bush goes! At a time when part of the European Economic Community wants to give economic aid to the Soviet Union, the United States links that aid to a halt to economic cooperation and the supply of weapons to Cuba . . .

Cuba is a country constantly threatened by the imperialists and they don't want us to receive a single weapon or bullet. They establish those humiliating conditions which have received a fitting rebuff from the Soviet government. They said they weren't begging and political strings could not be attached to economic cooperation.

Appendix 3

Revolutionary ideas are not obsolete

The following excerpts are from a speech delivered by Fidel Castro on the 30th anniversary of the Committees to Defend the Revolution (CDR) on September 28, 1990.

We have worked for 30 years at the task of defending a revolution which will soon be 32 years old. We have come through difficult times: those of the first few years, of the struggles against bandits in the Escambray Mountains and the Bay of Pigs invasion. Then later came the Missile Crisis, which will also have its anniversary in a few days and of which there has been a lot of talk lately. For two or three days I have been reading international wire dispatches reporting the excerpts of a supposed autobiography or notes by Khruschev being published in the United States. It is claimed that I had advised Khruschev to make a preemptive nuclear attack on the United States.

Perhaps Khruschev interpreted, or could have interpreted, some of my messages in that way, but it really wasn't like that. I'm not going to explain now, but fortunately I still have the messages I exchanged with Khruschev during the most difficult hours of the crisis and on subsequent days. I still have them because I thought that one day they would be interesting as historical documents. But since lately so many indiscretions have been committed and so many papers have been published on this matter, perhaps I'll find it necessary to publish those messages now, so that people will know what was said and to make clear what my viewpoints were on this matter at the heart of the Missile Crisis. I want today's generation to understand what Cuba's position was at that moment.

This may disturb the US government, which is always looking for ways to create hatred and animosity towards Cuba among the US public. I repeat, things are not as they say. The positions which I held then are those that I hold now, and what I said then I would say now in just the same way. I do not regret one word of what I said or one bit of what I did. Nevertheless, in the midst of all this gossip and scandalmongering, it's a good idea to make public some of these documents. Look how the Missile Crisis is still in the news, that period our people lived through, an extremely difficult period which we confronted calmly and level-headed.

Since then we have lived through all kinds of threats in these years. We have carried out extraordinary internationalist missions which will remain eternally in the history of our people's spirit of revolutionary solidarity . . .

At certain moments some have called us a satellite, some have even believed that we take orders from outside the country — many times they wanted to humiliate us with such offensive assertions. But solidarity is a principle, to be brothers and sisters in revolution is a principle; it has been, it is, and it always will be. As for those who think that we were once satellites, I hope that they realize beyond the remotest shadow of a doubt that we never were, nor are we now, nor will we ever be, anybody's satellite.

We have to say that we made this revolution on our own — nobody made it for us, nobody defended it for us, nobody saved it for us. We made it ourselves, we defended it ourselves, we saved it ourselves, and we will continue to defend and save it as many times as necessary.

However, as we have said many times, it was a privilege, a stroke of good fortune, an extraordinary fact for our country, for our revolution, that the October Revolution took place. The thousand times glorious October Revolution!

In these days when some people want to smash statues of Lenin into pieces, we feel the figure of Lenin growing in our hearts and our thoughts.

Lenin and his ideas have meant so much to us and still mean a lot to us, we who have interpreted his ideas and those of Marx as they should be interpreted: in an original manner, unique to each country, to each revolutionary process. These ideas retain their validity in our revolutionary process, at a time when some are frightened to call themselves communists.

Lenin's work has endured throughout history and has helped to change the world. Lenin's work meant the emergence of the first socialist state in human history, and this state saved humanity from fascism. Without the blood shed by the Soviet people, fascism would have been imposed on the world, at least for a period of time, and all humanity would have known intimately the horrors of fascism. That first socialist state meant an advance for the peoples' liberation movements and the end of colonialism, and it meant so much to us when the imperialists wanted to destroy our revolution, when they blockaded us and tried to starve us out . . .

It's shameful to see the extremes to which the imperialists have gone, asking the Soviet Union to please help them destroy the Cuban revolution. They ask the Soviet Union to join their blockade against Cuba. The blockade — which determined in part the close relations between the socialist camp and Cuba and the Soviet Union and Cuba — still exists against our country and is more rigorous and merciless than ever. And now the United States which has not been able to defeat us is asking the Soviet Union to join the US blockade against Cuba . . .

What are we trying to do and what are we actually doing given the situation? We say that if we confront a special period in peacetime, a tough special period, our task must not only be one of survival but also of development. First, it would be a period of adapting ourselves to the situation, maintaining the country's basic development programs, the essential things such as the food program . . .

The second program is biotechnology, the pharmaceutical industry and research centers, because these offer a world of resources to our country — a whole world! If we only had enough cement and steel cables for that and only enough resources for that, we would use them, because except for the food program this program is the most important . . .

The third most important branch is that of tourism, which can also bring in large revenues for our country, because this is a country which has clean air and pure seas. This sun which cracks the stones is the same sun that Europeans and Scandinavians love in the winter, because it is very good for relaxing. It's not great for growing sweet potatoes, but it's excellent for recreation . . .

However, comrades, there is one thing I want you to keep in mind: only a socialist system could confront these problems. In a capitalist system, what they would do with electricity is double or triple the price and that's that. The poor and people with low incomes would be without electricity and that would be it. Only a socialist model can confront the problem differently and is capable of rationing electricity instead of solving the problem by raising prices.

What do the capitalists do? What are they doing in a lot of Latin American countries? Every day we read the news and they haven't yet begun to feel the effects of the approaching fuel crisis. Thousands of people are being thrown out on the street, prices are multiplying, the people are harassed and only a minority of the very privileged can solve their problems.

No, we will not abandon a single person. This is characteristic of our socialism, our system. We challenge the capitalists to solve their problems and confront their difficulties in this way.

If we have to reduce the days worked, we will reduce them. If we can't work five days a week, we'll work four. And if we don't have enough raw materials and fuel in the industry to work four, we'll work three and there will be plenty of free time left which can be invaluable when put to good use.

We are now asking the country to carry out an extraordinary internationalist mission: saving the revolution in Cuba. Saving socialism in Cuba. And that will be the greatest internationalist service that our people can render humanity.

Revolutionary ideas haven't become obsolete or anything like that — they're going through difficult times but they will return with added strength. And they will return sooner if there is more injustice in the world, more exploitation, more hunger, greater chaos in the world. Revolutionary ideas will return and it's up to us, the standard-bearers of those ideas, to raise them up high, for that's the mission history has assigned to us. And as I said, we have the intelligence, the moral virtue, the courage and the heroism to fulfil this mission.

We've been greatly concerned over the past few days about the fate not of Cuba but of scores and scores of Third World countries. You've all had the chance to see how our representatives at the UN Security Council have acted in regard to the Persian Gulf crisis. We've had the privilege of being able to act totally unselfishly, with total dignity and a total spirit of justice, and we've made extraordinary efforts on behalf of peace, to find a solution to the problem — a just solution, without war.

We didn't hesitate to reject and condemn the occupation of Kuwait and the annexation of Kuwait, on the basis of principles and considerations of international law that we feel must rule in the world. And accordingly, we didn't hesitate to support resolutions that condemned those actions which, in our opinion, violated international law.

But at the same time we have strongly opposed everything we consider unjust, and one of the most unjust things is the attempt to bring a whole people to its knees through hunger, which is what the blockade boils down to.

A political solution, in our opinion, necessarily implies an end to the occupation of Kuwait and the reinstatement of that country's sovereignty . . .

We feel there must be guarantees for all the countries in the region; and we feel that if the United Nations can come forward with a political solution, it could produce guarantees for all countries in the region through the withdrawal of Iraqi forces to their border to their territory and with the withdrawal of US and NATO forces from the Persian Gulf region.

Failure to reach a political solution would be a defeat for humanity. We have set our sights on a political solution and have worked and are still working towards that end, although we realize that time is running out. It's not just because of the political inclination of our people, and our revolution, not just to do our international duty. It's because it hurts very much to see a catastrophe looming over the world and nothing done to prevent it . . . Such a war would not only mean heavy loss of life on the battlefield; it would be a catastrophe for the international economy and especially the economy of the developing countries, for the Third World countries that don't produce oil, which are the great majority. Some will swim in money, but others will wallow in misery, sacrifice and suffering of all kinds. For every life lost on the Persian Gulf battlefields, a thousand people will starve in the Third World. Such a fate is inevitable.

Index

Also from Ocean Press

Changing the history of Africa

Why did more than 300,000 Cubans — of all ages and professions, men and women, black and white — volunteer to help defend Angola from repeated South African invasions? Was the presence of these Cuban forces in Angola an obstacle to Namibia's independence?

Contributions from Gabriel García Márquez, Fidel Castro and Jorge Risquet help to provide a background to the events in Southern Africa. For the first time in such depth Cuban leaders discuss Cuba's participation in Africa.

175pp plus 32pp photos.

A new society — Reflections for today's world

Has socialism a future? Che Guevara's perspective from the early years of the Cuban revolution on the transition to a new society as presented in this selection contributes to the discussion in the world today on the future of socialism.

Fidel Castro has said that "as a man of profound thought, Che had the exceptional opportunity during the first years of the revolution to delve into the building of socialism."

This book is the product of Che Guevara's experience as the President of the National Bank, the Minister of Industry, and as a central figure in the revolutionary government.

234pp plus 16pp photos.